STO

4.8.80

ROCK-A-BYE, BABY

Popular music is one of the most sensitive indicators of the state of popular culture. It is a mixture of business, technology, and mass media with the values and concerns of the record-buying, concert-going public. Popular music is not just entertainment, but an image of the American Dream.

ROCK-A-BYE, BABY is as much about culture as it is about music. In her look at the female singer from the days of the Hit Parade to the present, author Aida Pavletich profiles the stars and styles of every genre from folk to funk, from bubble gum to blues. She also analyzes the cultural and political influences on their work, and their own considerable impact on modern sensibilities.

What emerges is a portrait of women adored and abused, publicly placed on a pedestal, and—too often—privately pushed around. In ROCK-A-BYE, BABY there are perceptive observations of such different women as Joan Baez, Dolly Parton, Linda Ronstadt, and others, revealing how they have dealt with the pressures of stardom and found their voices as individuals. Some, like Janis Joplin and Cass Elliot, found the conflicting tensions too much to handle; others like Helen Reddy, Aretha Franklin, and Carole King succeeded in expressing passion, pleasure, and pain for millions of people.

Symbolic because of their vast audience, they are no less human; fan and feminist alike will find ROCK-A-BYE, BABY an enlightening and fascinating tour of pop culture.

ROCK-A-BYE, BABY
Aida Pavletich

Doubleday & Company, Inc.   1980   Garden City, New York

This book is dedicated to everyone I've ever met.

ISBN: 0-385-11207-6
Library of Congress Catalog Card Number: 76-23790

CONTENTS

I
ROCK-A-BYE, BABY

SHE sings of love, the voice of your mind, the singer of your heart. She sings the melody that turns and turns in your head.

She sings to you.

She sings for you.

For you she beseeches every lover, she protests every betrayal, she begs all forgiveness. She takes your part, gives words to every hope and vision to every dream. She is supplicant, friend, lover. Of women, she is all you could wish of her or wish to be, she is the woman of the songs, the bird of bright feather, the lark of hope, the brazen-throated thrush, the Emperor's nightingale of the legend without whose song he lost all will to carry on.

She sings to *you*, the you of the songs who is everyone and no one, a thousand people and only one. For you alone are the songs of love.

If there be a queen of the western world, she is a popular singer. Her reign is brief. Heads roll readily in the unstable dominion of the popular heart, and yesterday's queen may be banished to oblivion tomorrow.

But if you hear and listen, the singer is voicing an awareness of now. Like the masthead of a ship who does not plan, propel, or command the voyage, she seems to lead; she is a charm against misfortune, the figure of the soul of the craft.

The singer is the image of the spirit of a people. She's the woman, mother, sister, lover of your first affections. She's the woman who might have cradled you in her arms and sung a lullaby, and held your life in her hands, and sung rock-a-bye, baby. Your first singer.

Men have not sung the lullabies. Women have, and have nurtured the will to live as human beings; and so their voices have come to symbolize the gentle and the good in our civilization.

A man's highest falsetto is no peer to the voice of a woman, it reaches neither the hair-raising heights nor the poignancy of the feminine voice.

The female range, voice, and texture will never be assimilated to the male's, and the difference is an advantage so clear that it cannot be challenged, claimed, or fought for. A female vocalist is supreme. In singing women dominate. By consent.

A popular singer is an ally. Actresses may play a villain, but a singer strikes too close to the heart to ever take on that character; she does not attack us because she is our own errant human selves, fashioned of the same moss and dirt of our creation. If she sins, her sins are of the all too human flesh, crimes of indulgence. She is our martyr, she is our doll.

She is a dumb image to be adored and despised. We imbue her dumbness with every virtue, chastise her for every fault, dismember her with our attention, and, for lacking qualities we may wish her to possess, put her away and never look at her again.

The greater her popularity, the more our illusions surround her, fantasies that are tempered by just one fact: she must be able at some time in her public life to sing.

Her value is the dreams she gathers around her. The more she leaves to the imagination, the easier it is for the hearer's dream to encompass her. There is a cultivated vacuousness in singing (sometimes it springs up naturally) that has no connection with intelligence or sophistication, a dumb quality in the sense of "dumb blonde," and also in the sense of mute. The "dumb" singer suggests a myriad of emotions supposedly beyond her ken and ability to articulate them.

4

Billie Holiday left connections to be made by the listener. No mystery enraptured her audience, it was the attraction of the void, the "dumb" sound, with its simplicity, defenselessness, vulnerability.

Anna Russell once aimed a barb at her favorite target, singers, by saying, "Of course—one of the reasons you have such a great voice is that you have resonance where your brains ought to be." To sing, Cynthia Weill mused one day, "It helps not to have too much up there."

It's a joke. It's also funny that the most vocal of women must have the ability to say nothing at all, that "dumb" quality that so effectively captures hearts.

The popular singer is the singer of our songs that are like all the songs of humanity, hunting songs, since we are the arch-predator of this planet. Unlike our hungry ancestors, for us the only spoor worthy of our chase is each other. Our singer sings love songs; all our popular songs are songs of love.

The songs express an idea of woman, whether she writes them or not. Some songs are true reflections of a female sensibility, and some are moon-June-croon tunes with all the significance of a bonnet. More women are writing songs with a personal point of view than formerly. Some write brilliantly: Joni Mitchell, Buffy Sainte-Marie, Nona Hendryx, Dolly Parton, Janis Ian, Dory Previn, Cynthia Weill, Carole Bayer Sager.

Popular music goes from an emphasis on songs to singers, and then returns to songs, and the pendulum continuously shifts. Eventually singers began to have an idea of what they were singing.

Song is an illusion. It twines itself around the consciousness with insidious force, working its wiles subliminally, seeping out of unseen speakers in an elevator, blaring out of a storefront radio, carried in a box on the streets by a media addict, insinuating itself among the chatter in a bar, leaping out of a jukebox with its message from the haunting shadows of human experience and of love. There is no defense for anyone who has intact hearing and understands the language.

But what is the message? It does carry a message, and it does influence the thoughts of people. Song embodies a culture's beliefs: I'm proud to be black; I'm happy to be free; My boyfriend is going to save me; I want to be Bobby's girl; These boots are going to trample you; Respect me. A life could be ruled by the jukebox by going from song to song, for the cheapest advice to be found.

Songs are so sensitive a barometer of what goes on that they pick up vibrations of fraud, bad faith, and self-delusion. They may express a chic mentality of what people believe they are supposed to think. Song expresses also what people feel, which may differ from what they may admit to thinking. Songs are for comfort and courtship.

There are songs certain singers would choose not to sing. Phoebe Snow would not sing about politics or government. Dionne Warwick wouldn't sing the praises of a New Orleans hooker, Patti LaBelle would. Linda Hargrove wouldn't sing or write anything like "I'm going to kill you and put your body in a box." Dolly Parton says there is no song she would refuse to sing, and thereby seem to say, "I am above that."

Performers take part in political, social, and humanitarian issues, lending their celebrity to campaigns and causes, they already have one kind of vote for a sort of office; each singer represents something to someone, and probably many things to many people.

A great performer can outshine any but the most highly placed politicians on a public platform if for no other reason than she looks better, and she has always been associated with the pleasure of music and not the duties of authority. For Linda Ronstadt to be an item with California's Governor Brown brightened the spotlight on him, for who has the greater light, a governor of a state or the queen of rock 'n' roll?

Barbra Streisand lent Senator George McGovern's candidacy for the presidency her support. Tanya Tucker was honorary chair for the Save the Seals Organization. Olivia Newton-John and Helen Reddy canceled tours to Japan in protest against the slaughtering of thousands of dolphins by Japanese fishermen. Joni Mitchell's involvement against nuclear energy goes far back to the ban-the-bomb issues of the fifties; Joan Baez, Bonnie Raitt, Buffy Sainte-Marie, Nina Simone have always let their political ideas be known. Women who have sung and written songs are not necessarily mute on issues.

Song fantasy creates such an aura around a woman that it transforms her even to the point of reflecting back into the audience and revolutionizing its concept of female beauty, as Barbra Streisand, who once remarked that she had succeeded in her career without capping her teeth or fixing her nose, did for the ethnic Jewish look.

But most performers are pressed into a decorative mold. Names need changing from Cardona to Carr, Egstrom to Lee, Barbara to Barbra and from some hell came the idea of abandoning the sonorous name of Constance Franconero to go by the insipid moniker of Connie Francis. Thank heavens for Lori Lieberman, Helen Schneider, and Phyllis Hyman.

Part of a performer's job is to maintain the image she has placed before the public. It is all they ever see of her and they would recognize nothing else. Marlene Dietrich's image was so well defined that when she fell into the orchestra pit at the end of a performance, she refused to be helped out of it and remained in the pit, thence to wave goodbye to all. Her gown was ripped up the back and by no means would Madame present that unfamiliar facet of her persona to her starry-eyed fans.

Piaf forever sang in something like the ugly black street dress she'd been discovered in when she sang on the Paris streets.

If our performers are more than themselves, it is because they are building on the legends of our culture, their debts are to Lady Godiva, Joan of Arc, Messalina, Eve, and Pandora. They reply to the need for people to adulate, an impulse that even in our enlightened society is inaccessible to reason. The performer is deluged with the putative love of that volatile infant that is an audience.

A crowd of people is a real expression of a society, because it states its needs without the complexities and refinements found in an individual of the same culture. A crowd is an idiot-savant, a baby. It can express pleasure and displeasure, very little else. An audience has little patience. A performer dealing with a crowd is dandling a very large baby, cajoling it, trying to elicit a smile, a coo of pleasure in the form of applause, half-fearing that it may break into hisses and boos, which means failure.

The displeasure of an audience, unlike a baby's, may be dangerous, since a crowd is not as helpless as an infant; there is a capacity for real malice by its members when the solitary arm of the crowd

may step over the footlights, across the mirror that is the proscenium, into the other dimension, the reality of the human being who
is a performer.

A Performer belongs to her audience sometimes too literally,
being assumed to have no personal existence outside of their minds.
Janis Joplin complained that all her records had been taken; people
who visited her house would help themselves to her belongings. Some
of Loretta Lynn's fans bring scissors to cut off locks of her hair, or to
take a swatch of her dress. Buffy Sainte-Marie was followed cross-
country by a persistent jerk who knocked at her door at 3 A.M. every
morning. Martha Reeves eventually decided to go hungry rather than
eat delicatessen food after having found it laced with drugs so often
on the way to her table. The Jefferson Airplane had a food-taster in
their entourage.

There is a dismal groupie scene for women; it is usually the case
that the kind of men who come backstage to meet the artist are not
the kind whose attentions a woman enjoys, the balance sinks heavily
in the direction of creeps.

But the occasional importunate individual is not representative of
the audience. The majority of the popular music audience is made up
of women and girls. They used to be easy marks for the appeal of
popular songs, the hope for easy fulfillment through love, because for
women, to aspire to love was to aspire to power, the only kind of
power women could get. A woman's power over one man was her
means to power in a world where power was wielded by men.

Now the music audience as well as the population is becoming
older. Music still affects the young very deeply; it is the last oral
form, it carries the messages of our culture and is the most accessible
popular communication. The Population Council in the United States
blames rock lyrics for the unmarried teen baby boom of the seventies.

A singer is now more sensitive to the consequences of the message
of her song, but there is no way that the subject matter of popular
songs can be changed so that certain messages could be disseminated
for the good of the public.

An audience for popular music is the most mercurial mass of humanity that exists. It is ungovernable. No sooner is it told "you shouldn't" than it replies "I did."

That audience makes its demands in incontrovertibly commercial terms. Artists of its choice are given the means to thrive, others disappear. This group of people is not to be punished, it can only be rewarded; it is impossible to intimidate an audience or force its choices.

Sales charts listing records by rank in music trade magazines, are the people's plebiscite. Charts may be manipulated, but since the price gets high, sales can't be kept up indefinitely on mediocre products. The trash will fall.

Courage, craft, commitment are respected. A singer cannot purvey trash and go for the cheap shots consistently and still survive. She can't repeat herself too often or listeners will turn away, having heard it all before.

There is a type of song that can be the kiss of death to a singer's career; it might be her biggest hit and still contribute to her eclipse. Patti Page found her Waterloo in "How Much Is That Doggie in the Window." Excellent singers can be done in when they too obviously pander to the "dumb" appeal. Patti Page is an exquisite vocalist, and she grew heartily sick of singing "Doggie." Melanie is one of the bravest voices, but she blew it with the dopey innuendo of "Brand New Key." Another low blow was Teresa Brewer's "Music! Music! Music!" wherein "nickel in" is rhymed with "nickelodeon."

The nemesis of a female vocalist is the cutsie-poo ditty that draws ridicule and that for a while everybody seems to want to hear: let's see you put that lampshade on your head again.

When the novelty has worn off, people will say, oh, Brenda Lee, isn't she the one who sang "Dum-dum, Doodle-de-dum," or was it "Sweet Nothin's"? They forget that she sang "Johnny One Time." With a giggle, they'll remember that Sue Thompson sang "Sad Movies (Make Me Cry)" and that Lesley Gore, an excellent singer, sang "It's My Party (I'll Cry If I Want To)."

Only the very greatest can escape the consequences of the absurd. There was nary a ripple when Peggy Lee sang "The Siamese Cat Song" or when Patsy Cline sang "Tra-la-la-la Triangle," they simply passed like ships of state dragging behind them a few balloons. But for the others, the singer became identified with the song, and her popularity faded along with the song's.

Singing is a rite, at root a Dionysian rite. There is something of the inebriate in every singer. People are accused of making a spectacle of themselves when they are drunk, and what better can a singer do than make a spectacle of herself. So much depends on acting uninhibitedly on a stage that it's a temptation to help enter the performance trance with alcohol or drugs, to be desensitized, to achieve "dumb" simplicity by artificial means.

The love of a thousand people for a performer expressed in the space of a concert hour is a disorienting high that leaves a heavy depression in its wake, making anything on human scale minuscule by comparison. Drugs and alcohol are a danger in the celebratory atmosphere that surrounds a performer. With the synergy of drugs, alcohol, and with stress, she can snuff out her life like Dinah Washington, Janis Joplin, or Cass Elliot.

There are other dangers, like falling from a badly placed set as Ann-Margret did, getting retinal damage from following an arc lamp on a television show for several takes, following a director's instructions as Dusty Springfield did, falling off the stage and breaking her neck as Patti Smith did.

But the greatest threat to a singer's career is love, love, love, that stuff she sings about, and should be immune to, as a snake charmer to venom after having suffered many bites. Love, in all its forms. She may give up her career to do something that will bring her closer to a lover, since like most ladies, she's been trained to subsume her own needs to someone else's way of life.

Rise to stardom, and then chuck it all for the proverbial night of love. Undertake the burdens of a needy lover. Become helpmate to a husband. A husband may, like Roberta Flack's, say that show business puts a crust on a woman, as Richard Lee reported. The woman herself may, like Brenda Lee, consider nonchalance about her work a point of pride and say, as she did to Christopher Cabot, "Unlike many people, I don't put my career first," putting the face of virtue on what is actually a lapse.

Emotional blackmail can be a stumbling block. Chi Coltrane quotes a typical ploy:

"If you go on the road, don't blame me if I find another woman. I can't help it."

One time on the road, making those awful calls—calling at three o'clock in the morning and finding out they're not there—is enough to make a woman avoid the next tour.

And so, women are subject to marital bliss, a condition which is encouraged by society, fostered by families, and is an alternate source of self-esteem. The duration of this state encompasses the most productive years of a woman's life.

The performer who is wife and mother has to make space for herself. Minnie Riperton wrote songs, but not under the best circumstances:

> I write in the bathroom, I write in the bedroom . . . usually away from the kids. They usually don't bother your things, but you never know when the baby wants to color something you're writing on.

A husband can figure in a woman's career as a manager, musician, agent, or producer, collaborating with her. Helen Reddy with Jeff Wald, Cleo Laine with John Dankworth, Loretta Lynn with Mooney, Tina Turner with Ike. It would be unfair to speculate on the careers of either partner in the absence of the other.

Sometimes one member of the partnership is dragged along on the stage where their styles don't mix, their personalities are incongruous. Kris Kristofferson and Rita Coolidge, Waylon Jennings and Jessi Colter, Nick Ashford and Valerie Simpson, John Lennon and Yoko Ono. They probably would be better single performers.

Bad duo acts fall into the worst mistake a duo can make, relating to each other on the stage instead of to the audience. This never happens with legit duos, Tammy Wynette and George Jones, Loretta Lynn and Conway Twitty, Ike and Tina Turner.

Partnerships can be unequal. Johnny Cash, with an unbeautiful voice that rings like a kicked stovepipe, sings along with June Carter Cash, his wife and heiress to the Carter family voice. Their album comes out titled *Johnny Cash and His Woman*.

It is not for the sensitive flower to aspire to a life on the stage. If she fears to expose herself to an audience, or is flustered by the impudence of the press, offended by the demands of the business to the extent of it all becoming too much and she withdraws, takes a hiatus, she may risk never coming back.

Fleeing the world of commercial music from 1972 to 1976, Laura Nyro found that during her absence her audience had consoled itself with other talents. Laura Nyro, once considered a genius and the most exciting talent to appear on the American scene since Carole King, was easily forgotten. When she returned, she had it all to do over again. Dues never cease to be paid.

Recording songs that will follow her around for the rest of her life is one of the singer's toughest jobs. The strain shows. Linda Ronstadt gains weight, Bette Midler drifts around like a zombie, angels turn into bitches, and everyone is paranoid. Setting something so ephemeral as a song into permanent form is difficult enough without trying to act normal, but the studio situation may seem as a bizarre environment littered with surreal occurrences, as Rita Jean Bodine describes it:

> The place is like a spacemobile. It's very fuzzy with electronic happenings, and the room is very hollow with wooden floors and high ceilings like a sound stage.
>
> I knew that there were about thirty-five people in the booth; I couldn't see them but they could see me. I couldn't compare it to anything else except for fucking when you know somebody's looking through the window but you can't see them. It was great.

For a performer who knows herself to be the focus of every eye, the problem of ugly elbows can take on monumental proportions. A studio situation can magnify every phobia. More than one fine singer has driven producer Jerry Wexler quietly insane in the studio, but one in particular had

> . . . this neurotic overconcern about what songs she should sing and how she sounds! She would worry it to death. It would be a continuous jesuitical argument—it's Jewish too, the casuists—endless self-analysis till I wanted to throw up, honey, come on—here's the song—let's go in the studio, make some music . . .

In reality a singer is neither saint nor goddess, she's working. She may be an evangelist, capable of swaying a crowd to laughter or tears, but under the aureole of stage presence, she is a person of markedly human proportions. Singers are assumed to be statuesque, but few of them are taller than five feet three.

She doesn't have to be conventionally pretty. It was a disadvantage for Olivia Newton-John; she got her break, it was assumed, because she looked good. It escaped notice that she had tried to be part of the folk scene in the early sixties and her pretty face got her nowhere, and before she became an overnight sensation in the seventies she had worked for a decade in obscurity.

No successful singer has an ugly mouth, and she is said to be an oral personality. She usually has a substantial jaw; to look at some, you would swear they are capable of biting off the leg of an ox. She has a bull neck, great lung capacity, strong shoulders, back, legs. Singing is a sales job where you stand up on your feet. No singer who sits down is worth her salt, unless she sits down for an effect, as Helen Morgan sat on top of a piano.

She usually has the physique of an athlete, though more amply insulated with resonant flesh; since she must have a constitution that bears up under stress with little rest, she must have endurance. Not all do. Phoebe Snow knows herself to be an exception:

> I'm not athletic at all—that's not me. I just sit around all day. You know how if you leave Silly Putty out of the egg, how it melts? I'm Silly Putty. I've been out of my egg for years.

But when she is faced with a performance:

> I go into something like a training regimen. I have breathing exercises, and hot water with lemon, the whole mishpocha. I take thousands of vitamins.

A singer's psyche must withstand the emotional vagaries of success and failure, and her personality must countenance the sudden mindless hostility of a mob. She stands alone onstage.

Backstage, she can display the temperament that makes juicy gossip everywhere from La Scala to the local honky-tonk; she can spin off the adrenalin, a side effect of performing, in brawls, like Bessie Smith, Bonnie Bramlett slapping somebody's bad mouth, Dusty

Springfield throwing food, to the mortification of a British critic who demanded to know how Britain could have as its ambassador to the world someone who hurled teacups down corridors.

On the stage, there are few limits to self-expression, since the audience, for all its numbers, are considered intimates, which allowed Judee Sill to belch, Patti Smith to spit copiously on the stage.

Elsewhere there are accounts of those who slash their wrists, pop the pills, hit the bottle, and do cocaine. There are stories of the cruel, the religious, the psychotic, the down-and-out. Here are the ones who have remained in the public eye, who are the most successful; their careers are the measure of their sanity and strength.

Each genre of popular music has a different ideal of womanhood which is part of the female mystique of this girl singer who is wife, lover, mother. She is the fallen angel of country, the glamorous fatale of pop, the sassy fox of R&B, the sister of folk. She's tramp, bitch and goddess, funky mama, sweetheart, the woman left lonely, the hapless victim of her man, left with pride enough to protest, and that's what singing is all about. All songs are protest songs.

Each genre of popular music has created one of these ideals of womanhood. This book is about these ideals, these icons and divas of popular music. Gospel is absent because it does not focus on the singer, but as a religioso genre it is centered on a male deity. Jazz is absent because jazz vocalists are instrumentalists and composers, and because jazz is a classic, not a popular genre, and is not accessible to a majority with its message because of its reliance on melody in preference to lyrics. As a melodic genre jazz is better heard than read about. Jazz vocalists are treated in connection with their contribution to the pop genre.

Once the singers have caught an audience, a certain amount of loyalty accrues to them. They are not, as Florence Greenberg, founder of Scepter records and responsible for launching the Shirelles and Dionne Warwick, says, to be seen as objects of pity when their time has come and gone:

> I don't think I feel very sorry for them, because they perform for another twenty years successfully . . . records give them advertising

that they get paid for. They stay as performers, and as concert performers they make money for the rest of their lives.

I'm not feeling very sorry for them. On records, tastes change, and their particular sound, people are tired of it after ten years.

The business is egalitarian. It treats everyone with the same lack of regard like the rain that falls on rich and poor alike; men, women, minorities, have the same slim chance of making it; perhaps a handicapped woman has a smaller chance than a man with the same handicap, since there are blind male performers, and even a paraplegic one, but since Connie Boswell there have been no handicapped female artists.

The business is not as harsh as Bette Midler once commented to a press conference:

> The very nature of the business breeds fear. Everywhere there is bitterness and jealousy. The worst part of having success is to try finding someone who is happy for you. You don't really find that, not in this business.

Harsh words, and not true, but they reflect the isolation that a performer can feel even in the midst of success. The job of performing may exhaust emotional energy, and there is a marked contrast between the concentrated attention a performer gets on a stage and the neglect afterward.

Helen Reddy was not known till 1972, but she arrived in the United States from Australia in 1966. She knew no one, and professionally the times were hard, since psychedelia and acid rock were then popular. There was very little opportunity for a pop singer. She told music writer Kobe Atlas:

> Sometimes when I was working, the only conversations I'd have all day were with people in the audience while I was performing. The show would be over, and I'd go back to the hotel room and put the baby to bed, and sit there looking at myself till morning.

Some of the limitations on a woman are inhibitions that she has acquired that work subtle prohibitions on her. They may be perceived as opportunities missed, prerogatives waived, positions relinquished willingly, fights not waged, invitations not extended. Since the music business like most other profitable enterprises is run by men, a certain modesty is expected from women. Dusty Springfield wanted to produce her own albums, and was credited with co-producing later work, but it was not always the case:

> Nobody said, "You can't do that, you're a woman." I put the restrictions on myself. I did most of the production work on most of my records, I never got the credit . . . It would have been unthinkable for me to have had on the record label, "Sung by Dusty Springfield, produced by Dusty Springfield . . ."
>
> I was prepared to swallow my pride and let somebody else's name go on the label.
>
> It was very hard to put up with the amused, tolerant smiles from certain musicians when I scowled at them. They, over a period of time, came to respect the fact that I really wanted things musically right.
>
> But initially they just either thought I was a nuisance, or that I was a spunky kid: "My word, look at that little girl really trying—isn't she cute."

Many of the hardships faced by women are likewise faced by men, but women are not taught to overcome them but to withdraw from conflicts, which is a factor that has made women a minority in the ranks of every lucrative endeavor.

It does not seem as if it would be difficult to sing. Pop music favors the simple open-throated voice, a sound close to speech, evidently an untrained voice, a style that anyone could master.

Try it. Try singing for three minutes, if you are not accustomed to do more than hum along the first three bars of a song. Can you stay in tune? Can you remember the words? Can you follow the beat? That's nothing. If you can do these three things for an hour three times a night for a week, it will still take you ten years to develop a style.

Each genre has its conventions of vocal frills. There are warbles at the end of a soul phrase, dying wails within the country verse, jazz twists, blues moans, ways of phrasing a lyric that are not written into the music. The most bland pop singer adds an indelible stamp of her own to a song.

Genre loyalties, contempt for the culture which fostered the style, account for the fury some people feel on hearing songs in a style they do not feel is their own. Critics, as well as audiences, are often intolerant of genres they are not familiar with. They can be unfair to a singer simply because she does not fulfill the roles they are accustomed to in the genre they favor. It is a question of age and background and class. There is no style that found easy acceptance at its inception, or that eventually will not be scorned by someone.

The funniest voice on the pop circuit, and not the easiest on the ears, is the stageshow quack, a superannuated style that has as its fountainhead and sole survivor Ethel Merman, though it echoes in the voices of Barbra Streisand and Liza Minnelli, and it was brayed out by Judy Garland.

The stageshow quack influenced the sound of the musical theater and spelled the death to thin-voiced sopranos, since it cuts through an orchestra and the hubbub of a musical show, and carries as clear as a bell to the back row of the balcony.

Ethel Merman combines the stageshow quack with the most perfect diction Ira Gershwin, Jerome Kern, or Cole Porter could hope for. Hers is a feisty sound that when imitated by dishwater voices is one of the most infuriating noises ever to offend the blameless ears of an assembled populace.

The best singers are not necessarily the best voices. It took years for Anne Murray to learn how to sing with her beautiful voice. It was long before she developed the craft, the emotional sensitivity to carry a song, though it was worth the wait. Billie Holiday's voice was a monotone, but no one could fault her singing. Joni Mitchell has an hourglass-shaped voice that she has learned to use to telling effect. Linda Ronstadt only plied the emotion in her voice properly after ten years of performing.

Pop voices can have a cutting edge like Barbra Streisand's, or a smooth coolness like Roberta Flack and Carly Simon's, the brassiness of Helen Reddy, the husky, wrecked texture of Bette Midler and Melissa Manchester when they're playing cabaret Camille, or a Kim Carnes corn husk, the gravel of Gale Garnett, Bonnie Tyler, Nicoel Barclay.

Gospel-based singers like Aretha, especially Aretha, may shriek.

Rock singers can belt with the driving intensity of Grace Slick or Buffy Sainte-Marie, Rickie Lee Jones, Donna Summer, Chaka Khan. They can be smoothly sensual like Stevie Nicks of Fleetwood Mac, Ann and Nancy Wilson of Heart. A disco singer like Anita Ward can choose to sing sharp to stand out from the instrumental.

Some have astonishing ranges. Yma Sumac of eld sang like a jungle bird and passed for a Peruvian exotic (read her name backwards, she's from Brooklyn). Morgana King reaches ethereal heights in barely audible voicings. Minnie Riperton sang flute-like notes. Flora Purim sounds like a synthesizer. There are sonic booms from Odetta, doppler effects from Grace Slick. There are vocalists of stunning craft: Terry Garthwaite, Betty Carter. There are beautiful voices: Anne Murray, Esther Satterfield, Cheryl Ernst, Lori Lieberman, Donna Godchaux, Bonnie Koloc, and Marty Gwinn. Craft, beauty, musicianship do not necessarily guarantee popularity.

Popular voices are not necessarily pretty. They can be annoying and yet people will want to hear them: Buffy Sainte-Marie's vibrato-you-can-plant-corn-in, the wobble like a spinning top as it nears the end of its cycle that Melanie once affected, or early Joan Baez's thin high notes we winced at in the fifties.

Popular voices hardly need to be voices. A whisper, a very croak will do to get the message across. Some singers try to mar the smoothness of their natural voices; Janis Ian smokes plenty, and is pleased to have her voice show the effect, prematurely taking on that cracked character.

The wrecked voice is a hoarse, passionate, bordello style. Too much hardship, too much suffering and real despair takes away the gift of expressing emotion, you will notice if you ever listen to the voice of a brutalized Tijuana street singer whose eye has just been blackened by his pimp.

But the wrecked voice can be had by swallowing poison, smoking, alcohol, an accident to the pharynx such as being choked by a mugger, and probably in other ways. It is possible to sing with only one of a pair of vocal cords, lacking the other, as Nancy Nevins does. Too much singing, improper vocal technique, laryngitis will bring on the gravel, and one study found that five out of five pop singers had callused vocal cords.

What accounts for the popularity of the wrecked voice, when it is obviously an unhealthy sound, is that the hoarseness suggests the weariness of post-coital exhaustion. It is the post-coital croak you are hearing. Smile.

A woman's voice improves after she is thirty, adding pleasant lows and gaining fullness. A pop singer is only really through when bitterness crawls into her voice, darkening it to the point where it sounds dead, like Edith Piaf's sounded at the Bobino in 1962, a year before her death.

Popular vocal ranges are concentrated at the upper end of the scale, arresting soprano frequencies with a plangent sound whose drawn-out notes trigger a distress signal in the human ear, and call for attention.

Outside of Anne Murray, Tanya Tucker, and Karen Carpenter, there are few altos in popular music. Odetta, Rosemary Clooney, Vera Lynn, Sammi Smith, and Mary Travers are in the minority, and Julie London did a wonderful "Cry Me a River," but her acting ability, and not her singing, made this record.

It would be profitable for the business heads to predict the success of a record, and don't think they're not trying. The Consumer Behavior Center in Dallas and Preview House in Los Angeles are contracted to test the appeal of records.

The Dallas company gauges the commercial potential of a record by determining "subconscious responses" to music. Yes, they wire people to a machine to find out what they're feeling. It is a surer method, they say, than asking direct questions, since people often give the answers they assume the interviewer wants to hear.

Record research is a business tool, and probably can help to reinforce the status quo that is so comfortable in an industry where there is so little stability, though promoting sameness by predicting what will be liked by people is inimical to the nature of human beings, while they are alive, they are always looking for something new.

Popular music of the West has for this century been dominated by the United States. In the late fifties and early sixties there was a trend toward European singers, which eventually culminated in the British invasion. The females were Caterina Valente, the Singing Nun

(Soeur Sourire), Ginguiola Cinquetti, Rita Pavone, Mireille Mathieu, Dalida, and others.

Some of them were seen on the screen of the short-lived novelty invention, the Scopitone, a jukebox that showed three-minute lip-sync performances along with the song. They had some pretty silly production numbers on seamy sets that did nothing but highlight the greatest drawback of European acts: their dancing stinks.

The choreography was so ridiculously affected, the acts so predictable and cheaply made, showing no more imagination than the worst of the fifties live TV variety shows, that the invention disappeared, presumably dealt a coup de grâce by color television.

The international trend brought the Singing Nun to America for Christmas, 1963, with "Dominique (nique-nique)," the biggest religioso hit since "Ave Maria." She had written the song and sang it with a sweet chapel hootiness as tepid as holy water. Sister later doffed her frock for a show business career, and wasn't heard of in the United States again till years later, when the Belgian revenuers caught up with her for unpaid taxes.

Internationals were a novelty, even the best of them like Caterina Valente, who is known in the United States for "The Breeze and I" and schmaltz like "Malagueña." Clear and buoyant though her sound was, there was no place for that style of Europop in the States, particularly since Europop can pass so easily for a spineless imitation of the American pop of the early fifties.

There are popular singers who have not traveled well between western countries for cultural reasons. British rock acts can share a stage with music hall acts, but in the United States the traditions do not mix. That may account for the limited success in the United States of singers like Maggie Bell, Lynsey DePaul, Cilla Black, and Lulu.

Each nation has singers who are successful in their own country and barely known outside of it: Gagoosh, the most popular female vocalist in Iran, the brilliant performer Misora Hibari in Japan, who for forty years has been ichiban, number one. There is Lata Mangeskar in India, who between 1948 and 1974 recorded twenty-five thousand songs in twenty Indian languages, and scheduled up to five recording sessions per day. There is Amalia Rodriguez, the greatest singer of the blues-like Portuguese fados, and in Latin America there are countless others who in the United States are only known in the urban barrios.

France has Barbara, the mysterious singer who sings with icewater in her veins, the polar opposite of Piaf, word of whose performance of "Non, je ne regrette rien" from the Eiffel Tower went far beyond the Champs Élysées.

The artists discussed in this book are the best we have: creators, innovators, and classics. They've had, and will have, enormous success. There are others who have been overlooked.

There is no definitive way to portray a living and changing scene such as popular music. One hopes to catch it on the wing to have some idea of the direction it is going.

It is true that the essence of music cannot be arrived at by means of words, because music exists in time, and the written word does not. This book is about our popular music in the only way I believe that I can interpret it, by what it may mean to the people who live with it.

I am lucky for having been able to speak to the makers of this music who are alive in my own time, who between 1973 and 1979 made their comments to me. A handful of the remarks are from interviews published by other sources. I have tried to imprint on these pages the music of their voices, in the hope of understanding the force behind their music. There is more music in their voices that can't be rendered adequately in print; Thelma Houston's contagious laughter, and how it ends on a high note, the slow, thoughtful pace of Peggy Lee's speech, its measured and balanced proportions, the precision of Dusty Springfield's diction, the put-ons in Grace Slick's manner, or the speedy, unpunctuated stream of words in Vicki Sue Robinson's conversation.

I had resource to interviews, which made me an ally, at least for the space of the interview, with the subject of my interview. There are always some contretemps in interviews, which consist of two strangers who must speak to each other. People dread interviews.

While waiting for Dory Previn to arrive, I read a clipping of another interview where she had confided to Ralph Keyes that on her way to interviews she drives her car screaming, *"I don't want to do this!"*

If my heart sank at this, it was because I try to listen with tolerance and compassion, and interviewing is for me like walking down a well-kept street and having a flowered door open suddenly to reveal a mummy.

Rock-A-Bye, Baby is based on interviews. It is an attempt to explore the background of our popular music. It is a book of egos. I've tried to be the articulate cell of the audience, its eyes and ears, moving among the musical indigenes like a Margaret Mead.

There may be remarks in the verbatim comments that are axe-grinding, grandstanding and self-serving, that some may recognize and some not. I offer them for your delectation along with the truth and the insights, in the hope that more may be revealed to you by your interpretation, or they may cast more shadows for their own mystique. Though I have tried to slight no one, I know that many worthwhile artists have been neglected whose day I hope will come.

I have concentrated on female vocalists who are primarily recording artists and who perform in concerts and smaller venues. Back-up vocalists and television personalities are beyond the scope of this book.

These are our singers.

Nothing is as old as yesterday's love song, and yesterday's singer. Not hearing them for a few weeks, months, years, you may forget how good they are.

In the ups and downs of their fortunes, when they're off the charts, without a hit for years and without a booking, when they've disappeared beyond recall, don't forget how good they are.

Don't forget the singers of your heart, the nightingales who are the voices of your mind when your own voice is silent, the ones whose words and melodies lifted you when you despaired. Don't forget how good they are.

II
CANARIES, FRAILS, AND
GIRL SINGERS

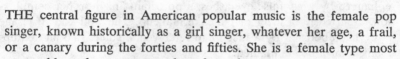

THE central figure in American popular music is the female pop singer, known historically as a girl singer, whatever her age, a frail, or a canary during the forties and fifties. She is a female type most acceptable to the greatest number of people.

Other singers rise and fall with their musical genre or go out of favor with all but the most rabid loyalists of their cult, but the pop singer survives even the most revolutionary changes in popular taste. The pop genre is a catch-all for performers who arrive from other genres once the vogue for their style graduates from a cult following or dies down from a major fad. The center of pop music shifts to accommodate every new style so that it includes a corner of every musical genre, or at least a watered-down sample. The stronger a singer's style, the more the style of pop music evolves.

The pop singer fulfills the expectations of the audience by offering a classic, easily recognized stage character. Her persona is impersonated by transvestite acts because it represents a hyper-female fantasy, preferably one in full decay.

Peggy Lee, Barbra Streisand, and Dionne Warwick have distinctive, easily mimicked styles of dress and singing. Their material is identified with them, so that if a tall black transvestite should appear in a tasteful gown, with a few leggy steps, a toothy smile, and sing "Don't Make Me Over" the audience would recognize Dionne Warwick. A platinum wig, some finger-snapping, a sly, come-hither smile with a few lines of "Fever" will identify Peggy Lee. A wide-open mouth, a pained expression, and a braying "People" will conjure up Barbra Streisand.

Certain locales are the pop singer's territory: supper clubs, major hotel lounges, Las Vegas showrooms, and when she is at her peak, large concert halls such as Carnegie or outdoor amphitheaters like the Hollywood Bowl. She plays cameo roles in Hollywood epics and appears regularly on television.

Costumed in beaded gowns, surrounded by dancers, backed by an orchestra, she never fails to purvey glamour, elegance, and deliver a high quality show, well polished and slickly timed, to her audience. It is expected of her, since she is at the center of the American dream of womanhood. Usually she is an Aryan type blonde whose reality is enhanced by wigs, false eyelashes, a porcelain finish on her complexion imparted by a layer of pancake makeup. The well-known visage is perhaps boosted by a facelift in later years, since, like any equipment, it must be maintained.

Since a pop singer is acceptable to a great number of people, she is not usually a pioneer who originates musical ideas. She takes the most amenable facets of new trends and presents them to the pop audience in a form they will understand and accept, which may sometimes rob the material of its uniqueness.

This habit arouses the indignation of music genre loyalists, who recognize the source of the pop singer's material, and justly or not may slough her off as a milksop, preferring in rebellious spite a lesser singer of their favorite cult. Conversely, a finer singer with a small cult following may be denied the limelight by having her material or style appropriated by a pop singer. Though material is fair game for all, the difference between success or failure, if success is measured by the number of people reached by a singer's voice, is sometimes only a matter of exposure, and a pop singer brings a song to a large segment of the public.

To become a household word, the pop singer sometimes indulges in another small artifice. She changes her name to suggest a more arresting character, creating a mythical femme. Not many members of their audience would recognize Frances Gumm, Ethel Agnes Zimmerman, Maria Magdalene von Losch, Morgana Messina, Ruth Jones, Norma Delores Egstrom, Constance Franconero, and Clare Ann Fowler as Judy Garland, Ethel Merman, Marlene Dietrich, Morgana King, Dinah Washington, Peggy Lee, Connie Francis, and Patti Page. But this is not feminine coquetterie, these are masques, as Elton John, Bob Dylan, and Engelbert Humperdinck will attest, themselves having found Reginald Dwight, Robert Zimmerman, and Arnold Dorsey would be drab weeds to wear in the light of fame.

Since the pop audience, though loyal, is slow to change, the pop singer's career is predicated on blandness and conservatism. But there lives not a critic so cold who innerly may not harbor a secret, burning passion for Patti Page, Peggy Lee, or Jo Stafford, an enduring respect for the ability of Barbra Streisand and Dionne Warwick, and personal tastes aside, no one can belittle the unquestionable talent of Brenda Lee, Timi Yuro, Doris Day, and Connie Francis.

The roots of the pop singer extend through the musical genres to all musical eras and audiences: minstrel shows, blues, jazz, big bands, radio, recordings, and the hit parade are all sources, but there are three basic types of singers: the diseuse, the chanteuse, and the rhythm singer. The diseuse goes for the lyrics, the chanteuse concentrates on the melody, and the rhythm singer opts for the cadence. Each genre has all types of singers.

The pop singer who is closest to the American audience is usually a diseuse or a rhythm singer. She delivers the message and the beat of the song to the audience in the most accessible form, the rhythm. Rhythm predates melodic structure in human awareness. Rhythm is comprehensible, more so than melodic structures, to an untrained ear, since music is not the universal language it is touted to be, as anyone who encounters the classic structure of any culture's music may realize. The pop singer deals in language, idioms, and ideas based on values that her audience is prepared to accept.

The most melodic singers in American pop music are the jazz vocalists. At their best, they are at the top of their craft. Billie Holiday,

Ella Fitzgerald, Carmen McRae, and Sarah Vaughan are consummate, sophisticated vocalists who bring out every nuance in a song, and qualify equally as creators of a song as the composers and the instrumentalists who back them.

The jazz singer has a built-in inferiority complex which stems from the instrumental hierarchy of the bands she associated with; she attempts to be an instrument, which is a redundancy, since the human voice is capable of reproducing the sound of every instrument in the orchestra, almost every sound comprehensible to the human ear. In attempting to become an instrument, she casts away the one uniqueness of the human voice that sets it apart from the machinery, however intricate, of an instrument; more than in its sensual, emotional, and melodic appeal, the human voice can articulate thoughts through words. A singer who disdains lyrics wastes an entire facet of her expressivity.

The human voice has disadvantages when compared to instruments, which should discourage competition; it is subject to pain, colds, fatigue, mental depression, and other accidents that no horn ever risked. Also, it cannot produce the sustained volume an instrument is capable of.

In the outer reaches of jazz, the aficionados of least discrimination approve the use of a human voice as an instrument with no lyrics whatsoever, which is an excellent idea when the singer might be at a disadvantage with English lyricism, as is true with the Brazilian vocalist Flora Purim and the Polish composer Urszula Dudziak.

The use of a vocalist as an instrument will allow breathy saxophone textures that retain the character of the human voice and produce whining flatulent sounds, which taken out of the context of the structure of the music sound simply stupid. Flora Purim produces hissing, percussive sounds, and the wordless improvisations of Urszula Dudziak sound like the vaguely terrifying blitherings of the insane. Lacking the expressiveness of English skat syllables, improvised nonsense syllables that still retain basic utterances tied to the logic of the language have a chilling effect, something like the vision of a woman without a face. Dudziak and Purim are nevertheless excellent vocalists.

Lyrics of jazz songs are usually exquisitely crafted, since they would fall in the way of the melody if they were not. A good lyric has a rhythmic structure of its own that can be used by an astute singer as another facet of her technique.

At the farthest extreme of what might be termed jazz, every piano bar has its warbling chirp with a wrecked voice from drinks and cigarettes she has ingested torching her way to the witching hour.

The jazz singer is set apart from other vocalists by her improvisations around a melody line; she never sings a song the same way twice. When singing "You've Changed," Billie Holiday sings the title phrase nine times, in nine ways. Traditionally, jazz singers read music, their training enabling them to pick up a sheet of music and perform a song at once like a studio musician.

She tends to use her voice like an instrument, as Billie Holiday approximates the sound of Louis Armstrong's trumpet. Occasionally she will do away with lyrics in favor of skat, which is Ella Fitzgerald's forte and a favorite caper for Sarah Vaughan. She may also syncopate musical phrases, throwing the stress of the music out of balance, as Carmen McRae does. The jazz singer is usually sure of her pitch, diction, and tempo.

Jazz blended with the blues to produce the style of Billie Holiday, whose major influences were Louis Armstrong and Bessie Smith. Her career began by chance while she desperately tried to find a job when faced with eviction; she was engaged as a singer in Harlem's Log Cabin on 133rd Street.

In the 1930s she made light, Satchmo-style musical jokes when she recorded with Benny Goodman and Teddy Wilson. Lester Young christened her Lady Day, and she appeared wearing a gardenia in her hair. The comedic touch was a hallmark that became more poignant as the years wore on. Personal unhappiness, hardships inflicted by race discrimination, the heroin habit that landed her in jail and caused her to be harassed by federal narcotics agents for the rest of her life took their toll.

She wrote a few songs, most notably "God Bless the Child," "Don't Explain," and "Billie's Blues." Toward the end of her life in the late fifties, there was still a wisp of the joking tone in her songs. Her voice had a wrecked timbre, trumpet vibrato, Satchmo's dirt and gravel on the bottom. Even though her voice sounded dry, threadbare in spots, the charm of the cajoling, confiding tone was hard to resist.

A technique copied by some of the worst singers in the business is her vibrato, that she herself used with taste so that it never seemed to be out of her control. One of her most enthralling facets as a singer was her choice of songs, such as the difficult "Strange Fruit," a song about the lynching of blacks in the South, and other material that could have been the most depressing collection of songs ever written, songs that should not be attempted by novices either to singing or to life since despair and depth are not synonymous; they unquestionably reflected her experience. She sang reflecting familiarity with heartbreak and pain, and a quizzical bewilderment that was almost numbness; songs about unrequited love: "The End of a Love Affair," "Glad to Be Unhappy," "You Don't Know What Love Is," "I'm a Fool to Want You." They were songs of elegance under duress.

At her deathbed in the summer of 1959 of complications leading from heroin addiction she was cornered by the authorities, who had found drugs in her home, and placed under arrest.

Billie Holiday tried to produce tones like Louis Armstrong's trumpet and Lester Young's tenor sax. Her rival Sarah Vaughan's vocal quality is nearer an oboe or a 'cello, with textures ranging from rough to velvety. Where Billie Holiday was witty, Sarah Vaughan is sassy. Her disregard for lyrics, which she often forgets, is a quirk she turns to good account by skat singing.

Like the singers of her generation, Sarah Vaughan began by singing with big bands, with Earl "Fatha" Hines and Billy Eckstine. She then went the pop route successfully with her sly versions of "Make Yourself Comfortable," "Whatever Lola Wants," and "Broken Hearted Melody." Possibly the only other vocalist she seriously listened to was the mistress of skat singing, Ella Fitzgerald, the paragon of jazz vocalists. Ella Fitzgerald, forever daubing at her sweat and tears with a hanky when she appears, has a lightly swinging style that makes her singing seem facile, and an affinity for the songs of Irving Berlin and Duke Ellington.

In the same class as Ella, Sarah, and Billie Holiday, Carmen McRae also has an instrumental approach to songs. As her voice thickened with time, her mature range developed chilling low notes.

Before Greenwich Village became a haven for the folk movement, it was a center for jazz clubs frequented by a similar class of serendipitous intelligentsia, but a decade older. Morgana King was among them, singing at the Old Bohemia and the Open Door. In her time, she also sang in the type of place where the boa constrictor almost choked the stripper in the act.

Morgana King's voice is liquid, pure, and sweet at the top of her four-octave range and tough at the bottom, a voice she produces with an ease that makes it seem as if she were humming to herself. Her free-form improvisations when she takes off from the melody of a song bear the trace of influences in the classical vein as well as jazz.

A tribute to Helen Morgan in 1955 was her first album. She shares the delicacy of attack with the torch singer, but differs in her choice of material because of the responsibility she feels in perpetuating the ideas found in songs:

I look for truth—you know, what's happening. The truth. Lyrics are most important, 'cause you can always work with the melody. But that message is so important, because those people are waiting for someone to say something. They want somebody to help them. When people are really disillusioned and depressed, they go home and listen to sounds, man.

For a while I really resented those downer messages performers were laying on people. They were really putting them on bummers, because they were making such heavy statements . . . I think there's another approach. It's a very big responsibility.

Music is going back to a kinder approach. You can program people through kindness, instead of that "You better listen or I'm putting a rod up your ass, man!" You don't need that—you really don't.

The jazz influence in pop has been a sobering one, giving the singer an awareness of technique and a paragon of craft to work toward. The newer jazz singers are usually remarkable stylists, as is Nancy Wilson, a singer of warmth and classic style connected with Cannonball Adderley who discovered her. Maxine Weldon is a newer singer with a wide range and sensitivity. Marlena Shaw is a different style of jazz-flavored cabaret entertainer with a limited voice, but with taste, feeling, and conviction.

31

The big bands of the forties swing era carried vocalists with them on the road, among them Helen O'Connell, Helen Forrest, and Margaret Whiting, who halted their careers when the big bands went out of fashion. There were those who, like Kate Smith, made their biggest impact fronting a big band on the radio. There were others who continued as solo performers, as did the late Dinah Washington, who sang with Lionel Hampton, then went to a recording career, where she remained on the rhythm and blues circuit till she was recognized by a pop audience. The distinctive catlike voice of "I Won't Cry Anymore" and "What a Diff'rence a Day Makes" found its echo in the style of her friend Diana Ross, whom she influenced.

There were harsh realities faced by early black singers on the road long after Bessie Smith had died when she was refused treatment at white hospitals. Billie Holiday was snubbed and refused service at restaurants when touring with Artie Shaw's all-white band.

The rigors of road life were not the only circumstances that were difficult for black singers; the film industry was no more enlightened than the weakest links in American society of its time. Lena Horne, who began performing with the all-black Noble Sissle band and sang with Charlie Barnet's band in 1940, did not bow to the pressures placed on her when she was discovered by Hollywood. To avoid racial complications, plans were made by MGM to promote her as another Carmen Miranda, a "Latin American Discovery." She refused, and was given roles in all-negro cast films, *Stormy Weather* and *Cabin in the Sky*. Her occasional songs in mixed cast films were shot so that they could be deleted for southern distribution. Her marriage to white bandleader Lennie Hayton also created pressures on her. Finally in the fifties she was blacklisted during the McCarthyite Communist witch hunts, and for seven years there was no work for her in television or in films.

A different factor eliminated Anita O'Day, who sang with Gene Krupa and Stan Kenton. She was jailed for possession of marijuana in 1953, an experience which catapulted her into heroin addiction from the time of her release till 1968.

The band singers changed drastically when the bands broke up. With recording technology and the record industry beginning to come into its own, and Hollywood promoting them in the brainless but appealing musicals of the fifties, women singers became independent performers. Of the younger singers, Doris Day and Peggy Lee came to their peak in that period.

Peggy Lee began as a band singer with Benny Goodman, and usually appears at supper club dates in a turquoise, pink, or other pastel colored satin gown, or a classic songstress' white-on-white beaded dress with chiffon panels.

The crooked smile, the polite come-on, the casual air is a matter of precise planning. Her aura of calm is brought on by a control of the variables in her stage performance, since she carries with her a looseleaf notebook of detailed notes on every show she has given during the past two decades. Songs, costumes, hand gestures, sidemen, and comments on the treatment are included for every show.

Morgana King is credited in part for bringing the Bossa Nova beat from Brazil in 1960, but before her, Peggy Lee introduced Latin rhythms to American music. She had used Latin rhythm earlier, but her impassioned reinterpretation of Richard Rodgers' "Lover" opened up the music scene:

> We had everything in "Lover," two, four, and six-eighths, everything mixed up. We had eight percussionists . . . There were thirty-seven or -eight men, and four singers that just went aaaa aaaa aaaa . . . It did start a resurgence of interest in music right then, because arrangers were having trouble thinking of new ideas, new ways to do things. This was a question of changing time values. At first Richard Rodgers said, "Oh, my little waltz, my little waltz!" (laughs)

He later used her version of "Lover" as an example of creative interpretation needed for a song's survival when lecturing at colleges.

She has written songs in collaboration with her husband, Dave Barbour, with Sonny Burke, Cy Coleman, Dave Grusin, Quincy Jones, Johnny Mandel, Victor Young, and others. Her best known was "Mañana," a charming piece, which in hindsight, from the social standards of the sixties, is a mildly presumptuous statement about the laziness of the Latinos: leaky roof, broken window to be fixed "mañana."

The real importance of the song was that it presented a new concept to the American music scene, that a singer is capable of writing and singing her own material successfully, and particularly that this ability was possessed by a woman. The latter fact was noted at the time by Jackie De Shannon, one of the earliest of the late sixties movement of women singer-performers in the United States.

As the grande dame of the pop world, Peggy Lee weathered the changing tastes of the pop audience and recaptured their imagination repeatedly by innovating, while the trends toppled her less venturesome contemporaries. While in 1958 the only solo females with any following were Connie Francis, teenaged Laurie London with a fluke religious recording that became popular, "He's Got the Whole World in His Hands," and Doris Day, Peggy Lee was present with "Fever."

Long after a singer's career is usually finished, she still contributes to popular music. Peggy Lee had recorded more than five hundred songs by the time she returned in 1969 with Jerry Lieber and Mike Stoller's "Is That All There Is" for which she won a Grammy award for best contemporary female vocal performance category against Brenda Lee, Jackie De Shannon, Dusty Springfield, Dionne Warwick, and Vikki Carr. "Is That All There Is" was a perfect marriage of material and interpreter.

She had been searching for a song that carried with it an identification for her own experience, a quality the song possessed:

> I knew I wanted to do it, immediately. I'd play it for people and they'd say, "That's weird, what does it mean?" And I'd say, "I'm not sure yet what that means, but there's something in it that I hear from 'way back someplace."
>
> It wouldn't let me sleep. I'd hear it over and over and over in my mind. At first, because I have a great sense of responsibility about lyrics, I didn't want to sing something that was hopeless or morbid, because my personal belief is that there is more, much more . . . It just happens that the song fit my life.

A totally different career resulted for Doris Day when she left the music scene after her beginnings with the Fred Waring and Bob Crosby bands for involvement in the film industry musicals of the fifties.

Her Ipana smile, her corn-fed good looks conjured up all that was good and pure in the girl-next-door image for the female vocalist, which she led in the fifties. Most of the positive image was a sappy one created by her roles in Warner Brothers musicals. She hit her stride in *Calamity Jane,* a tale of a competent woman, a sharpshootin' lass from the hills reduced to a sissy by Hollywood *love. Calamity Jane* altered the girl-next-door onus and supplied her with the 1954 hit record, "Secret Love."

The following year, the clean-cut athletic champion air was laid to rest for ae by her role in *Love Me or Leave Me* as Ruth Etting, the unhappy torch singer of the twenties. By then the gay Technicolor musicals were being replaced by biopics that beat the American work ethic drum and depressing slice-of-life drama films, and she sang less and less.

The overground hit parade of the fifties became an important indication of the nation's musical taste as the recording industry gained prominence. During the early part of the decade, a record usually held the top spot on the sales charts for several weeks. Later, the charts changed each week as more records were released and the number of recording artists grew.

The charts were shared by remnants from the jazz age and the popular radio singing trio, the Andrews Sisters, Dinah Shore's southern elegance, the novelty sound of Teresa Brewer, Eileen Barton singing "If I Knew You Were Comin' I'd 'Ave Baked a Cake."

There were the multiple-tracked overdubs of Les Paul and Mary Ford, the molten harmonies of Patti Page, "the singing rage," Rosemary Clooney, a heavy, comedic alto known for the clearest diction of all the pop singers, an expertness that tied her big voice to novelty dialect songs like "This Ole House" and "Botch-a-Me" although she was also capable of the tenderness of "Hey There." The voice of Kay Starr, originally a country style singer who had a riveting snarl in her throat, could be heard, and Vera Lynn singing "Auf Wiederseh'n, Sweetheart," her nibs, Miss Georgia Gibbs, giving her all in a passionate tango, "Kiss of Fire," and former band singer Kitty Kallen's pleading "Little Things Mean a Lot."

The simple perfection of Jo Stafford's "You Belong to Me" was really a call to escapism in foreign parts, part of an undercurrent that longed for faraway places during this period, as did a strain of songs in foreign languages. Joni James's pathetic "Why Don't You Believe Me" shared the air with the Chordettes' calliope styling of "Mister Sandman" and the almost religious sincerity of Doris Day's "Secret Love."

The young voices of Patience and Prudence singing "Tonight You Belong to Me" were harbingers for later girl groups. A different sound from the McGuire Sisters, who soon sang a cover version of the Moonglows' "Sincerely," or the old dreamy style of the Andrews Sisters, popular during the Second World War.

Cathy Carr's beseeching waltz to a cold lover, "Ivory Tower," and Gogi Grant's dramatic "The Wayward Wind" shared space with Silvana Mangano and Debbie Reynolds. As the sounds edged each other out, in 1958 there were no solo pop vocalists making any impact, with the exception of Connie Francis, and by the following year Della Reese, Dinah Washington, and Sarah Vaughan had captured the pop audience.

The stately pop singers of the fifties fell into characterizations of nobly poised insouciance; they were innocent or saucy, little sisters with something cute to say, done-wrong sweethearts of a type dear to the country genre, or sympathetic barmaids without the slatternly overtones that the later rock women acquired.

Of the little sister variety, Brenda Lee sang romantic ballads with countrified vigor. When she appeared at the Copacabana in New York she was eighteen years old and her show called for a burst of trade paper hyperbole from *Billboard,* which called her a teenaged Sophie Tucker. Later in her career she went country, but as a pop singer, she was one of the best, with "Sweet Nothin's," "I'm Sorry," "I Want to Be Wanted," and "All Alone Am I" challenging the primacy of Connie Francis in 1960.

A voice with a similar timbre but with less poignancy was Teresa Brewer's, whose songs were decorated with squeaks and squeals that fell on tempo and were in tune. A lively young voice that never really matured into a fuller texture stood her well for the 1950 "Music! Music! Music!" a rag tune that became an annoyance on the radio, and "Ricochet," another fast-paced gimmick. Her best record was a sensitively sung "Till I Waltz Again with You," worthy of Patti Page, and coming in on the coattails of the fad for heartbreak waltzes in the early part of the decade. Later in her career she became a country singer, as did Brenda Lee and Patti Page, the only refuge for the soft pop singers where their sentimentality was welcome, but none of them achieved, with the country audience, the acceptance they had had in the pop scene.

Kay Starr, one of the few singers to come out of the country field to sing with the big bands, Bob Crosby and Charlie Barnet, was of the more worldly persuasion among pop singers. Her most distinctive recording was "Wheel of Fortune," which she sang as if she were riding a roulette wheel. Evidently caught willy-nilly in its circular motion, she seems to draw nearer and farther away: "THE-e WHEE-eel O-of FOR-or-or-tune . . ."

Another of her literal interpretations of a lyric is her double tracking on "Side by Side," in which she sings a robust country harmony with herself, conjuring up a feeling of closeness as she and herself march down the road of life. In 1956 her version of "The Rock and Roll Waltz" was a clever idea to try a blend of the waltz appeal of Patti Page and the new genre rock 'n' roll which soon was to swallow up the girl singers.

An excellent singer at the start of the sixties was Timi Yuro, whose voice was in the deep range. Timi Yuro's tough "What's a Matter Baby" was a gut relative to the style of singing that LaVerne Baker and Etta James had developed in the rock 'n' roll camp.

Timi Yuro had a huge voice, but she was criticized for a dreadful stage manner. Reviewers urged that her expressions be toned down and reported that during an ill-fated engagement at the Copa, she hammed it up with her deep, husky voice by singing a baritone aria from Puccini's *I Pagliacci,* the stentorian "Vesti la giubba."

The most successful female recording artist of the fifties was Patti Page. Her version of "Tennessee Waltz" in 1951 was the second largest selling single record, surpassed only by Bing Crosby's standard "White Christmas."

No other female singer had as many hit records as did she. She sang as if the words melted into the melody, in a voice that was everything expected of a woman's voice, warm, flexible, pure, and a trifle sad. From the beginning of the 1950s till 1957 were the peak years for the bittersweet softie ballads she was known for. Appearing always in a white gown, she sang "I Went to Your Wedding," "That Doggie in the Window," "Allegheny Moon," "Old Cape Cod," and others.

At the same time as Les Paul and Mary Ford, she pioneered multiple tracking in the studio, and what began as an economy measure to fill out the harmony of "Confess" in 1948 when money was not available for backup singers became her trademark and a widely used recording technique of the fifties.

The greatest lead singer of a group in the big band era was Jo Stafford, who sang with Tommy Dorsey's band and at one time matched vibratos with Frank Sinatra in the Pied Pipers. She had the unusual capacity of singing on key. Like Kay Starr and Rosemary Clooney, she recorded a number of novelty dialect records, which tied her to ephemeral material, "Shrimp Boats," "A-Round the Corner," and "Jambalaya," though she had the sensitivity to sing "You Belong to Me," the worldliness for "Make Love to Me!" and the quasi-innocent suggestiveness that was the forte of Doris Day for the laid-back pillow drama "Teach Me Tonight."

In the late fifties rock 'n' roll era, there was a moment of trauma in 1957 when the Russian space probe Sputnik went up. An intellectual inferiority complex in the American awareness caused a surge of energy and a new respect for competence of any kind which took in cultural matters, and gave more importance to hardware such as instrumentals and beefy rhythms to the detriment of the female vocalist. Most female singers went unheard, with the exception of Connie Francis, who had gained popularity on the Dick Clark "American Bandstand" television show.

The most distinctive part of her style, which was sweet, warm, and sentimental, was a slight shiver when she let go of a note, a suggestion of a shudder as she descended the scale at the end of a phrase, releasing the syllable with fond regret. She glossed gently over "Who's Sorry Now?" "Everybody's Somebody's Fool," "Mama"—an Italianate gem of that heartrending theme—"Where the Boys Are"— and where indeed were they in March of 1961?—"Don't Break the Heart That Loves You," and others with similar sentiments were in her compass from 1958 to 1962, with her greatest emotional diapason a light, crooning lament.

There were other good singers who had limited commercial success; Jaye P. Morgan, a bubbly blonde who later had a complete change of image when she became a dramatic actress, Julie London, with a soft, weak alto voice, whose career consisted of "Cry Me a River," Felicia Sanders, a tasteful singer whose greatest impact was with "The Song from Moulin Rouge," the Singing Nun, Soeur Sourire from France, whose great success with "Dominique" at the end of 1963 caused her to doff her habit for a show business career that subsequently was not smiled upon by le bon Dieu. Caterina Valente, another international influence, a polyglot whose buoyant style traveled on the wave of internationalist feeling in the pop mode during the end of the fifties.

In a different class from the pop recording artists, whose base was the big bands, the radio recordings and films, were the performers who clove to an earlier tradition of live shows, cabaret and stage singing. Eartha Kitt was one of the most developed personalities in the supper clubs. She would begin her act among the tables, a pinpoint spotlight tracing her progress toward the stage, wearing what were then eye-popping outfits: a bright scarlet gown, or a leopard throw with a matching slinky floor-length dress split to the hip, or an ermine gown and floor-length cape trimmed with chinchilla.

Eartha, who had begun as a dancer in Paris with the Katherine Dunham company, played her feline flirtatious role with grandeur, sauntered onstage to sing from a chaise longue. Very boudoir.

Her torrid image overlaid with a sprinkle of frost, she sang "Santa Baby" in a languorous meow, addressing Santa Claus as a sugar daddy, enumerating the items on her opulent Christmas list: a convertible, a mink coat, Tiffany decorations for her tree.

At her most approachable, she appeared as an affable lioness, a creature not to be crossed, which is part of her piquancy as a performer. Eartha Kitt has one of the strongest and most consistent images of any female singer, a deluxe aura of sophistication, but the private person is another matter:

> I'm not interested in big mansions and big cars and big diamonds, even though I sing those kind of songs. You see, I only work in show business, I don't live in it, and neither do I think in it. Only

when I'm onstage or when I have to get an act together . . . But I never forget the feeling that you are trying to connect to that person, that audience . . .

People's feelings, my feelings, are connected with another human being's feelings, whether it's sorrow, happiness, a joke, tongue-in-cheek as everything I do mostly is, with the mink coats and the bijoux jusqu'ici et toutes les choses comme ça, it's fun.

I have a lot of fun being Eartha Kitt—nobody has more fun being Eartha Kitt than I do.

Another personality was Judy Garland, essentially a film actress known for her Metro-Goldwyn-Mayer musicals and boy-girl films with Mickey Rooney with a darker, self-destructive side to her personality which came to light in later years. Until her death in 1969 she was the reigning gay cult heroine, a favorite for transvestite acts, and possessed one of the unhappiest of female images.

It is a moot argument whether her unhappiness or her great talent were a stronger draw, but a gay cult does form around female performers who offer febrile, neurotic traits, and if any identification exists between gay sensibility and the less stable emotional elements ascribed to femininity, it is part of the helplessness both segments of the society feel at being pressed into passivity.

Like a luckless woman, a gay male may be mistreated by men, with even less recourse than women have to a sense of fair play in a man. Since society does not defend the feelings of homosexual partners, a man is even more liable to being emotionally exploited and betrayed than the historical helpless woman.

Judy Garland presented overblown emotionalism, portrayed a neurotic need for love and acceptance, and expressed a nostalgia for a never-never land where there was a place for her in "Over the Rainbow," a piece of material from *The Wizard of Oz* easily transformed into a gay metaphor signifying a world where the outcast is accepted, expressing a malaise with the world as it exists.

In upbeat moments of her stage shows, live appearances that took on the traits of cult rituals—one of the most auspicious was immortalized in the 1961 album *Judy at Carnegie Hall*—she was as jaunty as a waif on the road to Oz, the paradise identified with her. She took the microphone cord, and with carefree panache swung it casually over her shoulder. For heart-to-heart songs, such as "Born in a Trunk," she began seated at the edge of the stage, confiding in her audience. There was always the nostalgia theme, in "Swanee," "Blues in the Night," "The Man That Got Away," or a hint of coyness, singing "You Made Me Love You" with a break in her voice that never surfaced. Her timbre (the stageshow quack) and the emotional wobble in her voice (that always seemed near tears) were as distinctive as they were unmusical.

Judy Garland was not the only proponent of the stageshow quack. It was perfected beyond reprieve by Ethel Merman for her roles in *Annie Get Your Gun* and *Call Me Madam,* and found its way into the voices of many lesser singers. Even Barbra Streisand falls into it during moments of excess. Though it carries well beyond the proscenium arch, that timbre has an edge that even the normally affable critic Henry Pleasants found not only unforgettable but unforgivable when Streisand deployed it in the closing notes of "People" at her Central Park concert.

Streisand is the pop workhorse who continuously puts out new films and new records, offers a large, easily attacked target because she overextends herself; chutzpah, she doesn't know her place. There are few aspects of performing she will not attempt, and, more mud in the face of her detractors, succeed in. Her own opinion is that she is more actress than singer, and she has performed some convincing portraits of women in musical films: *Funny Girl,* based on the life of Fanny Brice, for which she won an Academy Award in 1969, and *Hello, Dolly!* as well as appearing in several nonsinging roles.

More than an actress or singer, she is a personality whose force makes her a leader. As a singer she can be moving, poignant, or embarrassing, but she does not take embarrassment upon herself; she has made it evident that there is no need to apologize for aspirations, a factor even her fiercest critics must respect. A fine voice compensates for her excesses, a voice that cannot be mistaken for anyone else's, even though she often takes her style wherever she finds it. It is a voice with more character and range than the singer whose material she appropriates.

Considered Brooklynese, lacking taste and class, ostentatious in her singing, costumes, and personal style, she gets occasional sniggers from the press. The press is required to report upon her. By sometimes designing her own gowns, she leaves herself open to comment. One of her dresses was found by Rex Reed to resemble a cut-up parachute dyed in Rit, while to Henry Pleasants it suggested a female Batman outfit.

Her singing melodrama was adjudged vulgar, but vulgarity is the essence of popular music and, vulgar or not, Barbra Streisand is both popular and musical. Popular music is the most accessible music; it is the expression of the masses, because it appeals to the most common denominator of a group of listeners. If vulgarity is the criterion for a pop singer, then she surely is at the top of her class. Vulgarity, with no overtones of crassness, is as essential to the pop genre as social concern is to folk, as dumb conviction is to teen. Where Barbra Streisand breaks down is when she reaches for "something better," for what is called by its adherents "serious" music, which is only a survival of an older genre from Europe. The only true failure she has encountered is in trying to be accepted into the classical music world.

Otherwise she has been honored in film, television, and recording: with an Oscar for her first film, *Funny Girl,* an Emmy for her first television special, "Color Me Barbra," vocalist Grammies in '63, '64, '65, '77, and one for songwriting in '77.

In those years there was little competition from other female vocalists. The other women did not seem to be taking themselves seriously in comparison with Streisand's efforts. Weighty contenders for the female vocalist award in the National Academy of Recording Arts and Sciences balloting were involved either in lightweight numbers, as was Peggy Lee, whose entry was Lieber-Stoller's "I'm a Woman," and Eydie Gormé, who sang Cynthia Weill and Barry Mann's "Blame It on the Bossa Nova," and the other candidates were exotics, Miriam Makeba and the Singing Nun. For the awards in '64 and '65, Streisand bested Petula Clark, Astrud Gilberto, and Nancy Wilson, each twice, and ran against Gale Garnett in '64, Jackie De Shannon in '65.

From the beginning of her career, Barbra Streisand's uncompromising attitude resulted in unprecedented deals, since she places a high price on her appearances. Her Las Vegas fee was $8,000 for

DIONNE WARWICK

BESSIE SMITH

NANCY WILSON

PATTI PAGE

ODETTA

JUDY COLLINS

BONNIE RAITT

MARY TRAVERS

JOAN BAEZ

one night at the end of 1963, then after five gold albums, two years later it rose to thirty-five grand. Even after her flop classical debut concert in September 1968 she set a million-dollar deal for Las Vegas performances, and by 1969 she was receiving a hundred thousand dollars a week.

In a profession where so many are underpaid, Barbra Streisand is a woman who knows her worth, to the extent of asking to be paid for placing her feet in wet concrete at the forecourt of Grauman's Chinese Theatre in Hollywood. How not to applaud this woman?

She revolutionized thinking about how a singer should look, since she has an unusual face by the old pop singer standards, never in her life having been cute. She was a non-Aryan, she was not a white, Anglo-Saxon Protestant, but had her own authentic beaked nose and wide mouth.

In the summer of 1963, when she drew the largest opening night crowd to the Cocoanut Grove in Los Angeles since Judy Garland, note well, the cult was forming for her, the initial reactions to her were surprise. She was an original, something new, prettier than expected. She had a broad Brooklyn accent, an overwhelming commitment to the songs, a quality that overcame the occasional brays, yelps, and bleats her style was prey to. With good diction and phrasing, by treating songs as if they were small dramatic vignettes, she sold them.

Streisand is a performer who works on a large dramatic scale. For Laura Nyro's "Stoney End" she supplied the grandeur and abandon that Nyro herself, when she wrote the song, was too timid to approach. But for Carole King's songs, Streisand is extravagant. When Streisand opens her mouth, an express train roars out. Carole King's transparent ditties are drowned in the gush of Streisand's emphatic emotions.

When she isn't caught mimicking the greats—Lena Horne, Peggy Lee, Ethel Merman, Judy Garland, or Joni Mitchell—she is one of them.

Starting at about the same time as Streisand, Dionne Warwick is another archetypal pop singer, and, like most black singers, her background is in gospel: "born and raised in the world of gospel, and will die in the world of gospel" she says. Along with members of her family she was one of the Drinkard Singers before her pop career began, and the sweetness of gospel surfaces whenever she sings pop.

She plied the professional music route by singing backup vocals and demo records, and while her personal friend Shirley Owens was sidelined by a pregnancy, Dionne Warwick took her place with the Shirelles at the Murray the K shows in the Brooklyn Fox. For six weeks she sang "Soldier Boy," "Mama Said," "Dedicated to the One I Love," and "Tonight's the Night," till the record that started her long collaboration with Burt Bacharach and Hal David was released, "Don't Make Me Over," and in 1962 she was signed to Scepter records, the company that Florence Greenberg had created for the Shirelles.

Gospel, backup vocals, girl group singing were her background, but that experience alone did not add up to one of the most original pop styles of the sixties. Dionne Warwick was trained at the Hartt College of Music in Connecticut, and also counts among her influences Johnny Mathis and Gladys Knight. But as the performer who gives the most valuable insights into her craft she chooses Lena Horne:

> It may not be the way she walks on a stage that I would do, but it's the approach she uses to get out there that I have used; the authority of knowing that's my stage and I'm going to go out there. She's the pro of all pros.

> Two ladies who I have to say have conditioned me, the way I look, the way I act, the things that I say, and that's basically the fundamentals of becoming an entertainer—that has been Lena and Marlene Dietrich. There has been an invaluable amount of experience I have gained from watching both of these ladies just handle an audience—and I mean handle them.

> They take them and ply them and pull them and push them and pinch them and squeeze 'em and slap 'em and do whatever they like with them until they're finished, and then they say okay, you've got yourselves again.

> That period of time when you're sitting in the audience you are absolutely theirs and nobody else's.

In her own performance, she carries herself regally, moves little and well; with hardly any more animation than a ladylike East Orange slop, she covers the stage from side to side. Her style is best in slow ballads, the definitive versions of Bacharach-David material that she has made hers. Her aplomb weakens fast numbers but strengthens gospel tunes, where the mood is exaltation. Dionne Warwick does not boogie, and her only flaws are some rare off-key notes.

The dynamics of her voice are its most outstanding feature; she finishes a line by letting it fade away. She finds her style has changed since her career began in the early sixties:

> I've gotten older, more experienced. I've utilized those things. My "style" has veered very far from where it was when I started singing. Just my method of approach has changed, matured drastically, because I've lived a lot longer . . . You do things and you go places and you see things and say things, and that becomes as much a part of you as your everyday life, and certainly it's reflected into everything that you do professionally.

Dionne Warwick has been the definitive interpreter of the songs of lyricist Hal David and composer Burt Bacharach, and considers herself fortunate, since she esteems Hal David as the perfect lyric writer:

> He writes about things that people want to hear about. They want to hear about their problems, and how to solve them; and he writes from the heart, and that's where it's at. That's what I'm all about, about living, and that's what he writes about—life.

Experience with lyrics that were meaningful to her set her standards for being involved with a song. She would refuse to sing lyrics that did not express her personal beliefs; an example would be material contrary to her religious tenets, or a popular song about a New Orleans hooker. Outside of stylistic considerations, the song would also not express her point of view:

> I wouldn't sing "Lady Marmelade" even if they guaranteed me the minute I opened my mouth that it was going to be platinum, be-

cause that's just not what I want to say . . . no way. Too easy to get permanent laryngitis—know what I mean?—No voicie, no songie! (laughs)

The idea that a pop singer would refuse to sing a song that would guarantee her a million sales is unusual in the commercially minded record industry. It implies that Dionne Warwick's contribution to popular music is of a piece; she stands behind every song she sings, and the listener can be reasonably sure that what is heard expresses the sensibility of the artist.

It takes confidence and a modicum of faith for an interpreter to take such a stand, but these are the factors that set off Dionne Warwick from a number of run-of-the-mill chirps who can be pressured into singing material they may disbelieve, even hating it and holding its sentiments in contempt, yet singing it repeatedly, and if it is successful, hearing it broadcast in their own voices as many as once in every half hour of top forty radio programming.

Fear of reprisals from irate producers, composers, lyricists, and other members of the recording industry would make a singer hesitate to reveal songs they've sung for meretricious reasons. A song may be a success and make the career of a singer; even though she may not be committed to it, it yet may catch the fancy of a large group of people. Pressures from producers and record executives is always strong to record certain material, particularly if the individual owns part of the publishing rights to the song.

A successful song may benefit a singer's career, and also limit it, since success with a certain type of song carries the idea that the singer will do well with similar material, which is true if the success is based on the nature of her style or personality, or her ability to express certain emotions more effectively than others.

The canaries, frails, and girl singers who were popular in the early fifties were pigeons for the pot shots of the rock 'n' roll of the midfifties, of Bill Haley, Elvis Presley, the Everly Brothers, Fats Domino, Chuck Berry, Jerry Lee Lewis; rock 'n' roll was a dance form dominated by strong rhythms. Their melodiousness was outdone by the quasi-operatic timbres of the new folk singers in the early sixties. The women known as girl singers were replaced by the teen genre singers who were real teenagers with girls' voices.

The largest blow to the solo female pop singer was the great popularity of the male instrumental groups carried into prominence by the British invasion. During the height of this movement, few women were heard at all, since the new singers were working in the obscurity of the new genres that were to break forth at the end of the sixties.

After the fad for rock groups settled, there were no new American pop singers. Pop singers became foreign to the American sensibility. Later again, there were more American women singing pop, but not until the fragments of the genres of American popular music began to coalesce once more into a cohesive American musical culture.

But the pop genre is a constant, the center of U.S. popular music. Eventually the outspoken rebels of the teen, rock, and soul genres, the clannish country genre partisans, the individualistic singer-songwriters, and the singers of disco will be the new pop singers of a later era.

III
FOLK MADONNAS

THE aura of a saint surrounds the female folk singer. She is a madonna. Adoring students hover around her playing guitars, dulcimers, and autoharps. She holds aloft the torch of freedom, shelters the oppressed behind her billowing robes, and with her foot she crushes the head of the snake Injustice. She reigned in the pantheon of female deities during the early sixties folk protest period.

The folk madonna was not a huntress like the teen girls or an amazon like the rock women. She was an earth goddess, a defender and cultivator. To some she appeared like an avenging fury, to others she was a crusader for a holy cause. Her virtue was simplicity: no artifice, no kitsch, no get-down funk.

Popular singers altered songs to accommodate their sex or changed lyrics or disqualified themselves from singing material that would not suit their role in life. But the folk madonna placed the song in the foreground and remained modestly detached from it. She could make any statement, if she delivered it in a ladylike way.

Folk blurred the male and female territorial distinctions that were strong in the pop music of the fifties. Since folk songs were period pieces detached from contemporary values, a singer could be a male narrator and sing songs with what were considered masculine attitudes.

That freedom allowed Odetta to sing sea chanties and ox-driver songs. Joan Baez could be the "Rake and Rambling Boy" of the broadside ballad who becomes a highwayman to steal for his wife. In "East Virginia" she sang of courting a fair pretty maiden.

After coyly altering "Man of Constant Sorrow" to "Maid of Constant Sorrow" Judy Collins went on to sing in the character of sailors and miners.

Mary Travers took that freedom with her in later years when she left the Peter, Paul and Mary trio to become a solo pop singer, and sang ballads that might have been meant for men. Buffy Sainte-Marie translated that freedom directly into her own songs.

Folk is the populist genre, the haven of liberals, freethinkers, and socialists. True to their belief in a classless society, the performer and the audience at a folk concert are one. Folk singers invite the crowd to sing with them as a gesture of unity, a way of breaking down the barriers between people.

Early in the folk movement, there was barely a difference between performer and listener in the coffeehouses. Anyone who mastered three chords on the guitar that was passed from hand to hand could sing the basic folk repertory. There was no mystification surrounding folk technique. The field was not restricted to technically proficient men, as was the case in rock. Excluding women or limiting their roles would have violated the unwritten laws of the folk movement.

A folk performer expected the audience to meet her halfway. The audience came to be enlightened, not to chat or dance. This encouragement and good will, and uncritical compassion for technical lapses, were not present in pop music circuits. A folk stylist would fail there because the pop audience does not participate in the performance. The ideas in folk songs are usually dated, topical, or concerned with political or social issues. The touch of reality is not welcomed in the carefree atmosphere of pop supper clubs where glamour and tinsel are the usual fare. On television, another pop stronghold, folk singers were in bad odor for their attacks on the government, and their demands for social justice.

The importance of folk songs lay in their lyrics. All the passion of the genre lies there. The songs are reports of sorrows, crimes, and derring-do set to a convenient melody with no great care to suit the mood of the tune to the lyrics. Words are in the foreground, not obscured by the action of the music.

After the meaningless chants of fifties rock 'n' roll and pop banalities, folk songs were the key to a world of truth and beauty by comparison. To carry the message of the lyrics, vocals were controlled and diction was precise, which gave the folk singer an air of detachment. A singer's personality always deferred to the lyrics.

Folk took the idea of rebellion from the teen genre and transformed it. The object of dissatisfaction was no longer the parents, a notion that could dissipate with time. The entire social and political system had to be changed.

Though folk bears resemblances to country and shares common sources, folk is the polar opposite of country. The folk madonna is a leader, Joan of Arc. The country queen is the keeper of the castle. Country is rural, folk is urban. Folk expresses middle-class liberal ideals, while country has elements of the lumpen working class proletariat. Country is regional music from the South and Midwest of the United States, while folk chooses from any ethnic tradition.

The folk genre is distinctly American. Britain had skiffle groups during the same time period, similar to the U.S. jug bands, but they did not have the politically engaged folk protest movement that was raised by the inner conflicts in the United States. Since the folk genre was a training ground for singers who wrote their own material, lack of a folk movement put Britain at a disadvantage when the popular music scene was taken over by singer-songwriters at the start of the seventies.

Folk singers traced their lineage from the medieval troubadours and, like the bygone itinerant musicians, their songs were an oral news medium. Since it is difficult to report without judging, topical songs became songs of protest.

Folk changed from pretty legends to songs of social concern and then to protest. There were songs that assigned guilt, pointed out abuses of power, snarled in righteous indignation. Folk did not beat its own breast as country does. Folk was judgmental, country is penitent. The country lyric throws the narrator at the mercy of "honey" or "Lord" with all humility. The folk lyric is underscored with pride.

With pride comes princely noblesse oblige. Since it claims cousin to the wandering minstrels of the Middle Ages, it subscribes to a chivalrous code of honor. In folk's knightly code, the strong must temper their power with virtue: they must aid the downtrodden, protect the weak, and champion the righteous. Folk is the crusading genre.

New York's Greenwich Village was the most active folk center where the main folk revival took place in a triangle bounded by Washington Square on the north, Bleecker Street on the south, and Sheridan Square on the west. More people gathered around the dry fountain at Washington Square each weekend, bringing guitars, banjos, bongo drums, and songs. When police clamped down on their noise, the folk singers were forced into the back rooms of coffee shops like the Caricature and the Folklore Center and Kent Sidon's guitar shop on Macdougal Street.

Clubs with cabaret licenses set up hootenannies: Gerde's Folk City, the Gaslight Café, the Bitter End. Later in the full decadence of the folk cycle the Café Bizarre and the Café Wha? opened. Folk clubs opened in every major city. San Francisco had the hungry i, Chicago had the Gate of Horn, Boston had the Golden Vanity. They created a subdued continental atmosphere by a combination of espresso coffee, mulled cider, and candles stuck into Chianti bottles.

One of the first folk singers to become prominent in the folk movement of the late fifties was Odetta, who has a distinctive voice even for the folk genre, which is noted for the prettiest voices in popular music. Odetta's voice is unmistakable. On top she has exquisite highs, jazzy, ethereal tones like Morgana King. Her lower register plummets to a female baritone unmatched for its strength by any popular singer's voice.

To any artist who ever sang folk, Odetta was a touchstone, an inspiration to women singers, a bulwark against the fey style of female warbling. Odetta's bellow, her whanging guitar, her cast-iron timbre were a welcome change from the dulcet pop of the late fifties. When

Janis Joplin first stood up to sing at a party, it was no accident that she rolled out an imitation of Odetta's huge "Take This Hammer" voice. Grace Slick, who had no female models in the rock genre, counts Odetta as an important singer in her background.

Odetta was recording in 1956 when she came from Los Angeles to join the folk movement in New York's Greenwich Village clubs, after having played in San Francisco's Tin Angel. She helped popularize the genre by appearing at the Newport Folk Festivals and Harry Belafonte's television show.

Unlike the later folk madonnas, she was a trained singer with a degree in music and musical comedy. She suffered setbacks when protest overtook folk music in the early sixties, and she also did not fit the stereotype of the folk madonna that caught the audience's imagination.

Even though it was made up of young liberals, the folk audience had strict dogmas; the folk purists were as parochial as any genre snobs. In their zeal for authenticity, they set standards of indigence that performers with any ambition could not meet. Odetta was no Moms Mabley, and she would not cater to folk pretensions:

> We're trained in stereotypes. I know there have been an awful lot of people who have been disappointed with me because I didn't have runover heels and my slip hanging down in front of my dress . . . I figure that's their problem.

Odetta sang negro spirituals, "Joshua Fit the Battle of Jericho," "He's Got the Whole World in His Hands," "What Month Was Jesus Born In," a repertory that fell into disrepute when black consciousness was at its height in the late sixties.

Since she was of an earlier generation, her songs of social consciousness were songs of concern, not protest or revolution. She chose from material available at the time on issues such as the inhuman conditions on southern chain gangs, the labor-management struggles, the mistreatment of blacks.

The ideas in "All the Pretty Little Horses" were shocking. The lullaby took the point of view of a black slave who nurses her mistress' baby while her own infant lies neglected in a field, prey to insects and crying. It portrayed slavery in basic terms, with a resigned humility that cried out to be vindicated.

Mary Travers, Peter Yarrow, and Paul Stookey, combined in the folk trio Peter, Paul and Mary, made their debut before the exposed brick wall at the Bitter End Café in 1961. They were brought together by their manager, Albert Grossman, who also led the careers of Odetta, Dylan, Janis Joplin, and others, and who managed the Newport Folk Festivals.

To the folk purists. of Macdougal Street, Peter, Paul and Mary were plasticized popularizers of folk style who sang ersatz Appalachian and Child ballads written by Paul Stookey and Peter Yarrow. The trio displayed streamlined good looks and a polished vocal style. When they met with commercial success, the street's opinion of them was confirmed.

When she was part of the trio, Mary's hard-edged alto was offset by the harmonies of Peter and Paul. Her voice alone is flat, strident, and unwieldy. At a time when folk music could have floundered in sweetness, Mary's raging energy powered the songs. She forged ahead of the beat, seizing the initiative while the two men's voices filled out the background.

Peter, Paul and Mary had their greatest success from 1962 to 1967. They began with Pete Seeger's socially conscious "If I Had a Hammer," and took a side trip with Peter Yarrow's "Puff the Magic Dragon" a song about a boy's imaginary friend that was interpreted as a marijuana pipe dream by the new drug culture. In the fall of 1963 they sang Bob Dylan's "Blowin' in the Wind," a song that became a rallying cry for the antiwar movement. "Don't Think Twice," another Dylan song, followed. They slid off with a brief stab at the contemporary market, "I Dig Rock 'n' Roll Music" in 1967.

By then the rock genre had taken over protest, and was speaking of revolution with a force that folk could not muster; its gentle blandishments could not compete.

Peter, Paul and Mary were active in the student peace movement, appearing at the Washington Monument with Martin Luther King and supporting John F. Kennedy and Senator Eugene McCarthy for the presidency.

They remained together through the hard rock period in the late sixties, although their folk approach was outflanked by the sophisticated harmonies of the Mamas and Papas. The mellow tunefulness of Cass Elliot's alto helped eclipse Mary Travers' sound in 1966.

In 1970 Mary Travers went solo. By then Carole King was surfacing as a solo artist, as was Cass Elliot. Mary Travers could not make the transition into the seventies because she neither wrote her own material like Carole King, nor had she developed a strong personal identity as a singer, as Cass Elliot had.

Writing became a survival skill for singers in the early seventies. Buffy Sainte-Marie was a songwriter at the outset, but Joan Baez and Judy Collins learned to write. Odetta and Mary Travers, major figures in the early period, did poorly during the singer-songwriter phase. While their influence waned, the career of Joan Baez bloomed.

Baez is the compleat folk madonna. The fantasy follows her even as she dances the Wah-tusi in discothèques, or croons "Cry Me a River" or "Earth Angel." It is considered suspect by right-wingers, it is satirized by the *National Lampoon,* it is no less a source of amusement to herself:

> . . . that image people have of me, sitting crosslegged on the railroad tracks waiting for a train to run me over, holding a pot of organic honey.

Her music is occasionally slapdash. She may confound lyrics, allow commonplace arrangements to be cast around her voice, and perform with no frills, as none of the other folk-based performers have done since the early times, alone onstage with a guitar, a spartan minimum for the more elaborate staging of the seventies. Her greatest fault, as she acknowledges, is that music is not her central concern:

> I've never been fair to my music. I've always felt for some guilt reasons that I had to put it in second place and go on doing everything else in the first place.

Joan Baez's voice is the finest in folk music. The thin reedy soprano she wielded at the early Newport Folk Festivals became warmer and richer with age:

My voice has changed since I was fifteen years old, approximately lowering a full octave. It's much fuller. It's developed a funny little crack . . . I always thought that little sound came from smoking or whiskey, but I don't do either, so I think it may come from twenty years of singing.

When she began, her upper range was a piercing soprano distinct from the rest of her voice. Her habit of whooping to a high note divested anyone of the delusion that her voice had ever been trained. She had an affected vibrato that sounded as if she were being shaken by the neck. Later her voice knit together smoothly, and she controlled her vocalisms. Her own opinion that as a singer she is the best cannot be denied. She may be criticized for lacking commitment to her music, but her commitments are elsewhere.

More than any other popular singer of her stature, she has involved her life and her career in political issues. She believes that a performer's political, moral, and ethical leadership is partly an illusion. An audience converted by her song will find another faith moments later with another singer, another song. Her personal leadership is not her bid for immortality:

Hopefully, no one will have to remember me, but if anything is done, if I contribute anything—it'll be there—something that meant something to someone.

She could not be dismissed as a political force. Her rhetoric was measured, her tone reasonable. Groups tried to humiliate her only to cover themselves with ridicule. Jailed at the Santa Rita Prison with her mother and sister Mimi Fariña during a draft demonstration in 1967, she turned the stay into a consciousness-raising session. The three women were an embarrassment to the penal system, which discharged them prematurely, claiming that their rehabilitation had been accomplished.

When in the summer of 1967 the Daughters of the American Revolution decided to penalize her for what they regarded as "unpatriotic activities" by not allowing her to perform in Constitution Hall, a 3,800-seat hall which they control, she held a free concert at the base of the Washington Monument for a crowd of thirty thousand.

Less direct means of checking her activities had to be found by the government, whose war policies she flouted openly, particularly since she based her war resistance on her Quaker religious principles.

As a symbol of the peace movement, she could only be pressured when she was isolated from her followers. While she toured Japan, the Japanese press protested that the CIA had threatened to refuse her Japanese interpreter any future U.S. entry visas unless her political remarks were toned down or mistranslated.

When she refused to pay the portion of her income tax that would go to finance the war in Vietnam, an amount reflected from the federal budget as 60 per cent in 1963, that escalated to 80 per cent toward the end of the involvement, the Internal Revenue Service attached her bank account, and claimed her house and car.

Her most direct confrontation with the United States Government came while she was visiting North Vietnam. The U. S. Air Force held an eleven-day bombing attack while she was there.

When she returned from Hanoi, shattered, she tried to share the harrowing experience by recording tapes from the Hanoi bombing on one side of her album *Where Are You Now My Son*. The record was not successful.

The press found a more fascinating revelation. When she mentioned in an interview after her return that she had had a relationship with another woman, the story was seized. Negative responses came unsigned, from the nebulous "stamp out Communism" fringe with envelopes that bore the imprint of a snake twirling around the American flag, choking it.

The positive response was touching; groups wrote and thanked her for her support.

The furore did not undermine her madonna status. Since she was not running scared, she braved the controversy, refusing to discuss her private life while the important issues she stood for were ignored; bodies still floated down the Mekong delta.

She consistently steered the press toward her social and political concerns while it would have preferred stories about her liaison with Bob Dylan, her marriage to antiwar activist David Harris, the birth of their son while Harris served time for draft resistance, and their divorce soon after his release.

The causes she stood for read like a catalogue of the oppressions of America. Her Quaker beliefs tempered with Ghandian nonviolence involved her in social and political issues: southern school desegregation, the movement to end the war in Vietnam, supporting Cesar Chavez and the striking United Farm Workers union, resisting compulsory military service, protesting capital punishment, supporting the Greek resistance movement before the fall of the military junta in that country, and supporting the homeless Chinese boat people. She founded the Institute for the Study of Non-Violence in Carmel, her home community in California, and joined Amnesty International, an organization formed to abolish the torture of political prisoners.

An extension of her resistance to arbitrary power is the stand against large corporate profits made at the expense of individuals. She applies this principle to herself, considering it indecent to pile up capital while many people go hungry.

Her audience felt the results directly. In 1969 she reduced the admission price of her concerts to the lowest feasible amount. The low figure benefited the majority of her audience, who were either students or not particularly affluent. Charging one admission price to all allowed those who arrived early to sit closer to the stage. Usually the richer members of an audience buy the better seats, and they were not necessarily the group most interested in her music.

Joan Baez is less sure of her writing than she is of her singing or her politics. Her writing first came to light in her fanciful 1968 autobiography, *Daybreak,* a densely written collection of autobiographical vignettes.

Daybreak is set in various styles, too exquisite an ornamental style with flaccid Oriental imagery like Kahlil Gibran or Rabindranath Tagore: "My life is a crystal teardrop." Other passages are confessional or reportorial. The warmest passage is a pleasant portrait of her mother at the Santa Rita Prison among the inmates.

Her songs are an extension of this autobiography. The source of her writing is passion:

> Whether it's passion that I'm missing, or passion that I'm involved in, or political passion . . . "Bangladesh" was all written from one

italic headline in *Newsweek* about Bangladesh. I wrote it in a day and a half. Another one would take a week.

"Bangladesh," the story of army officers in that country who called for volunteer blood donors, then drained every drop of blood from their bodies, is one of the most harrowing songs of protest she has written. Her audience was as unprepared for it as they were for her Hanoi experiences. The ugliness of its topic is repellent. Despite its pretty melody, "Bangladesh" only succeeds in numbing the sensibilities of its listeners.

The most often requested of her songs is the sultry "Love Song to a Stranger," two days of an affair that unrolls in a lilting waltz tempo. Though it is a glowing account, it isn't the song of a woman of reckless abandon. No sooner does she threaten to go careening off on a flight of torrid emotion than she checks herself, and transforms the feeling into elegant lust. Another song in that exquisite style is "Diamonds and Rust."

The sentimentality that opens her poetry to attack is one of its most endearing traits. She turns a piquant wit on herself in reaction to the supposed inviolability of the "madonna" and "the girl on the half-shell." The madonna, she tells a lover, "was yours for free" in "Diamonds and Rust," the nostalgic ode to an old love affair.

Where she once urged Bob Dylan, for pity's sake, to rejoin the movement in "For Bobby," she later chastised herself for self-righteousness in her attempt to judge his choices, "Winds of the Old Days."

Buffy Sainte-Marie made her first impact on the folk scene of the early sixties at a guest night hootenanny at the Greenwich Village Gaslight Café. She sang folk songs, but finding their subject matter limited, she wrote her own, which made her a suspicious quantity among the folk purists of Macdougal Street and the Newport Festival. They also found it odd that she wore high heels and tight dresses while the mode tended toward sacks and sandals. It was a characteristic of her personal style to be unconventional even in the unconventional confines of a cult.

In any group of Buffy songs there are decorous waltzes, lyrical efflorescences weighted with imagery which does not exclude an occasional glimpse of a steel mind. Her French style torchers have all the gripping qualities of that superannuated mode, combined with unconventional love song lyrics. Other love songs are warmly sentimental, with haughty and forbidding undercurrents. One quality they all have in common is their lively tension.

Buffy's songs have a variety that makes them seem written by women from different backgrounds:

"No One Told Me," from *Quiet Places,* is lush—too lush for the seventies. It's only when you have a certain feeling that you can listen to that song. Most people will say to themselves, "I'm too tough for that!" It's a French style song . . . A lot of my songs are French. "Until It's Time for You to Go," the music is French.

Her identity changes with each song. The womanly ballad singer of "Until It's Time for You to Go," "All Around the World" is not the same woman who sings "Now That the Buffalo's Gone" and "My Country 'Tis of Thy People You're Dying" in a hacksaw tremolo.

The corn row vibrato warbles through country style rockers like "Piney Wood Hills" and "Cripple Creek" and soars in "Tall Trees in Georgia" and lilts in the minuet of "Carousel."

Her voice is younger when she sings "Sweet Little Vera," a song about a thirteen-year-old groupie, than when she sings "Generation," a song about the new generation of the American Indians. Gutsy, gelatinous, piercing timbres carry her songs in different directions:

Each song of mine comes from the same place but goes in a different direction . . . Some of the music I write is pitched very low, to the thirteen-year-old in me. It's dumb: "Sweet Little Vera." A lot of people have a hard time putting together the fact that anyone who would think so strongly and clearly about something like "My Country 'Tis of Thy People You're Dying" or "The Universal Soldier" or "Now That the Buffalo's Gone" could possibly have the audacity to have a heart inside, and write "Until It's Time for You to Go," let alone "Sweet Little Vera."

They wonder if one side must be fake, if the other side were genuine, not realizing that all of us are this way.

The most carping criticism comes from the genre loyalists whose boundaries she crosses. The pop audience has little patience with a writer of songs of social concern. They accept her ballads. The folk-protest group disdain the ballads but applaud her antiwar and socially conscious songs, "Now That the Buffalo's Gone," "My Country 'Tis of Thy People You're Dying," and "Suffer the Little Children." She is unacceptable to the country audience personally because of her antiwar stand, but her "Piney Wood Hills" was brought into the country audience by Bobby Bare in 1967. Glen Campbell, Bobby Darin, Donovan, and Elvis Presley took her songs beyond the folk audience.

The self-assured lust she expresses in "97 Men in This Here Town (would give a half a grand in silver just to follow me down)" and the broadly comic "Don't Call Me Honey When Your Mother's Around" delivered in honky tonk country style was a goodtime Buffy that gave her serious followers pause but was consistent within herself:

Our multiplicity is one of the better mutations of the human race. Multiplicity is a joy and a privilege . . .

A lot of people are afraid that it's sick, or betraying or lying, to develop all of yourselves. In my music, the same person who wrote "My Country 'Tis of Thy People You're Dying" and "Suffer the Little Children" and "Native North American Child," that person split also into the one who wrote "Sweet Little Vera" and "She Used to Want to Be a Ballerina."

While exploring other styles of writing and more personal themes, she dealt a blow to the folk purists when she wrote the pop standard "Until It's Time for You to Go" in 1965. It passed into the mainstream of pop veiled in the decorous waltz of its melody. Alarms were not sounded by anyone who realized that the lyrics held a message that was new to pop music; equal partnership between lovers with no promises of permanence.

It was love without illusion, a temporary arrangement between equals with their own lives to fulfill. It is indeed a woman's song, written to be sung by a woman, even though men did not hesitate to sing it.

Women's myths and roles as wives, mothers, sisters, and lovers are amply stated in popular songs. Buffy's intent, when writing songs from a female point of view, was to create material devoid of conventional female masochism. One step was the equal relationship of "Until It's Time for You to Go."

Buffy was shunned by the majority outside folk circles, as were most folk singers, for antiwar sentiments. "The Universal Soldier," a moving indictment of war, was banned from the air for two years. Her pro-Indian stand was equally unpopular.

Although she champions her heritage in the cause of social justice for American Indians, she speaks as a performer, not as a politician. Her songs express her views directly, so that she does not repeat her statements in speeches.

For different reasons than Joan Baez or Judy Collins, she feels that the presence of a celebrity at a political event detracts from the validity of the issues by drawing attention to the personality. The issues are paramount. Indigence, unemployment, and infant mortality among Indian tribes in America are abnormally high, along with the highest suicide rate of any group of people. She will appear at benefit concerts and support the native American movement financially.

There are constant battles to insure native American rights and enforce treaties. She has funded the Nihewan Foundation, a group she started to provide scholarships for Indian students of law, and she formed the Native North American Women's Association, a group that sponsors Indian arts projects. But she does not consider her Indian heritage an exotic jewel in her performer's diadem, another source of fascination to be bartered for applause.

Buffy Sainte-Marie developed the greatest artistic scope of all her contemporaries, from the righteous indignation of the protest songs to the velvety romanticism of her ballads, and beyond, to the unexpected silliness of her rock 'n' roll ditties. She refers to her songs as marks of passing through the carnival midway of life: "bruises, scars, lipstick smooches, and cotton candy stains."

A great contrast in her views on death sets her apart from the social and political concern of the other folk artists:

> I used to think I could heal anyone, or that anyone was healable.
> But that was just a wish. I don't think life is a compulsory art. Sui-

cide is a valid option. Although I am a survivor, some people would prefer not to, and I don't think they should be forced to hang around . . . I think death is one of our finer options. It's like love. It can be abused, it can be ennobled.

Duality, contradiction, and isolation are characteristics of Buffy as a person that crop up in her work. Mysterious origins and an unusual background heighten her mystique. Born in 1941 at the Piapot Cree reservation in Canada's Saskatchewan province, she was adopted by Albert and Winifred Sainte-Marie, who named her Beverly and raised her in Maine and Massachusetts. Her stepmother was part Mic-Mac Indian, half bred like Buffy herself:

I'm a half breed. I don't know what the rest is . . . I was raised loosely in touch with the people I came from, but I never knew my parents. I know a lot of my relatives. I know I'm half Cree and half something else, I keep speculating on what. It depends on how I'm feeling that day. My tribe would come from the plains to Ontario every summer, and we'd all meet.

While at the University of Massachusetts, she studied Oriental philosophy and sang for five dollars an evening at off-campus coffeehouses. After graduation she appeared in the Greenwich Village coffeehouse circuit: the Bitter End, the Gaslight, and Gerde's Folk City.

She makes a distinction for herself as a performer. She is not a musician, she is an artist. She possesses a basic folk technique on the guitar, and does not read music. She composes it.

She plays the mouth bow, an Indian instrument that combines the attributes of the Jew's harp, the musical saw, and the wah-wah pedal of an electric guitar. It is a simple instrument made with a stick and a string, after an expedition to the countryside to find a proper stick:

I make a lot of them. When one breaks I make another one. This one's guava. It took me five hours to find this right stick. I had to go out with a machete into this pasture, crawl over the barbed wire.

Here's a herd of cows and horses looking at me—they don't even like the idea of me being in their pasture . . . You have to get one that's just the perfect bend, because the bend is curved by the wind, and by the way the sun sets in relation to where the tree grows. You have to get one that's curved in the right way, because the string isn't holding the curve. The flexibility is important. Then I put any string I want on it, big ones, little ones, all different sizes.

At the end of an eight-year stint with her first record label, Vanguard, an association that resulted in an artistic stalemate ostensibly between the company's folk leanings and the development of her music beyond that genre, she joined MCA for one album, *Buffy,* that fetched the strongest blow to the folk purist's sensibilities that they had borne since Joan Baez's return from Hanoi.

Buffy was photographed laughing on the album cover, giving a cub scout salute, wearing a bandleader's jacket that was open to expose one breast. She had shucked her demure madonna robes and thrown them in the faces of her followers; madonna gone tart.

Critics and clergy claimed she had cast her integrity to the winds. They might as well have tried fitting a loincloth to an offending landscape. Buffy was unrepentant. Her reply was a giggle.

When Sears Roebuck took the record off its racks, Rick Frio, head of MCA's marketing arm, sent instructions: "Put a pastie on the boob."

Buffy was destroying one stereotype with another. The bared breast represented her own right to her body as a woman, and the right to sexuality as an Indian.

Buffy's penchant for flashy costume was evident in her first sorties in Greenwich Village. That was not the facet of her talent that gained her the imagination of her audience, which regarded it with suspicion since they had rejected the discipline of costume.

Costumes, makeup, and glitter are reserved to women, transvestites, and performers. It is an art form, and its canvas is a human being. Buffy creates fantasies of herself in feathers and silks, although warpaint might have met with greater approval among the purists. The fantasy image is a performer's discipline; at times it is a form of bondage. But it is for a purpose. A performance is a ritual to exorcise the demons of the human spirit.

When feminine finery is used by choice, it is a freedom. The same woman who goes through the fields with a machete wears a maribou feather coat and paints her toenails with wisteria sparkle.

The softness, the refinement, and the weaknesses of the folk genre are combined in Judy Collins. The simple elegance of classical proportion orders her singing style. It is unadorned and stark as American Puritan.

Her voice is exemplary, it is free from the nasty excess of early Baez's high hoots, the uncontrolled warble of Buffy, without Odetta's beefy punch or Travers' flat honk. Her voice has an even texture that does not thin out or strain at any level. Though lacking Buffy's intensity, Joan Baez's heat, and Mary Travers' brittleness, she is the greatest diseuse of all the folk singers.

Although her voice can be flavorless, she is ultimately a theatrical singer. She has a quality of phrasing that makes her the best interpreter of songs with limited melodies such as those of poet-novelist Leonard Cohen ("Suzanne"), which she has interpreted definitively. She is also excellent with Jacques Brel, Randy Newman, Brecht-Weill, Dylan, Joni Mitchell's thoughtful sophistries, and Sondheim.

Her versions of poetically styled songs like the pretty setting of Yeats's "Golden Apples of the Sun," Sandy Denny's "Who Knows Where the Time Goes," and the dramatic "Marat/Sade" set her style in a direction that suited her personality.

As a thirteen-year-old she was destined for a concert pianist's career, since she was then adept enough at that instrument to make her debut playing a Mozart piano concerto with the Denver Symphony Orchestra.

Although she decided that she was temperamentally unsuited to the discipline, the classical background affects her approach to popular forms. That training left her with one of the finest pianistic touches in popular music. She has an affinity for European pop composers, themselves rooted in classical styles.

The tastefulness of a classical background is reflected in her concert style, from the simple flowing dresses she wears to the air of polite formality when performing. Unfortunately, the main attribute of good taste is that it is predictable. It works against her when she needs gusto and fire, keeping her on the middle course of vaguely mauve sentimentality. She sings through a rosy haze that prettifies every harsh angle; sorrow becomes wistfulness, anger becomes reproach. Emotional implications of a song are thrown away for fear of exaggerating them.

The impressionistic lightness Judy Collins attains depends on maintaining distance from disturbing emotions. Her placid style won't stretch for emotions that ladies have been untaught to express.

Collins did not change her style to go with the times for the sake of maintaining an audience. Although she was not strong enough to lead any trend, particularly the trend to classicism, a move the mass of the pop audience balked at, she did not follow fads.

At the start of her career she sang sea chanteys, old songs of political concern from the folk repertory, a few spirituals like the rest of the folk madonnas.

Her choice of material is one of her most valuable contributions to popular music. She expanded the pop repertory by popularizing songwriters like Jacques Brel, Joni Mitchell, Leonard Cohen, and opened options for a wider choice of styles by bringing out the delicate songs of Mitchell and Sandy Denny.

As she draws further from the folk influence, her choice of material reflects influence from dramatic sources, show tunes from the new style Broadway musicals, *Marat/Sade,* Stephen Sondheim. On a standard ballad, she is exquisite. She sells it with the schmaltz of a torcher draped over the piano in a Bogie film, flicking ashes on the folk madonna's broken halo.

By 1966 she had hit her stride in popular music. Pressure for singers to write their own material was growing at the time, and she wrote her first song, "Since You Asked." She began writing comparatively late, and averages one song per year, hardly a prolific output.

The natural comparison falls between Collins and Baez, since both are exquisite singers, politically engaged, and not overly prolific writers. Baez writes more sensually, with darker, more emotional topics. She is more direct than Collins, who writes in metaphors.

Collins goes for lightness. Her Gothic style lyrics in "Secret Gardens of the Heart" are arty. There are unbearably lax spots in her songs where melody drags lyric around by the nose.

It would be unlikely for anyone not already established to get by with as sweepingly corny a song as "Albatross" and expect it to be performed. It is heavily encrusted with images, and floats in an atmosphere as murky as the moors in a Brontë novel.

"Albatross" fulfills all the conventional notions of what female writing should be, save one. The woman in the song feels she is trapped in a design.

Her songs do not reflect political concern, she chooses from other writers to express her political leanings. At the beginning of her career she campaigned for the southern blacks' voter registration and equal rights. She supported prison reform, and Senator George McGovern's try for the presidency. She was jailed in 1972 while protesting the Vietnam war, and visited Paris to meet with the delegations at the Vietnam peace talks.

Later she withdrew from protest movements and changed her style of political involvement. Singing to the already convinced at rallies was an action she considered preachy, divisive, and not expressing any emotional depth. The concert was only a means of bonding a group together briefly in a union that falls apart after the performance. A show is a spell she casts; it does not change an individual's life dramatically afterward. She considers politics in its lowest terms the relationship of love or hate between two people, a microcosm of the state of the world.

From the Italian community in Greenwich Village, Maria Muldaur crossed into the coffeehouse folk culture by becoming a member of the Jim Kweskin jug band, a group managed by Albert Grossman.

She might have become part of the teen girl group phenomenon. At sixteen, she haunted the Brill building with her Hunter High School group, the Cashmeres, who wore ponytails and matching outfits like the Shangri-Las or the Crystals. A deal was pending with Artie Butler and Gone records when:

> My mother came screaming into the studio that she wasn't going to let *her* daughter become a white slave and that was it . . . total heartbreak, but now I thank her because I could have just gone down the sleazy trail behind JoAnn Campbell.

The Jim Kweskin jug band, exponents of a folk style that was an offshoot from folk that coexisted on the same streets with the Child ballads and other laments, were popular at Village hoots, colleges, and television's folk music program, "Hootenanny."

For five years with the jug band, Maria Muldaur stayed in the background, carrying her daughter Jenny on the road in her tote-a-tot and nursing her between sets. She emerged once with Jerry Lieber-Mike Stoller's "I'm a Woman."

The original version was Peggy Lee's, but Maria's was definitive for its jaunty exuberance. The song was a charming fable, a catalogue of a super materfamilias' virtues that had her wash a scout troop's entire collection of socks and shirts and had them pressed and starched in an instant. Only because she is a woman, she can accomplish dozens of household tasks in a jiffy. The song was a charming novelty with the appeal of tall tales.

Maria Muldaur absorbed different musical styles from the Village folk scene, the jug bands, and afterward as a duo with her husband Geoff Muldaur. She learned country folk music at the source in Appalachia, while visiting with Doc Watson's family in North Carolina. Watson's father-in-law, Gaither Carlton, taught her to play fiddle, which had a deep effect on her vocals. She sings with the smooth flowing lines of a violin, to the enchantment of jazz loyalists.

After her divorce, she began a singing career that revealed an unusual fluid and rangy vocal style, a taste for funny, no-message tunes, and a sensitive approach to ballads.

She hit her stride a decade after her debut with the Jim Kweskin jug band when she found the proper blend of musicianship and jazz-tinged material for her voice. Her approach to Dolly Parton's country songs is a knee-slapping city facsimile tantamount to a white performer's wearing blackface where she retains the high spirits but not the emotion. She is best with more sophisticated melodies where an instrumental approach is needed. She stepped squarely into the pop scene with "Midnight at the Oasis," a romantic puff of desert perfume that typed her as a dreamily suggestive pop singer.

Folk roots for singers who began in later years were indistinguishable from rock and country influences. Bonnie Raitt has strong connections with the last outpost of East Coast folk in Woodstock, New York. She developed the most advanced guitar technique of all the women folk singers. Her acoustic, bottleneck steel, and twelve-string guitar playing is respected in any circle of musicians. Vocally, she has sweetness, finesse, and not too powerful a voice. She is more subdued than her contemporaries Maria Muldaur or country-rock-oriented Linda Ronstadt.

Another folkie with a delicate air is Emmylou Harris, a protégée of the late Gram Parsons, an association assuring her of a place in the country-rock fold. Since she began her career singing folk songs, her vocals have a soft approach. She does not summon up the energy of the country or rock styles, but she's very good.

The Roches, Maggie, Terre, and Suzzy, are three sisters who had a surprising success with a folksy style when the genre had almost been forgotten at the end of the seventies. Kate and Anna McGarrigle are also a delight.

Maria Muldaur, Bonnie Raitt, and Emmylou Harris are separated by a decade from the earlier folk madonnas, Joan Baez, Buffy, and Judy Collins. The new singers present an idea of womanhood that is closer to romantic conventions. They are not closely identified with political or social issues. They do not sing socially significant songs but prefer love ballads or personal statements. The audience is prepared to accept their romantic ideals rather than the social commitment of the older folk madonnas.

Folk as a popular music style returned to the background when its purpose was exhausted. Some of its styles and attitudes flowed into the mainstream of popular music, but its issues and messages remained tied to the sixties. Protest was no longer popular when the problems of the draft, war, social inequities seemed on the way to being solved.

Folk singers had made their statement, and reached whatever solutions were to be found by singing. Some of them were too closely tied to dead issues to be able to make rapid artistic transitions. Had they been able to as individuals, expressing the change as artists would have made their motives suspect. Sudden changes would have made them unrecognizable to their audience and seemed like a commercial ploy to regain a following, rather than a reaction to a new situation. It was no surprise to anyone when Joan Baez and Judy Collins began singing pop tunes. They did it well.

IV
TEEN ANGELS

A number one hit in early 1960 describes one of the antiheroines of her time, "Teen Angel." It's a tragic tale of a teenaged couple who abandon their stalled car in the path of a speeding train. Suddenly the girl rushes back into the car.

Crash.

She's dead. Harp. Ave Maria choir. Why did she do this mad thing? The boyfriend tosses his anguished questions to the heavens. Does she hear them? Why was she found clutching his high school ring?

Melodrama. Romance? Teen Angel, the paragon of teenaged womanhood had a heart, if not a brain. But she left the boy to go get the ring. Maybe he should have given it to Judy, the little snot in English class who got all A's. Judy would have been too smart to dash into the path of a locomotive. But Teen Angels were usually dumb.

Their lives were not guided by reason but by passion. They were dumb. The "dumb" sound was an important part of teen songs. All good popular singers have it to some degree, but the Teen Angels had the very essence of the "dumb" sound.

Like soul, a singer either has it or does not. But the idea of soul was a mystification. The "dumb" sound was clearly audible. It was a nontechnique that sprang up naturally but was difficult for a trained singer to obtain. It has no connection with intelligence. Carole King, Ellie Greenwich, and Cynthia Weill all have the sound because they are not singers. Cynthia Weill assumes that it is helpful not to have too much "up there" to get the proper "dumb" timbre.

The young girl groups sounded "dumb" because they could not float a note on a column of air to achieve a full-voiced sonority; they sang like children. They also sounded "dumb" because they could not phrase or pronounce their lyrics properly.

The "dumb" sound was encouraged by lyrics that forced words into unusual patterns, with pauses and accents in the wrong places for the usual speech cadence. The flaw is elevated into a style for the "dumb" trick of the misplaced accent in the Shirelles' "Dedicated to the One I Love." The stress falls on the third syllable of "dedicated," which freshens the overworn phrase.

The "dumb" sound was as attractive as the idea of the "dumb blonde." The "dumb" are supposedly more approachable. The popularity of the "dumb blonde" myth and the "dumb" sound was due to their possible lack of artifice and shrewdness. The evanescent "dumb" sound was not bound by the rules of logic, and at times amounted to baby talk.

To the girls who listened, Teen Angel was a martyr of love. They would aspire to die for love. Love was a do-or-die affair, life without love an empty shell. Their highest goal was to get a boyfriend, the incarnation of love.

The boyfriend was the central theme. He was a panacea and a status symbol. A composite portrait of the boyfriend shows him to be handsome, tall, shy, sweet-talkin', a good dancer and swell kisser. His hair is wavy. Her parents hate him. Although he was as victimized as she was, together they could make it. They would strike out on their own and carve out a new utopia somehow. Indications grow vague after the last chorus.

For certain situations the boyfriend is a necessity, but the heaviest duty he had to perform was for the Angels, one of the youngest sounding girl groups. The Angels relied on the boyfriend to protect an endangered reputation. The ratty masher came 'round while the boyfriend was away in "My Boyfriend's Back."

The teen love cult worshipped abstractions, the symbols and trappings of teen love. Teen regalia was the ring, the sweater, the letter. The rituals were the date, the dance, the party, and the wedding. Locales were parties, dances, the school hallway, the street corner, the candy store (the teen equivalent of country's honky tonk), and the beach. Other elements were unlikely coincidences, embarrassing confrontations and accidents. In the teen genre, the bedroom was for praying, the church was for kissing.

The demons of teendom were the other girls, above all Judy, Lesley Gore's archetypal nemesis in "It's My Party" and "Judy's Turn to Cry." Teen Angel's rival envied, and was eager to run off with, her prize possession, the boyfriend.

Parents were another conflicting force. Her parents usually disapproved of Jimmy or Eddie or Johnny, and made vague but forceful class distinctions to keep the lovers apart. Their objections were met with either rebellion or death. Only Janis Ian capitulated in "Society's Child," breaking the mold.

Even in the best circumstances, the boyfriend's fickle nature had to be contended with. He was all too willing to run off with the school flirt or with Teen Angel's best friend. And he had a persistent fascination with Judy.

To adults, who were by definition incapable of understanding, teen songs and the enthroned personage of Teen Angel were irksome objects of great detestation. They were disturbed by what they judged to be the extreme, absurd, three-hanky morbid emotionalism of the death-rock ("Patches," "Tell Laura I Love Her," "Teen Angel," "Leader of the Pack," "Give Us Your Blessings") and true confession dramas. At the other extreme they objected to the mindlessness of the frenzied dance rituals with their repetitive shoop-shoop chants. They wondered seriously whether or not rock 'n' roll contributed to juvenile delinquency.

Parents drawn into the controversy saw the teen record makers as a bunch of sharpies who were exploiting their children and fomenting rebellion. There was no honor in the teen hit factories, no fairness doctrine. Whatever would sell was good.

The teen music phenomenon mystified even the people most deeply involved, who would offer lame explanations for its popularity. Statistics showed that young girls bought the most records. Murray the K, a New York disc jockey who was influential on the scene, theorized that boys become attached only to a certain sound. The girls are doubly attracted, to the sound and to the performers. Girls, he concluded, get emotionally involved.

He could have looked beyond their emotional involvement to the reasons for it, to the fact that girls mature emotionally earlier than boys, and that emotional outlets were limited for all teenagers, but specifically for girls. Expectations were less limited for the boys, who would have other opportunities when their biology caught up with their mentality.

The girls would shriek at performances by their favorite acts at the shows at the Brooklyn Paramount and the Brooklyn Fox. Shrieking along with the records or shrieking at a concert was one of the few emotional outlets. There were no rules governing appreciation, and no parents or teachers present.

In the late fifties, there was plenty to shriek about besides the aura of suspicion produced by the McCarthy hearings and the atom bomb scare. For girls, love was the only path to fulfillment. There was no other way to gain respect, for their lives to have meaning. There was no shrieking at their parents, teachers, classmates, or at the tiny world in which they lived. They shrieked from pure terror.

Teenaged girls accepted teen as a protest genre that represented their feelings. The songs expressed their goals, however limited they were. They spoke to their needs in their gee-whiz language, and in their voices, the "dumb" girl sound. Any three girls could reproduce the simple harmonies and effects of the teen sound in an empty subway tunnel. Although teen songs were written by teams of adult men and women, they were extrapolated from the code of teen society.

The people responsible for some of the teen songs were songwriter Luther Dixon, manager and Scepter records executive Florence Greenberg, and Shirley Owens, lead singer of the Shirelles.

The Brill building songwriting teams wrote material for the Cookies, Little Eva, the Crystals, the Ronnettes, and others. They were Carole King and Gerry Goffin, Cynthia Weill and Barry Mann, Howard Greenfield and Helen Miller, Neil Sedaka and others.

The producing and writing combinations of Ellie Greenwich and Jeff Barry with George "Shadow" Morton at different times wrote for the Shangri-Las with Morton or for the Ronnettes and the Crystals with Phil Spector.

Jerry Lieber and Mike Stoller were a music publishing, producing, and songwriting team. Don Kirshner and Al Nevins were publishers and executives of Dimension records. Brooks Arthur was then an engineer, songwriter, and singer.

The messages that the girl groups sang may not have fostered self-reliance, but they were in tune with the times. An embarrassment to Barry Mann and Cynthia Weill, "Home of the Brave," was seen as a significant work at the time. The song was about a boy who was ostracized because of his long hair. Phil Spector, who was often associated with them as a co-writer and producer, cut the song with Jody Miller, who later became country music's "sweetheart of the rodeo" and won a Grammy in 1965 for "Queen of the House" as best country vocalist.

There was advice and encouragement in the teen songs, and there were dreadful cautionary tales. There were pretty fairy tales with lines plucked from Andersen or Grimm that struck a familiar note to girls who were not far removed from childhood. Teen Angel could fancy herself a Cinderella whose Prince would come. He'd take her away, preferably in his car, but if he happened to be a motorcycle knight, his bike would do. Either way it would be against her cruel, misunderstanding parents' wishes. She'd marry the boy of her dreams and live happily ever after.

The hard and unfeeling parents were balanced by the stubborn capriciousness of their offspring. The Shangri-Las were curtly instructed to throw over the "Leader of the Pack." Jimmy died when his motorcycle crashed after Betty told him they were through. He asked why, she cried. He left. It was raining. She begged him to go slow, but . . .

It was also the parents' fault when Jimmy and Mary died in a car accident, after being laughed out of the house when they told them they intended to be married. Mary and Jimmy's last words echo back tragically from their rain-drenched graves, "Give Us Your Blessings." They wanted their parents to attend their wedding.

The Shangri-Las' Dad was a villain, and when paired with Mother, they were a double threat. Mama alone was a different matter. For the Shangri-Las, she was a source of remorse in "I Can Never Go Home Anymore" when she dies after her daughter runs away with a boyfriend.

The Shirelles had good luck with Mama, who is a benevolent figure in "Mama Said." They listened to what Mama said, unlike the Shangri-Las. Mama is a refuge and comforter in the Shirelles' "Mama Here Comes the Bride," a song that combines the Mama theme with the wedding theme, but with a twist. The newly wed bride is coming home to Mama.

The heart of the teen themes is the boyfriend, but the Teen Angel plays the game for the thrill of the hunt. Girl gets boy at the end of the song. The real motive force for the Teen Angel is torrid teenaged emotion. But all jealousy, possessiveness, and goggle-eyed devotion to love did not make the Teen Angels helpless gushing fools. There were a few Lucifers in the swarm of Gabriels. Women were expected to be gutless sissies. But girls were still close enough to basic animal nature to have guts, to rail against the inadequacies of their lives, to rebel against constraint and injustice.

At the dawn of the teen era in 1958, the Shirelles wrote "I Met Him on a Sunday," a song about the wheel of love that keeps on turning. The plot covers the space of a week.

Girl meets boy (hey ron, do ron do ron do poppa doo). She finds herself thinking about him the next day (hey ron do ron do poppa doo). She calls him up (she's not a shrinking violet who waits by the phone to be called) on Tuesday for a date on the following day, and by Thursday she's kissed him (do ron do ron do poppa doo). He gets cocky and doesn't show up for a day. Saturday he turns up, but she dismisses him; bye-bye baby (do ron, do ron do ron do poppa doo).

The Shirelles weren't about to carry a torch for a lukewarm Romeo. Clapping and singing, they fade off on an ooo ooo oo oo oo.

Although the world view of the girl groups depended on who was behind them, each group had a different leit-motif, provided they lasted long enough to establish one. The Shirelles were the oldest teen girl group. They were managed by Florence Greenberg, who founded Scepter records from the proceeds of "I Met Him on a Sunday" for the Shirelles in 1960. Although Luther Dixon wrote many of their hits, the Shirelles were the only girl group who took a hand in writing their own material. "I Met Him on a Sunday" and "Tonight's the Night" were two of their typically robust songs. Lead singer Shirley Owens had a punchy style, and the three dauntless backups were her friends from Passaic, New Jersey: Addie Harris, Beverly Lee, and Doris Kenner.

The Shirelles had a positive outlook, rarely playing on the teenagers' fear of rejection or bereavement. They offered snappy vitality even in a nasty song like "Foolish Little Girl" and breathed life into the wistful Goffin-King "Will You Love Me Tomorrow."

The Chiffons were a New York City version of the Shirelles. They were several years younger than the New Jersey group, and they began their career with a version of the Shirelles' "Tonight's the Night."

Like the Shirelles, the Chiffons had sass. They acquired their own character after the success of "He's So Fine." They then leaped on their own bandwagon with more "fine" songs, the Gerry Goffin-Carole King "One Fine Day" and "A Love So Fine."

They were at their best in bright, cheerful tunes, but they weren't as strong as the Shirelles vocally and in their message they were just one notch shyer.

They had more enthusiasm than romance when they scored with "Sweet Talkin' Guy," a cautionary tale about a two-timer that harks back to Patience and Prudence, 1956 sound in "Tonight You Belong to Me" but salvages itself by the tough-minded statement, warning to stay away from the boy.

Stubborn teenaged pride is a recurrent attitude in the teen catalogue, and the choicest paean to teen paranoia was the Chiffons' "Nobody Knows What's Goin' On (in My Mind But Me)." It is a triumph of will for the girl in love. She is determined that no one will change her mind, and nobody knows better than she does what is good for her.

Most of the girl groups were in their mid to late teens. They came into New York from Brooklyn, Queens, the Bronx, the cities across the Hudson River in New Jersey, Passaic, Trenton, and Camden, and from Philadelphia.

The Tri-State area, which included New York, New Jersey, and Pennsylvania, had a common language in rock 'n' roll. An urban sound had sprung up in the cities. The girl groups' feeling for the music had been cultivated by the local radio, which played rock 'n' roll during the fifties.

They were thrilled to be chosen to record the songs, impressed by studio routines and the mysterious paraphernalia, awed and intimidated by the grownup producers, and starry-eyed with the glamour of the music. They believed the lyrics they sang.

Although the teen writers claim that the girl singers were completely interchangeable with any other teen group, and the material counted most toward the success of a record, it did not seem to be the case.

"Chapel of Love" was cut by Bob B. Soxx and the Blue Jeans, but it didn't work till the Dixie Cups cut the definitive version. Girl groups sang each other's material and copied versions note for note, as audiences demanded, but the definitive versions of a song did prevail.

Since the writers in the simply organized teen hit factories often helped produce the records, they tailored the song to the group's capacities. "Chapel of Love," a collaboration between Jeff Barry, Ellie Greenwich, and Phil Spector that had Ellie's "Gee" trademark, succeeded for the Dixie Cups even though they sounded cold and detached. Two college girls and a friend from New Orleans, they had the "dumb" sound, but not the fierce conviction of the Tri-State area groups. They had no hardness unless they were on their own turf. They were at their best in their own composition, the creole samba "Iko Iko." Ellie Greenwich was enlisted to get the proper New York City street hardness for the yeah-yeah-yeahs at the end of "Chapel of Love."

It would have been a different song if the Shangri-Las had cut it. The Dixie Cups were from New Orleans. They developed a straightforward simple harmony à la the Andrews Sisters. The Shangri-Las were tough kids from Queens, big city girls who could take care of themselves. They were highly strung and had an extreme emotional range, particularly the lead singer, Mary Weiss.

The Shangri-Las rated special material, and George Morton usually provided it. If the "Chapel of Love" were rewritten for the "Shangs," Jeff Barry speculated he would have gone into the studio prepared to make a small-scale operetta of it. The Shangs were the last stand of radio drama on the airwaves.

The mood would be set by sound effects. The point of the song would be driven home by the teen genre device of the recitation, a Shangri-Las specialty. There would be wedding bells, the rustle of a crowd, the hollow ambient sound of a cathedral. Barry rethought the song for the Shangri-Las version:

> . . . a little finger-snapping thing, and voices humming—
>> hmmmmmmmmmmmmmmmmmmmmmmmmmmmmmmmmmmm
>> snap-snap-snap-snap

that would be soft. Then it would fade, and you would hear coming up, "Do you take this man . . ." and maybe you hear a little sob, way in the back. You'd picture a church—you'd feel the sound of it.

We'd come in on the middle of the ceremony, ". . . and since you now take each other to be man and wife . . . powers vested in me . . . I now pronounce you man and wife . . . You may kiss the bride," then you might hear a little breathing, and a little kiss. All the time—

>> hmmmmmmmmmmmmmmmmmmmmmmmmmmmmmmm
>> snap-snap-snap-snap

and after the kiss, a guitar thing, a piano sweep, and come in "And we'll never be lonely any more!"

Jeff Barry directed Mary Weiss and the others in the studio as if he were making a film. He sat on the dead side of the microphone and mouthed the words while she lived the part. Like all the other girls in the teen groups, she had never been in the studio before when she began singing. But she had a quality that he treasured, the "nyaaah" street sound.

Mary was capable of passionate abandon. She wept, shouted, and screamed. For the declaimed passages, a diseuse device later used by Dolly Parton, Loretta Lynn, and Tammy Wynette to the same devastating effect, Mary was a natural.

The recitations are banalities on the written page, but they came to life in the studio. The Shangs never questioned the recitations leading up to their songs.

The beginning of the classic "Leader of the Pack" was the song that separated the Shangs from all the other girl groups. The important elements are there: the girlfriends, the ring, the school, the candy store, the boyfriend from the wrong side of town, the disapproving parents, and the fatal accident.

The Shangs in the studio were as intense as they were on the record of "Give Him a Great Big Kiss." Betty Weiss, Mary's sister, and the twins, Maryann and Margie Ganser, friends from Andrew Jackson High School in Queens, put hands on hips and turn to Mary, and hey, ask what color the boy's eyes are. They're fishing for a true romance tidbit. Mary can't tell. He always wears shades. Oh yeah? We're wise to her, she's trying to put us off. Well, somebody said he's bad.

Bad was the best thing he could be, but you don't flatter a Shangri-La. She parries flippantly. The kind of bad he is, is the good bad. He's not the type to cut his initials on my arm. Never mind. He's a mystery man, and she wants him kept that way. Remember Judy. If Judy hears about him, she'll want him. A girl can't be too safe. He meets the other requirements well enough, he's tall, and he has thick wavy hair, an inch too long, and as for his dancing, all she knows is that it's real close.

The Shang's Mama song is a calamity called "I Can Never Go Home Anymore." The girl makes a sullen threat to hide, to run away. Before the words are even cold, the doomy voice of Mary cries out, "Don't!"

The word hangs in a shocked silence that recedes before the fateful pronouncement. You can never go home anymore. The story is devastating. Any daughter who ever so much as made a face at her mother feels the weight of the accusing finger.

The picture is stark. Everygirl leads an empty life, one desolate day follows another, loneliness, boredom. One day, guess what, a boy.

She runs off with the boy despite Mama's protestations. Bad. But the boy was just a passing fancy, she forgets him the next day. While the girl is gone, Mama dies of loneliness. Mary stumbles with "dumb" genius over the final recitation about the angels taking Mama. The girl has no home to go to, ever again.

The Shangs were sulky, passionate, provocative. They were no wimps. Their ecstasy was staunch.

Jeff Barry, Ellie Greenwich, and George "Shadow" Morton were the major creators of the Shangri-Las. Morton discovered them and brought them from Queens to the Mira Sound Studios on New York's West Forty-seventh Street. Barry, Greenwich, and Morton co-wrote many of the Shangs' hits, beginning with their first, "Remember/Walking in the Sand," an atmospheric piece that had sounds of seagulls and surf crashing. Brooks Arthur engineered the delicate ambience of the Shangs' songs.

They intoned one last dirge at a gathering of the clan, "Past, Present and Future." Betty Weiss was missing. Jerry Lieber, Artie Butler, and George Morton wrote the song. Artie Butler fashioned the arrangement, Morton produced, Brooks Arthur engineered. About the past, it was passion and heartbreak. The serene arpeggios of Beethoven's "Moonlight" sonata bear up the recitation. Strings. Clearly, she'll never love again. To unheard questions, she answers in a voice that is carefully controlled.

Love? She looks in on herself, strips away a few layers. What is love? Was she in love or was she mistaken? Maybe it was not love and she had been fooling herself. She answers existentially, love is what she called it, then quickly amends that to the teen pragmatic mode, that's what it felt like. That's safe. She will say no more about love.

Next, the present. You ask will she go out? Why not. She is not going out with anyone else. There *is* no one else. It wouldn't matter if she lived or died, so why not go out with you.

Does she like to dance? 'Course she does. Walk around the beach? Delighted. She is being extremely polite. But, she warns, suddenly ice-cold, don't you try getting to her, it can't happen. Never again.

Coolly, she initiates a grand, heady waltz. Her youth is over. So are her wayward days with the Leader of the Pack. She's at the debutante's ball for the briefest of interludes, then returns. And the future? It's all so far away. Maybe someday . . . but now . . . No . . . never.

"Moonlight" sonata, movie fade. The sun sets on the eternal coquetterie of the Teen Angel.

Other girl groups carried the messages of teen concern. The Crystals, under Phil Spector's production, came out of Brooklyn high school hops to sing the Barry-Greenwich "Da Doo Ron Ron." The Crystals were given lyrics with story lines, "He's Sure the Boy I Love," "He's a Rebel," "There Is No Other Like My Baby," "Then He Kissed Me," and the Barry Mann-Cynthia Weill "Uptown." Their sound was sweeter and had less punch than the other girl groups.

Spector saved the straightforward verse-chorus songs for his primas, the Ronnettes, who were at home with harder up-tempo styles, as in "Be My Baby." They were a New York City trio made up of two sisters, Veronica Bennett, Ronnie, the lead singer for whom the group was named, who later was married to Spector and even later divorced. Her sister Estelle and their cousin Nedra Talley sang backup. They were a good vocal group without the drama of the Shangs, but with plenty of power. They would vary the recorded versions of their songs when they performed, a chance that very few of the other groups were willing to take. They were booked at New York's twist palace, the Peppermint Lounge, and eventually became an opening act for the Beatles.

The emotional issues of the genre were sidestepped by the good-time escapism of the dance tunes. The dances were pure recreation, with catchy novelty jingles for a lyric.

Shirley Ellis sang and co-wrote the upbeat novelty dance song "The Name Game" with Lincoln Chase. The tune was catchy. Pig Latin was popular in high schools, and the suggestion of "fee-fi-fo-fum, I smell the blood of an Englishman" was a familiar hook.

Little Eva sang Carole King and Gerry Goffin's "The Locomotion" and, from Philadelphia, Dee Dee Sharp sang "Mashed Potato Time" and its sequels; the Orlons sang "Wah-Watusi."

The first song for the longest lasting girl group, Patti LaBelle and the Bluebelles, was the "Itty Bitty Twist." They later blossomed into a top female group, but it took them fifteen years to fulfill their potential. Eventually Sarah Dash and Patti LaBelle became solo acts, and Nona Hendryx a songwriter.

They were barely distinguished from the scores of girl groups in the early sixties. Patti, the lead singer, had a strong, piercing little girl's voice, but with more than the usual power and control. She got effects like a police siren, an improvisation the other girl groups had not attempted, and she had the de rigeur "dumb" sound.

Mediocre material, cheap production values, and bad management held them back, but they had some success with "I Sold My Heart to the Junkman," a never-again love song, "Over the Rainbow," and a marriage idyll, "Down the Aisle," where Patti sings lead.

Patti's rhythm & blues version of the folk song "Danny Boy" is a funny travesty. "Oh Danny boy, the pipes, the pipes are calling" sounds as if she were referring to a hash pipe, not the bagpipe signal.

Teen-style solo singers had a keen edge on their immature voices, the quality children have when shouting on the streets. Their major contribution was to the boyfriend literature. Marcie Blane's only hit was the most abject of all teen lyrics; they went as far as they could go with the boyfriend theme when the girl's only ambition in life was stated in the title, "I Want to Be Bobby's Girl." Little Peggy March had a hit with the wistful, plodding "I Will Follow Him."

The most accomplished single vocalist was Lesley Gore, a diminutive nineteen-year-old jazz singer from Tenafly, New Jersey. She had a talent for turbulent teenaged emotionalism and abundant technique. She was a precision machine capable of duplicating every note, twist, and pause of a vocal so that she could sound like a carbon copy of herself singing harmony.

There was a capricious note in her voice that struck hard during the teen era. Her material enhanced the impression she gave of the willful girl, but there were mitigating circumstances. The situation is unbearable when her boyfriend Johnny leaves her party holding Judy's hand, in "It's My Party." When they return, Judy is wearing Johnny's ring!

"It's My Party" had a sequel, "Judy's Turn to Cry," wherein the vamp got her comeuppance. The boyfriend is property, and she does not resent losing him so much as she resents the final blow: Judy's mean smile. It is keyed to the same emotion as the line from the Chiffons' "He's So Fine": She wants the boy to be hers, so that the other girls will envy her. The boy is a catch, the Teen Angel is a hunter.

Lesley Gore had more freedom to choose material with her producer, Quincy Jones, than any teen girl singer of the time. Her songs came together to present a clear picture of her to her audience. She led the field, instead of being pulled from one schtick to another to make hits.

Her message was direct. She demanded respect from "boys" for "Girl Talk" and chafed at the retiring female personality she was expected to play when her impulse was approach the boy, hug him, but girls don't do that. Her conclusion was the most shocking revelation of the genre. She sometimes wished she were a boy.

The logical course of her songs of disobedience and nonconformity led to the indomitably self-assertive "You Don't Own Me," the most pointed stab at independence of the genre, and among the toughest songs of female liberation ever written by two men in popular music.

The Teen Angel of Lesley Gore's "You Don't Own Me" was a new direction for the teen spirit. The girl was outspokenly rebellious, a quality that was admired in the ideal teen boy. She was not rebelling against her parents but against the holy of holies, the boy.

Not content to be a sullen, silent, and misunderstood victim, she was showing her mettle. This hymn to independence was not sung from the usual position of pouting defeat. She tells the boy she is not his property to control or to display.

She sang it with conviction behind every word, there was no ambiguity. Other versions of the song were cut with a pop sensibility, a softness that threw the meaning away, and turned the message into a flirting challenge, but the definitive version is the intransigent one, Lesley Gore's.

The lyrics foreshadowed feminist ideas that were formulated at the end of that decade. The song was a stronger statement for women's rights than any identifiably political song that got by the wary macho establishment during the women's movement at the end of the sixties. "You Don't Own Me" fought gamely for the top three positions on the music charts with the Beatles' "I Wanna Hold Your Hand" and "She Loves You."

No statement so strong appeared at the top till Helen Reddy's "I Am Woman" in 1972.

"You Don't Own Me" was not a complete statement. If it were, it would be an assault, a battle cry, a political message instead of an emotional one. It contained the seeds of its own dismissal, one of the causes of the demise of the entire teen genre. It fell down in reasoning, revealing its statement to be caprice, since the basis for it is "I'm young, and I love to be young!" The demands are therefore only temporary. The teen birthright is to be stored in some drawer when she becomes part of the adult world.

The public identity built by Lesley Gore's songs was as the outsider. She was the third person in "It's My Party," "Maybe I Know," "She's a Fool," and "Look at the Way He Looks at Her." Her character either takes the blame for the rejection or exonerates the boyfriend, while expressing a glimmer of hope that he'll eventually return to her. "You Don't Own Me" was an exception. She assumes that it had visceral appeal for its pulse and for its statement:

> Maybe they were ready to accept "You Don't Own Me" because I had been through such a miserable time before that. Maybe they felt sorry for me.

Evidently she expressed emotions that disturbed the young people in her audience. Her songs center around the frustrating constraints, limitations, and taboos in their lives.

Another appealing quality was her simplicity. She was a young girl with no pretensions to chic:

> People were able to relate to the fact that I wasn't gorgeous and slender and glamorous. I just came out looking very much like they did, singing about things they could relate to. I cared about what I wore, but I mostly took my mother's advice. Probably my mother dressed me like a lot of mothers dressed a lot of other girls.

More consciously than Mary Weiss, Lesley Gore had a taste for dramatic material, narrative songs in the diseuse fashion of recitation that made few inroads in American pop music. She favors a narration and development of a story:

> I like stories where you can show what's going on in your head when those revelations are happening. That's what a song is, a revelation—it's happening the moment you're singing it.

Outside of a few songs written by Shirley Owens and the Shirelles, Shirley Ellis' dance numbers, and a few songs Lesley Gore wrote after the teen vogue had subsided, the majority of the teen singers were interpreters of other people's material. An adult, predominantly male sensibility codified the teen genre laws.

George Morton discovered and produced the one exception, Janis Ian, the prodigious teenaged singer-songwriter whose folk-based melodies and social concern went beyond the pale of teen sensibility.

Ian was part of a new generation. She identified more with Bob Dylan than with the Shangri-Las. Since she was sixteen years old at the time, she was the first and only authentic teen composer and writer who singly created her own songs.

"Society's Child," the song that flung her to the attention of a large audience, was a statement that blended the social concern of the folk movement with the teenaged feeling of helplessness. The parent's disapproval in this case is backed by the clout of an entire society. The boy is black. He comes to the girl's house, to her mother's consternation, and the mother forbids her to see him.

The song was rough. The writer did not simplify an adult perception into teen terms, she was already there. She had cut through the fluff to a real problem, one that might not be solved by growing up, even though she does hold out the hope for change. It was a brilliant coup by Janis Ian that revealed an innate talent that would have surfaced even if the song had not become a succès de scandale.

"Society's Child" became the center of a controversy, the subject of a raft of hate mail and took the intervention of Leonard Bernstein on his television show to allow the song to be heard by a wide audience.

The adults who had formed the teen genre in the early sixties were tied to the Brill building formulas for hitmaking early in their careers. Competition between the writing teams was stiff. As sounds wafted across the halls where they worked, they listened and fretted that the other teams' songs were better than theirs. Most of them had just begun writing songs, and they learned from each other in the Brill building craft shop. Jeff Barry describes their inner thoughts when they were put under contract to music publishing firms:

Ohhhh—it's $100 a week and we're gonna be recorded and they'll publish our songs and there's an office and phonograph with speakers and ooo ooo!

Jeff Barry and Ellie Greenwich were writer-producers connected with the major teen hitmakers, Lieber-Stoller, Al Nevins and Don Kirshner, Phil Spector, George Morton. Ellie had a soft, attenuated teen voice, full of sweetness and pain, one that rarely rose to the bitchy heights of the tougher teen group singers, who regularly cast their manners aside. A short stint with Barry as a singer in the Jellybeans was her major performing sortie during the teen era.

Cynthia Weill was the lyricist of the Mann-Weill team, while her husband Barry Mann was the singer-composer. Since she was a non-singer, she had a natural "dumb" sound that went over well on her demo records during the teen period, and her singing career ended when the sound went out. But her lyrics are the most substantive of the teen genre, and of popular music. She is the best poet of them all. Her songs were set apart from the other factory writers by the social concern evident in their stories. "Uptown" was cut by the Crystals, who couldn't do justice to the song. The complexity of the Mann-Weill team's songs placed many of their songs out of the reach of the girl groups, since the concerns of the Teen Angels were less cosmic than the material. Weill treated her subjects in an adult manner, from the love song "You've Lost That Lovin' Feeling" to the socially conscious "Uptown" and "We've Gotta Get Out of This Place." Weill's habit of meaningful lyrics stems from an early interest in folk and hootenannies. Her later interest in show tunes blended with the folk influence and polished it.

The most important writer-performer to surface from the teen hit factory is Carole King. At fourteen she had formed a girl group, the Cosines, with high school friends in her native Brooklyn. She was brought to the Brill building by Neil Sedaka, who wrote "Oh Carole" about her when she was still Carol Klein.

While at the song factory, she made several attempts at performing and recording. Her demonstration record for "It Might as Well Rain Until September" was a small-scale hit, but her efforts were outdone by other interpretations of her work.

Little Eva, a waif from Bellhaven, North Carolina, who worked as Carole King's babysitter, had a hit with "The Locomotion." The Shirelles did well with "Will You Love Me Tomorrow," and the Chiffons had "One Fine Day."

When sung by the mild, watercolor voice of Carole King, her songs acquire a vapidity that did not carry across during the stormy sixties. It took the childlike commitment of Little Eva or the Cookies to give her songs energy. Even when they copied her phrasing note for note, other singers could outdo her. The warmth of Anne Murray, the dogged intensity of Dusty Springfield, the earnestness of the Shirelles, or the intellectual aplomb of Roberta Flack filled the missing values in Carole King's interpretation.

After the teen period, her short-lived attempt to enter the rock scene in 1968 with a rock group called The City folded after one record and no performances.

Carole King had a teen voice, but she lacked the conviction of the street-corner singers. The girl singers had a belligerent toughness, an edge of desperation in their voices that was not part of Carole's makeup. Her apprenticeship in the teen hit machine marked her vocal style. At a decade's distance, her voice singing in the mature masterpiece album *Tapestry,* one of the most successful records in popular music, the Teen Angel can still be heard pleading in her limpid voice.

Her involvement in music always ran parallel to her family involvements. When she was a nineteen-year-old mother and worked in the Brill building in 1961, her baby had a playpen in the office where she worked in a cubicle with her husband, Gerry Goffin. Every few minutes, she came out of the cubicle, checked the baby, and returned to work. That baby was the talented singer Louise Goffin.

During the teen period, Carole collaborated on most songs with Goffin. Later going her own way, professionally and personally, her collaborations produced songs that made different statements according to who else was involved in the song, since Carole concentrated on the music. "Chains, my baby's got me locked up in chains/But they ain't the kind that you can see" and "He Hit Me (But It Felt Like a Kiss)" are two extreme examples of Goffin, with whom she also wrote "Will You Love Me Tomorrow," "Smackwater Jack," "No Easy Way Down," "Child of Mine," "Up on the Roof," and others.

Toni Stern's were the most cutting lyrics, "It's Going to Take Some Time," "No Sad Song," and "It's Too Late."

Carole King's own lyrics are filled with soft-focus optimism, "Beautiful," "Home Again," and "You've Got a Friend." A pretty fable in a New York accent.

Other collaborations produced "Natural Woman" with Jerry Wexler, "Cloudy with Occasional Tears" with Brooks Arthur, "Hung on You" with Phil Spector. Through all her years as a songwriter she associated with the most apt men in the business but made no impression on the public, who only recognized performers.

When she surfaced at last in 1971 with *Tapestry,* the music industry went overboard for her. She won four Grammy awards: Album of the Year for *Tapestry,* Record of the Year for the single "It's Too Late," the songwriter's award for "You've Got a Friend," and the award for the best female pop vocal performance.

The most unusual part was the vocalist's Grammy, won against Cher, Janis Joplin, Carly Simon, and Joan Baez. Cher's vocal endowments were no particular competition. Even though Carole King had a small, weak voice, she had vocal technique to compensate. Janis Joplin was dead. Carly Simon was a newcomer who received the Best New Artist award. Joan Baez had the best vocal equipment, but she was an outsider, not an industry and establishment stalwart. She also did not have the track record of commercial hits that Carole King had.

Two albums after *Tapestry,* Carole King brought out *Fantasy,* a concept album that revolved around a simple, day-to-day point of view. As she pictures it, the life of a housewife leaves plenty of room for fantasy, since her own middle-class daily life has little of the soul-crushing drudgery that a poorer housewife's experience could be.

Fantasy's message urges using the imagination to improve the world. It is full of the sound of the city and daily life. For the first time, she dispenses with collaborators and writes her own lyrics.

The result is the first total statement from Carole King, words and music. The point of view is from a woman who is at the top of her craft and who also leads the usual family life that most women do, with home, husband, and children.

She is aware of herself as a human being who is sheltered from the real concerns of life but is aware of their existence. She appears as a beguiling, naïve Pollyanna who believes in the basic goodness of humanity and softly bewails its shortcomings.

Peace, quiet, and love are recurrent themes. The scope of her concern is personal, even when she sings about the end to war. Her ideals are peace of mind, the value of human dignity, the need for a safe place to create, a safe haven at her husband's side, and a certain amount of comfort in "A Quiet Place to Live." "Weekdays" is what happens after the "Chapel of Love," and what it's like to be "Bobby's Girl." It's not "The Locomotion." She takes care of the house and she's bored. But the teen turmoil is over. Anxious parties, stolen kisses, disapproving parents, nights spent on the corner are gone. No more chasing boys, and no worries about Judy. As a lyricist, Carole King is endlessly concerned with tending her own garden. As a composer she is one of the best in popular music.

The teen girl sound was squelched by the British invasion and the onset of hard rock. The Beatles' vocal harmonies owed as much to the Ronnettes as to the Everly Brothers, but male groups were the rule. The falsetto surf sound from California and the Motown girl groups that flourished during the thin years for female vocalists after the end of the teen sound also stood on the shoulders of the Teen Angels.

Teen was the voice of an oppressed minority of the young from the streets of New York, New Jersey, and Philadelphia. It developed from the doo-wop roots of urban rock 'n' roll. Rock owes the Teen Angels its rebellious attitude and its hard-driving dance rhythms.

When the Mamas and Papas hit with the Shirelles' "Dedicated to the One I Love" in '67, and Janis Joplin later sang the Chantels' "Maybe," it marked the return of American pop music to its own roots.

Teen Angels

Teen replenished the emotions of pop music that had withered during the fifties pop takeover. Teen's reckless abandon reappeared in rock and soul. The melodrama perfected by the Shangri-Las, with their heart-rending recitations, reappeared in country weepers, as did the poignancy of familiar objects and daily existence. Teen paved the way for the intensity of Aretha Franklin, Janis Joplin, and Tina Turner.

When time passed, the Teen Angels grew to be the age of everyone else. They had to find another form of protest. There are teen genres for other generations of teenagers, but there will never again be a girl known as Teen Angel.

V
SOUL SISTERS

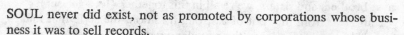

SOUL never did exist, not as promoted by corporations whose business it was to sell records.

Soul was a spellbinding fiction, a myth accepted by America after the British invasion as the True Word, a holier-than-thou tweak to white noses, anthems to the black spirit.

Soul was a hype like rock 'n' roll. Soul was sold to blacks as rock 'n' roll was to a generation of war babies in the fifties as "their" music. Though musicians who made rock 'n' roll were balding, just as some of the makers of soul music were white, the stunt came off okay.

Soul brewed where money was to be made. If the people bought the fiction it was only because they were gifted with no more sales resistance than normal.

Racial pride, only a kiss away from racism, was profitable, but soul music and the evanescent quality of soul did not exist merely as a musical form. It could only have appeared in the sixties; it reflected the spirit of that time.

Soul referred to a few individuals who like any great artist could communicate feelings to an audience via voice and rhythm derived from black gospel music.

Soul was not gospel, and contrary to the expectations of some entrepreneurs, it was not gospel that the new audience wanted; it was the fervor that went with it; the energy, joy, and conviction of the music had little to do with De Lawd, but soul was a fabrication with techniques borrowed from the superb marketing of the Church, a hustle from a commercial preacher.

Soul filled the need for a black cultural awareness when politics at last was recognizing the demands of American blacks, the flowering of a movement begun with the Supreme Court desegregation decision Brown vs. the Board of Education, 1954. Soul songs were on the march for change; give me what is rightfully mine: respect, freedom, love, the pursuit of happiness.

Like gospel, soul reaches for the greater love, or for what life could be, should be. Like country music, it is poor people's music; whites have country, and blacks have soul. Like "aw, shucks" country which drew together poor whites, soul is also exclusive. Soul says: brothers and sisters, we're all in this together (let's get out).

Soul grew from the root of a strong tradition, the style that makes American music dominate the popular music of the western world, the music of the American negro that brought its unfailing rhythm to popular music in the United States.

Black culture in America had to be strong, individualistic, and unburdened by European or African tradition to survive the enslavement of its people. A month spent in Europe listening to the best available pop forms there reveals Europop to be a bland, tasteless, rhythmless, undanceable, boring blend of mush more obsequiously derivative than the most unspirited middle-of-the-road pop played in a Stateside hotel lounge.

The quality of soul came from gospel roots and was suited to the times of great marches and demonstrations. Religioso black gospel exists as a separate genre, with its own artists: Mahalia Jackson, Clara Ward, Sister Rosetta Tharpe, Inez Andrews, Marion Williams. Gospel makes the congregation a part of the service, and is much like politics. Gospel is not so much religion as it is recreation, just as politics is not so totally idealism as it is social intercourse.

Soul Sisters

Traditionally, negros in America since the nineteenth-century slaver days were allowed religion as a calming influence. Religion took hold of the minds of people as it always does when there seems to be no other recourse for a better life. Poor and deprived people love the gospels that preach of an afterlife, that His eye is on the sparrow, that the reward of the good is not in this world. Beyond the pearly gates the Saviour forgives the sins of the repentant and rewards virtues long gone thankless in this vale of tears.

Because the sixties were a time of hope, because people in America were just that much above the mire to be able to see the sky, it seemed then as if great changes were possible within a lifetime. A revolutionary change could improve the world, and quickly. Justice for all seemed to be in reach.

Gospel training, a background common to all soul singers, is an advantage for a singer, since it is an improvised vocal style, yet still popular, not a classical discipline like jazz. Gospel-based singers go with the beat, rather than suspending their voices over it. They may be less precise than a jazz singer and go off key as Aretha Franklin or Dionne Warwick, who have gospel backgrounds, do. Roberta Flack, a classically trained pop singer, is damned if she will. If Sarah or Carmen do, it's a caprice.

Before the idea of soul was developed, music from the black community was called race music, sepia, rhythm & blues. The final change from R&B to soul took place when gospel and R&B fused to produce soul, the style with a new approach and spirit. The transition began with Ray Charles's blend of blues and gospel in the early fifties on Atlantic records. Taking gospel songs, he changed lyrics so that the love he sang about was the profane, not the sacred kind: "I Got a Woman" in 1955 or his version of Clara Ward's "This Little Light of Mine" that became "This Little Girl of Mine."

The sound based on Baptist, Holiness, Sanctified gospel singing exists. There is a common sensibility among people who share a cultural heritage and life experience. Soul on vinyl sold as an expression of blackhood is jive. Though the neat merchandising took a ride in the turbulent times on the back of the black movement and was propelled by its energy and did fill a need for a voice, it was not the ultimate expression of an entire race. Soul was a musical technique like any other. It could be learned; Bonnie Bramlett, Dusty Springfield, Maggie Bell, Janis Joplin could approximate the sound as could many white singers.

Soul was blackmail, though black people only marginally benefited from the proceeds of the artistic extortion on the conscience of America. Whitey in the sixties may have appeased some racist guilt by accepting that black music was the best music, accessible only to blacks who had soul, a separation as limiting to black artists as it was flattering and untrue. White guilt, black pride, cash flow.

The idea of soul caught fire so beautifully that anyone with a drop of negro blood in their body claimed it. The category of "blue-eyed soul" was invented for truly milkwhites, but they didn't really count, since no matter how hard they could try, none but blacks could have soul, and then only certain blacks. Blacks who bought too many "white" values along the path to success, the luxuries of glamour, sophistication, education, were out of luck. Unfortunately this left out some brilliant singers of the black experience, individuals like Nina Simone and Lena Horne who had certainly struggled for black rights and been strong, and paid heavy dues. Soul was only for the new singers of the sixties.

Some did acknowledge that maybe kasha varnishkes or spaghetti could be soul food as well as ham hocks, but there was no real definition of soul. Hairs were needlessly split over the question. Perhaps the only quality that could not be duplicated by whites was the actual cutting edge of a racially pure black singer's voice. Somewhere in her larynx, pharynx, or her bridgeless nose, she made a special sound. How about a Jewish voice: Barbra Streisand, Ethel Merman, Bette Midler, Lori Lieberman? Connie Francis, Timi Yuro, Morgana King and the pasta singers, an Italian voice? It gets stupid. And how did Bonnie Bramlett learn to sing so "black"? By singing backup for Tina Turner.

While the music goes 'round and 'round, singers express themselves in the style they care about, a style that reflects their background, taste, or education, whichever is most important to them. In a pinch, they'll sing in the style that feeds them.

If white singers were drawn to music through their churches, they would sing Schubert, Bach, Handel, and become classical genre singers. White singers found more ways to enter professional music, either classical or popular; they may have been given private lessons as children, a luxury in the black community. Gospel churches were, for black singers, the alma mater, the way to learn to sing. While there is racial separation, there will be a different cultural awareness between blacks and whites. There will be distinct musical styles built on different experiences.

Existing at the same time as gospel was blues, which began in the South as vocal music. The greatest difference between blues and gospel was that gospel is a free-flowing monologue. Gospel is an intense narrative form, storytelling, testifying, witnessing, a very old cultural form that predates theater with a central focus, a singer backed by a supporting chorus. Gospel is very individualistic, since the main focus is the preacher, the singer in the center who carries the message. Blues is a rigidly structured declamation, usually addressed to someone, the initial part of a dialogue, where the other person is absent, or listening without participating, and the singer is paced by a solid rhythm backup. Blues was recorded before country by Ralph Peer in the spring of 1928 when he captured the voice of Mamie Smith, a black vaudevillian whose recordings launched Okeh records and the boom for "race" music.

Between a soul singer and a blues singer, there are worlds, according to producer Jerry Wexler:

> Bessie [Smith] wasn't a soul singer. Bessie was a controlled blues singer. You don't have that abandonment. Soul, it's like being overtaken in church, possessed by tongues.

Rhythm & blues in the forties and fifties again set off black music from the pop music of the times, although there were black pop singers: Dinah Washington, eventually Sarah Vaughan and Della Reese, acceptable to a "sophisticated" audience, particularly Sarah, the most classic jazz singer.

The popular R&B singers of the fifties were energetic mistresses of innuendo, blues-based shouters like LaVerne Baker whose absurd "Tweedlee Dee" made baby talk suggestive, Big Maybelle, Baby Washington, and Etta James, who could have eaten a Motown girl group for breakfast and picked her teeth with a pop chanteuse.

Etta was a tough-mama blues singer whose career floundered when she became addicted to heroin. During the early sixties, she was shooting up her jugular vein, forgetting where she was, forgetting lyrics while onstage; she passed bad checks, was apprehended, treated, combined methadone with heroin.

She started in '55 with "Roll with Me Henry," a title later changed to "Wallflower," since it was considered too gamey for radio. She sings with joyous vindictiveness: "I've been in love with your man (hanh) for a long time (hanh)—you didn't know that, did you?" She riddles "Losers Weepers" with preachin' asides: "but let me tell you . . ." "now listen . . ." "sho' nuff!"

Methadone finally took over and while living in a psychiatric hospital in California, she was allowed to tour under a doctor's supervision and edged her way back into working, still a magnificent, explosive singer with irresistible power over an audience.

In the early sixties the popular style for black female vocalists became smoother. There were the three Barbaras; George, Lynn, and Lewis, who each sang and wrote their hit songs, "I Know (You Don't Love Me No More)," "You'll Lose a Good Thing," and "Hello Stranger."

Doris Troy sang "Just One Look." Betty Everett who sang in an elegant, restrained way, arrived with the peppery "You're No Good." Inez Foxx sang her version of the folk-based "Mockingbird" in a squeaky little-girl voice and Little Esther Phillips who was to return in the late seventies without the "Little" for a Grammy nomination opposite Aretha, was then only a child who had been discovered singing in the Sanctified Church and brought to commercial music to sing "Release Me" in '63.

At the end of '63 *Billboard* halted publishing R&B charts since pop and black music were the same market. When the British invasion alienated the black audience, who supposedly preferred "authentic" R&B sung by its own artists, not the pastiche the British were offering, the soul audience formed in 1964.

Between '65 and '66, when white female vocalists were getting the bird and American performers were being wiped out by the British, the only music that held its own was made by black performers, particularly the music of the Motown sound that had begun in Detroit,

1960, with the start of Berry Gordy's involvement in the music industry.

In the sixties, times of opportunity for blacks, Berry Gordy, who founded the company, developed talent from the local ghetto to make up what became the Motown empire: recording, management, and eventually films.

The Motown sound had a faster pulse than R&B, the accent on all four beats of the bar, instead of every other beat, popular in R&B and later in disco. The Detroit acts were the next step after teen for women. The Marvelettes, Mary Wells, Martha and the Vandellas, the Supremes took over the American imagination.

The Detroit talent was young, docile, malleable, amenable to being taken in hand by a paternal company, hammered into a mold calculated, yea, guaranteed to please.

The Motown girl groups were girls signed up after graduation from high school, Detroit ghetto flowers under contract, rough edges polished a bit by Miss Powell at the Motown charm school. Martha Reeves, along with the others, took advantage of the opportunity Motown offered:

> That's the thing I liked about them most. They supervised their talent, and whatever areas you wanted to develop in they'd not only find the source and the teacher for you, but they'd insist that you go and take these courses for your own good. They were more of a parent than they were a company.
>
> I'll always remember and be thankful that I was there at the time. We had instructions in the proper way to sit, a modeling course, more or less . . . We did this while we were not on the road, when we came back to Detroit. It wasn't like being idle, with nothing to do; it was going to the studio two or three days a week for either vocal exercising to prepare for future arrangements on songs, learning songs from different shows, just keeping interested in what you're doing, utilizing your idle time, never letting yourself become bored with what you're doing, keeping your act alive.
>
> It probably was the greatest advantage for Motown because most of us were babies just out of high school.

More than any other black-run enterprise Motown showed the world a new image of blacks. Motown's success was an economic as well as a psychological coup for black artists who for the first time, were accepted by a wider audience.

Motown's first success was the Marvelettes' "Please Mr. Postman," a teen song indistinguishable from music by the Shirelles or the Chiffons. The old-fashioned doo-wop fish of Rosie and the Originals' "Angel Baby" was then popular.

As the girl groups and their audience matured, Motown made a transition from teen to pop. The Marvelettes sang "Too Many Fish in the Sea," "Don't Mess with Bill," "The Hunter Gets Captured by the Game," and more through the sixties. Meanwhile, other acts developed at Motown.

Mary Wells' distinctive style, copied eagerly by some British chirps, was next to bring Motown attention: "You Beat Me to the Punch," "Two Lovers," "My Guy." She was a tasteful singer whose career faded when she married and had a child. Later comebacks did not succeed.

Martha Reeves worked as a secretary at Motown and baby-sat Stevie Wonder at the office before being given a chance to sing in '62. With "Come and Get These Memories," the sulky Martha Reeves style was established in '63. Quickly followed "Heat Wave," "A Love Like Yours," and "Quicksand." On their first tour, Martha and the Vandellas performed seventy nights running.

But Martha was Motown's Cinderella. She didn't have a style that was easy to define, recognize, caricature, and imitate. Unlike Diana Ross, she had no come-hither purr in her voice. She couldn't lock into any of the available sassy bitch, sex kitten, cocktail chantoosie jet streams.

Motown would have been poorer indeed without Martha and the Vandellas' "Dancing in the Streets," "Nowhere to Run," "Love Makes Me Do Foolish Things," "Jimmy Mack," "Love Bug Leave My Heart Alone," and "Honey Chile." Martha's sullenness gave her songs the proper touch.

Motown by 1965 had grown so large that Berry Gordy could not give his acts the personal attention he'd lavished on them in the beginning. He had helped with problems, decisions, and was available for 3 A.M. phone calls. Now some acts had to be set aside, and Martha and the Vandellas was one of them, although they continued to perform.

The most successful female Motown group was the Supremes, who sheltered Diana Ross and her mosquito-thin voice during her formative years in the Motown glamour mill, before she became the compleat entertainer, her diction, carriage, and moves planned with the thoroughness of a NASA countdown: a smile, a wave, a tear, an "oooweee" and take it from the top. She retained a hint of the plaintive girl group teen wail through all her "baby" songs, and through Billie Holiday's material on her soundtrack recording of "Lady Sings the Blues." Limited though her voice is, her technique is unflagging.

The Supremes survived many personnel changes, including the departure of Diana Ross. The Supremes sans Diana fared respectably on the charts, moving from Detroit material toward pop and disco. With Diana they had done well through the sixties: "Where Did Our Love Go," "Baby Love," "Come See About Me," "Stop in the Name of Love," "Back in My Arms Again," "Nothing But Heartaches," another of the patented "oooweee" songs, and "I Hear a Symphony."

Every song, every "oooweee" built Diana Ross a drama: "My World Is Empty Without You," "You Keep Me Hangin' On," "Love Is Here and Now You're Gone," then the bizarre "Reflections" and its sci-fi arrangement, and the strange put-off to a lover, "Love Child," with its fear of pregnancy! "I'm Livin' in Shame" was the ultimate mama song, where the college daughter pretends her rag-head mama doesn't exist, and is stricken when the old lady dies.

By the end of this period, the Supremes were ooos in the background. Diana Ross left to go solo in 1970.

Another Motown group, Gladys Knight and the Pips, was not made exclusively by the company as were the usual Motown acts. Gladys Knight had performed publicly by the time she was four, won the Ted Mack Original Amateur Hour at eight, and was a grownup by her first professional engagements as a member of the Pips. They were a family group, and the male members eventually settled down to three: Edward Patten, William Guest, Bubba Knight. The Pips touring performances in '62 were supported by a chart record, "Every Beat of My Heart," and culminated at the Apollo. Though they were used to working hard, the Apollo stint was the hardest, Gladys remembers:

> You talk about an experience! . . . when we finished that first show, we were packing our bags and going home.
>
> Everybody had a big laugh off us, because we were doing up our little uniforms and stuff and they said, "Where you guys going?" We said, "We're going home!" They said, "Man, you've got four more shows to do!" . . . We started at nine-thirty in the morning and went till one in the morning.

The Apollo shows booked ten or fifteen acts, lasted two or more hours. A typical program would open with the Staples Singers, go on with Patti LaBelle and the Bluebelles, the Four Tops, the Pips, the Temptations, the Marvelettes, Shep and the Limeliters, and several other acts.

Next, Gladys Knight and the Pips joined Motown. Since they were a family group, they were less dependent on Motown than other acts. Their career was neither built exclusively by Motown nor was it destroyed when they left the company. They were already professionals when they joined the label. Not created in the glamour mill, giving each other moral support and encouragement, they left Motown intact:

> A lot of the artists there had an insecurity about leaving the company. You've got to believe in yourself sometimes in order to make it . . . At Motown, it's very hard not to believe that the company is God.

Like most black singers, Gladys Knight had gospel singing experience, since popular music was considered sinful in her household.

> We were brought up Baptist Baptist. Not the Holy Rollers and the other kind of stuff, not the Sanctified, but really Baptist.

Influences on her style otherwise are the usual ones, Sarah Vaughan, Billie Holiday, influences that few popular singers could deny or avoid.

She also has come to exercise control on her choice of material:

I wouldn't sing a song about selling dope, or telling somebody, "Hey, c'mon, get high with me!" I don't believe in it . . . I have children, and I know what I want someone to be singing to them.

After leaving Motown, where their greatest success was the 1967 "I Heard It Through the Grapevine," Gladys Knight and the Pips entered a pop period with "Neither One of Us (Wants to Be the First to Say Goodbye)," "Midnight Train to Georgia," and "Imagination." Eventually the members of the group took on separate projects, but continued to maintain a group identity.

Gladys Knight is a pop performer, with an appeal to the broader American audience. Although through the political actions of the sixties the group was not involved with issues, they were a product of the black emergence of that period and were aware of it.

We just tried to live as we felt people ought to live. We always had black pride. We tried to carry ourselves in a way that we could be proud of ourselves and our people could be proud of us.

Motown left Detroit for Hollywood, changing its name to Mowest, in honor of the move, abandoning some of its more funky attributes and less successful acts. The glossiest product was Diana Ross, whom the company chose to develop, since she was the most plastic, the most old-fashioned "baby" girl singer, mistress of the dumb draw and of the "oooweees." She became Motown's star of the screen with *Lady Sings the Blues, Mahogany,* and *The Wiz.*

Out West, Motown signed more singers, Yvonne Fair, a former member of the Chantels and the James Brown Revue, Syreeta Wright, an exquisite singer who was not exceptionally successful, and Thelma Houston, who after many a year received the recognition she so richly deserved.

She had been nominated for an R&B vocalist Grammy award in '75, and in '78 she finally won for "Don't Leave Me This Way." She was brought up in Long Beach, California, and had been a gospel singer with the Art Reynolds Singers on weekends, but gospel was not her only musical background. Before then, in high school:

I used to sing—what do you call it—*Negro Spirituals* . . . yeah, that would be on the music, "A Negro Spiritual." It would be things

like "Steal Away" and "Swing Low, Sweet Chariot" . . . like that
movie, *Band of Angels,* where they had like black slavery, you
know, one of those kinds of movies, they had the slaves singing
"Ain't that great gettin' up in the mornin', hallelujah!" like they
were really thrilled and happy . . . It was really funny to me . . .
that's when I started to sing those Negro Spirituals—"Thelma, do
you want to lead this?"

After high school she began gospel singing in earnest:

I used to do a terrific tambourine number and dancing around
with the group. You couldn't look like you were enjoying it too
much, but you know what I mean. For the church thing it's a whole
different kind of thing, it's sacred holy goodtime. You can pat your
feet and you can clap your hands, and you can shout and you can
jump up and down, but you can't pop your fingers, or you can't
shimmy too much, because then it looks like it's another thing.

Thelma Houston is more versatile than the run of Motown singers,
good enough technically to perform on one of the first direct-to-disc
recordings made in the seventies, which are cut in one take, with
enough understanding to sing Motown girl songs, and also songs by
Dory Previn. She is clear on the type of material she will sing, and
what she will avoid:

I wouldn't sing a song that was blasphemous, because I do believe
in God. I wouldn't sing a song that questions the virgin birth, because that's treading on somebody else's stuff.

When she sings, it's with all the twists and turns of exaltation from
gospel and with intelligence. Hers is not a "dumb" persona. She is a
new style of singer, not in the R&B or the soul generation. Reflecting
the new freedom in American culture, she has chosen idioms that are
not exclusively from black cultural roots, though gospel is still her
most important musical lesson, her source of freedom.

That freedom, when you sing gospel, of not being locked in to
sheet music, as opposed to singing Negro Spirituals, that freedom
that allows me to move around on the stage, or to do the melody a

little bit different, to go with my instincts in my singing, which I got from my gospel background.

Motown had many more formula and nonformula artists. One of their ace writing teams, Valerie Simpson and Nick Ashford, began to perform live in the midseventies. Valerie Simpson is one of the most vibrant and dynamic performers, but the team doesn't make it because a softer foil for her could not be found than Nick Ashford, who is pure mush on stage. With sugar on it.

Motown through the years moved from the girl group sound that disappeared with teen, to the sweet soul style, its own patented Motown sound, adult groups, adult themes, pop status.

There were other voices during the Motown period. Dionne Warwick and Shirley Ellis were popular. Then came Barbara Mason, who in 1964, when she was sixteen, wrote and sang "Troubled Child." Later she had "Girls Have Feelings," "Yes I'm Ready," and others.

Fontella Bass sang "Rescue Me" in 1965, and Barbara Lewis, "Baby I'm Yours." The year 1966 was the peak for Motown, and while the Marvelettes, Martha and the Vandellas, and the Supremes were popular, and black was popular, the recording industry tried to follow that success by duplicating it.

There was criticism of white artists who were accused of aping, filching, covering, and deriving styles from black music, drawing from a tradition that did not rightfully belong to them. This was not a new phenomenon, since artists during all periods helped themselves from black sources: Patti Page, the McGuire Sisters, the British. There are white cover versions of black music, and American pop appropriates every kind of music, waters it down and predigests it for the pop public, throws out traits that are too ethnic. Every other culture has more or less become assimilated, but the black culture keeps striking off on its own, leading by innovation; but there is no copyright on originality.

It seems patronizing to defend the takeover of black music by artists who are not black. It is an affront to talent that when a white style (and what can that be?) is adopted by a black performer, other standards apply. It implies that the black performer is improving herself by singing white, while a white performer caught with black material has gone slumming.

Some British and European criticism, swallowing the soul myth without realizing how close the black and white musical influences are in America, is spectacularly venomous on the subject of supposedly stolen material. Their mistake is in interpreting the bastard American culture by purist continental standards, racist and separatist though they are.

There are different styles of black music in every part of the United States, different degrees of soul depending on the richness of the gospel mix. Refined and cool from Philadelphia, with political overtones, warm and sweet from New Orleans, reflecting creole culture, tough street sounds from New York City, blues from Chicago, mixtures from Los Angeles and other areas. Soul was based on gospel, but not all black singers shared gospel roots.

Though singers can pick up gospel turns from each other, their backgrounds will add individuality to their styles. There are black Catholics who sang Ave Maria in their church choir, Methodists whose choral singing is more controlled than many of the storefront sects, singers with classical training in opera or art songs, singers who tend more to jazz, R&B, Broadway tunes, rock, pop.

Freda Payne is black, but she is a pop singer, not part of the soul conspiracy.

Gospel style, that is just a way of singing. For Chrissakes, a lot of gospel singers can't sing jazz . . . In gospel singing they do a lot of shouting, and in the music world that I came from that was sort of frowned upon.

But it was like an opening, an impetus to the black movement. Gospel is sort of the grass roots of blackness coming out of the church. They used this gospel to break open, as a form of liberation. If you accept blackness, you've got to accept gospel as well, and that goes hand in hand with it. It's like soul food; ham hocks, greens and chitlins. It gets to be like an emblem you wear on your sleeve . . . It's all right, it's great, I love it, but hey, it's not me.

I wasn't raised that way. I'm not that crazy about it; it's not, to me, the essence of music. It's part of my culture and my background and I appreciate it, but I'm not going to eat hot dogs and beans forever.

Singers who had roots in gospel could reflect their backgrounds differently. Dinah Washington, Little Esther Phillips, Della Reese, Etta James all sang different sorts of gospel at one time, but their ultimate styles were far removed from their gospel base.

Gospel background among black women singers is so prevalent that whole life histories follow the same pattern. As a tot, she wowed the congregation at church by standing up on a box and singing. One of many children of a poor, religious family, a minister somewhere among them, she was discovered while making a foray into popular music by singing in a club where it was fated that a producer or manager with recording company connections heard her, convinced her to have a real go at it. With some variations, this story fits Barbara George, Valerie Simpson, Mary Wells, Esther Phillips, Fontella Bass, Aretha Franklin, Gladys Knight, Vivian Reed, Madeline Bell, Gloria Taylor, Rose Cornelius, Laura Lee, Judy Cheeks, Betty Wright, the Pointer Sisters, Delores Hall, Shirley Brown, Mary McCreary Russell, Lea Roberts, Lorraine Ellison, the Sisters Sledge, Thelma Houston, Dionne Warwick, Candi Staton, Odia Coates, and more.

In 1967 the most important soul singer arrived, Aretha Franklin, who set the standard for the black female singer in the late sixties. She sang with a new sensibility, but not by accident. She was not an overnite sensation.

Aretha had been signed by Checker in 1957, and, more important, by Columbia in 1960, where she recorded Al Jolson's hit, "Rock A Bye Your Baby with a Dixie Melody," and some relatively useless swing. Columbia had in mind a polished Aretha, hoping to fit her to pop singer specifications, some kind of snappy jazz negress, maybe a new Della Reese or Dinah Washington, who would snitch a few golden cookies from Dionne Warwick's ample buffet.

Aretha did not have the conventional beauty that goes in the supper clubs. She was chubs, she had no visible elegance to stupefy the eye, she seemed devoid of artifice, nice. Aretha then was a timid girl who had little idea where her power lay.

Her strength was revealed at Atlantic, where Jerry Wexler became her producer. Aretha could shriek in righteous indignation, in passion. She could rally a crowd, she had truth and conviction, she sang with faith, she personified the spirit of soul, the expression was invented as if for her alone. She did not suggest, insinuate, caress. She was not a dirty-voiced blues belter, her singing was leavened by gospel jubilation and lit with the glow of faith. Without trying, Aretha was a political figure, the voice of her people's yearnings.

She came when the political climate was favorable to black statements of every kind, and her message found the audience ready. Aretha made her statement with the blues styled "I Never Loved a Man (the Way I Love You)," a heady, lilting gospel waltz, then Otis Redding's 1965 "Respect," an important sum of the longings of the black generation of that period, the conventional "A Natural Woman," the driving, dancing "Chain of Fools," and then "Think" in 1968. Aretha was a protest singer, though the protest was lodged in her voice, not in her lyrics.

Aretha's message appeared only incidentally in her songs. Her intensity was the hook, the ideas could be heard or ignored. Aretha could not ignore what she was transmitting to her audience, Jerry Wexler witnesses:

> Lyrics are important with all great singers. These are not little rock 'n' roll rockoids, these are musicians, and sensitive, very sensitive women . . . Aretha will never sing a song, no matter how great it is, if the message at that moment that the song conveys is antithetical to who she is or what she is at that moment.
>
> You'll never get Aretha to sing a song about "you betrayed me and you made a wet rag out of me and you threw me away." It could be Gershwin's best. She would not sing a song that derogates her as a woman . . . Aretha regards every song she sings as her message to the world . . . She says: "These are my words—hearken!" Gets like her preacher father.

Then times changed and it seemed that Aretha was getting soft; singing Beatles songs, Elton John, Paul Simon, she always had that facet to her talent, just as she had a disturbing edge to her voice that appeared occasionally on an ill-considered gospel shout. The statement that had opened doors for her was no longer current. The pop-

THE SHIRELLES

ARLENE SMITH AND THE CHANTELS

BRENDA LEE

ARETHA FRANKLIN

MARTHA REEVES

GLADYS KNIGHT AND THE PIPS

DONNA SUMMER

THELMA HOUSTON

CHAKA KHAN

JANIS JOPLIN

EMMYLOU HARRIS

GRACE SLICK   LINDA RONSTADT

ular image had fixed her in that pose, expecting her to remain funky and "real" even though her reality in the intervening years had changed, as she had, as had the world, as had the movement for black equality.

When Aretha "went pop" it was as if the Statue of Liberty sat down to soak her aching feet in the harbor. Aretha added costumes and routines to her act, appearing for her opening number at Radio City Music Hall wearing a clown outfit, singing "That's Entertainment."

Tired of being fat, shy, dull, unattractive, she changed, varied her material. She did consider herself an entertainer, though the audience was not ready to see her as she saw herself. She was trying to get dolled up; they wanted earth mother. She saw herself as Judy Garland, though dozens of lesser singers were trying to be Aretha. Not even Aretha could continue to be Aretha. Life had been too tough. The energy required to be Aretha was superhuman.

There were fleeting glimpses of Aretha's reality in the papers, her troubles with a husband who humiliated her by publicly slapping her, Aretha hospitalized, Aretha performing in a wheelchair, Aretha canceling out, Aretha drunk driving, Aretha supporting Martin Luther King, Jr., putting up bail for Angela Davis, Aretha handing her Grammy award to Esther Phillips, whom she considered more deserving than herself.

Aretha had appeared, exposed herself as grand, and also as ludicrous. It was her burden as it was her charm to have in her scope everything from the absurd to the tragic, heroic proportions.

The old Aretha, or what was interpreted as Aretha at the outset, was a special performer. She couldn't be Dionne or Diana. Aretha had a nice face, warmth, and was best when she placed the least distance between herself and the audience, talking to them as if to one person, that one sinner in the congregation who believes the entire sermon is directed at *me*. Aretha was intimate, she was family. Other performers were theatrical, larger than life, stepping back from the crowd to entertain them. Aretha captured by drawing them in.

Aretha led the soul genre into the seventies. Pretenders to souldom couldn't come close, till the entire concept of soul began to disintegrate in the seventies and styles of singing changed.

Soul was questioned even in 1968, and not only by reactionaries who considered soul music a Communist plot to make America seem ridiculous in the eyes of the developing countries. *Time* magazine found soul everywhere from haberdashery to politics. The "Mona Lisa" had soul, but the "Nude Descending a Staircase" didn't. Mary Worth did, Prince Valiant didn't. Catherine the Great, yes; Frederick the Great, no. Later a New Yorker cartoon showed the magic mirror telling Snow White's stepmother that Snow White was the fairest of them all, then added, "But you got soul, baby." Hubert Humphrey claimed it by announcing to a group of college students that he was a soul brother.

While Aretha sang "Bridge over Troubled Water" and "Rock Steady" and "Spanish Harlem," Ike and Tina Turner had "Proud Mary," and Honey Cone, made up of a former Ikette, Shellie Clark, a Raelette, Edna Wright, and one of the Blue Jeans, Carolyn Willis, had "Want Ads" and "Stick Up." The Cornelius Brothers and Sister Rose sang "Treat Her Like a Lady," Denise LaSalle sang "Trapped by a Thing Called Love," and Betty Wright, "Clean Up Woman." Other black singers were gaining an audience in the pop area. Roberta Flack, who laid claim only to what she called "scientific soul" released *Chapter Two* and Freda Payne sang "Bring the Boys Home."

The Staples Singers, led by alto Mavis Staples went from gospel to pop in '68 and two years later sang "Respect Yourself," another successful song with that important message, and the dancing chant, "I'll Take You There." Mavis Staples is one of the rare deep-voiced singers in popular music, and is regarded as being excellent, though no match for Aretha's flexibility and passion. Mavis is also not a soloist, but part of the group, along with her sister Cleotha and her father Roebuck.

At the start of '72 Laura Lee sang "Women's Love Rights," not a statement committed to a mass movement for women's rights (go out there and have a good time, you know your man will; why sit at home?), yet a part of the new outspoken demands in the air for women at the time, and a break from the monotony of the thrashing "oooweee" and "baby" songs most singers specialized in. A small cult followed Laura Lee's career with interest, though she made nary a wave in the "dumb" sound of the status quo. Uncharacteristic for a female singer, she calls out the women in the audience in her live performances.

> I've always established a thing where I lead the women and tell them exactly how to handle a man, how to treat him, how to love him . . . not a women's lib thing really.
>
> Usually all my songs are geared like that, "Dirty Man," "Love Rights," "Love and Liberty" . . . now "Rip Off," of course, was saying if he mistreated you, wait till he leaves, go home and take the furniture out, the carpet off the floor, take the wall and everything and split. (laughs)

Changes came quickly in the early seventies. Black artists were blending into pop artists; they had broken the stereotypes of R&B and soul. Ann Peebles, a Memphis singer and songwriter, did not gain great popularity, but during her run with "I Can't Stand the Rain" in late '73, she was a different kind of black singer than usual; intense, introverted, she barely moved when she sang.

> What I'm doing really doesn't call for a lot of dancing. I just like to stand and just say what I want to say. Basically I move with my expression on my face, with my hands. I never did dance. When you're moving around you lose your will to think and words don't pop as fast as when you're just standing.

How black women sang, looked, acted, what they sang, horizons were widening for them on all sides. When they arrived, the Pointer Sisters were amateurs by most standards, exuberant, expending more energy on a show than was good for them, dressed from the thrift shop trash haberdashery in granny's favorite rags, singing as the old lady might have in her youth. Ruth, Anita, Bonnie, and June sang many of their own songs, "Yes We Can Can" and other fast-talking Lambert, Hendricks and Ross styled songs, and eventually crossed over with a surprise, "Fairy Tale," a country hit that earned them appearances on the Grand Ole Opry. When June was forced to retire from performing because of mental and physical exhaustion, a dent was put in the Pointers' career. The spirit seemed to flow out of them. Later, Anita and Bonnie reappeared solo.

People in America had danced either to live music or to a juke-box. In the early seventies a new idea arrived from France, really a way of stinting on entertainment fees and controlling the mood of a place, the discothèque.

Once in America, the discothèque changed into a major new trend in popular music. Disc jockeys at disco club booths played cuts from albums until record companies realized that special recordings could be made for this new area.

Atlantic records, in mid-'74 released the first special long play singles that were twelve to seventeen minutes long. By the following year *Billboard* began to publish disco charts.

Disco is the extension of rock fused with the street dancing of old rock 'n' roll and R&B, going back beyond the Peppermint Lounge, Cotton Club, to Saturday nights since the dawn of time, a mixture of gay, black, and poor influences, a product of the recession in the early seventies when people could not afford the cost of live enter-tainment but could shell out the buck or two to enter a disco, where they could entertain each other for an evening. Disco is the nonpareil audience participation show; everyone goes disco dancing to per-form, to be dressed, to be noticed, to shine. As Vicki Sue Robinson said, "They're all on stage when they're on the floor. Everybody's a star."

Disco dancers needed a different kind of music, strong rhythm, heavy accents, high energy chants, sparse, catchy lyrics. Pop artists; Al Martino, the Lettermen, rock 'n' rollers; Frankie Avalon, Motown acts; the Temptations, contemporary artists; Elton John, put disco cuts on their albums. But disco also created its own acts: Gloria Gaynor, Donna Summer, Carol Douglas, Anita Ward. Artists who might not have gotten exposure came to light in the disco scene: Vicki Sue Robinson, LaBelle, Janice Johnson and Hazel Payne of A Taste of Honey, Candi Staton, Maxine Nightingale, Andrea True, and others.

Disco was not limited to black performers, but it did build on the city rock of the sixties, Motown, and seventies' Philadelphia black music. Disco had a simple happy sound punctuated with horns like old-time big band dance music.

Disco was a commercial opportunity for singers, and at first even while profiting by it they thought of it as a fad. Dance halls, dance styles, and dance music come and go and there is little tolerance for yesterday's music in a crowd that wants to be out and moving. The disco artists wanted to remain popular and loathed being typed and dated by disco trends. The category of disco, they feared, spelled artistic death, sticking the artists with a bubblegum tag, branding them commercial opportunists who with the eclipse of disco would fall with it into obscurity.

But those philosophical questions can't concern a performer in the heat of the race for chart dominance. Donna Summer, one of the most successful disco singers, had begun in European theater, playing pleasant, light, innocent, and comic parts, in the Munich production of *Hair* and *Porgy and Bess* in Vienna. Her contribution to her first hit, "Love to Love You Baby" was moans, groans, and whispers; her image in America, she claimed, was based on a song that had no singing in it. When she arrived in the United States people said, "Groan for me, groan for me!" A Florida preacher burnt a pile of "Love to Love You Baby" records (they were "demonic") and the record was banned by the BBC.

Vicki Sue Robinson, who could eventually become one of the foremost popular singers in the United States—such is her talent and style while still a young woman—started in disco with "Turn the Beat Around." She had a background in rock musicals, listened to folk and jazz, hung around Greenwich Village, played the Café Wha?. For her the disco sound is a question of métier.

> The thing is, I don't have big tits, and I'm not a whole trip. I don't consider myself any kind of ideal from straight with anybody, and then when I come into the music business I'm not going to step aside you know. I'm good with people . . . It's all business . . . I'm really strong where I think I know what I'm talking about, if I don't I ask.

Another disco singer ("Right Back Where We Started From") with a background in rock musicals, the London *Hair,* the *Jesus Christ Superstar* production in Germany, Maxine Nightingale, was also initially embarrassed by the disco category. It cuts, to be tagged disco and placed in the company of nonsingers, for an artist who has ambition. Disco doesn't need a singer of any magnitude. One of the

119

earlier disco hit makers, Andrea True, who in "More, More, More" had a goodly "dumb" sound to her loose high voice overlarded with plenty of horns and rhythm, got her professional start in X-rated movies. In disco, the human voice need be neither voice nor instrument, but a rhythm device to repeat a phrase as if it were percussion.

Eventually, disco lyrics elevated the entire genre by carrying a more sophisticated message than "Shake Your Booty" to their audience. Disco became a form of protest and spoke for the poor, for gays, for women. Gloria Gaynor's "I Will Survive" showed that a woman need not perish when a lover departs. Donna Summer's "Hot Stuff" dispelled the idea that a woman should sit by a phone waiting for a call, instead of going out to boogie. Disco took the best of soul: its vitality, its call to freedom.

The time was late, in the later seventies, to cash in the soul chips. The idea was still a handy one to set off black singers from white ones, and to underline the continued existence of a separate black culture expressed by black singers. There had been many creative pioneers among musicians and singers who were black, who were at the top of their craft, unapproachable in their accomplishments like Aretha, or Stevie Wonder, who had created their own trends in music. The idea of soul is inappropriate when applied to the newer performers like Natalie Cole whose style is haut pop, scant debts to gospel euphoria or to the chitlin circuit.

Soul is not particularly useful to describe the style of Joyce Vincent Wilson and Telma Hopkins, the two Detroiters who made up Dawn, nor is it apropos when applied to most artists of the seventies, even though they at one time sang gospel. It is now pointless to conjure up soul to categorize Betty Wright, the Pointer Sisters, the singers of First Choice, the Emotions, or the oreo combination Hot.

The soul sister was no more in charge of her own damnation or salvation than anyone else is on the music scene, but a move upward for her, a claim for the respect she so passionately wanted was a step for her race, and for others. Black women who could sing were finding new ways to be artists in the seventies, and so the soul conspiracy had been worthwhile after all to allow new voices, who are always welcome, provided they can be heard.

VI
ROCK 'N' ROLL WOMEN

THE sentimental schmaltz of the fifties, the wistfulness of teen songs, and the social concern of the folk movement did not prepare women singers for the rock ascendancy of the late sixties that excluded them from popular music. The rock groups were strictly male bands who played rhythm music and had their own legends to build.

A rock band was a male team. They were also the boys Teen Angels sang about, supposedly tough, rebellious, lonely, indifferent to the future. They liked girls, but they could take them or leave them. One part of the rock genre formula was disrespect for women not only in the dearth of women in the bands but in lyrics of popular rock songs in the style of "Look at That Stupid Girl."

Rock was an attitude as well as a form of music: it was James Dean, Marlon Brando in *The Wild One,* and Elvis Presley. The men played guitar in splaylegged postures, a style that women, ever cautioned to keep their legs together, did not attempt till Suzi Quatro.

The rock 'n' roll women had to scream to make themselves heard; they were competing with amplified instruments. Janis Joplin produced fuzz tones and chords, like a guitar, Grace Slick a vibrating tone that took its place beside the electric skirls and wails of the Jefferson Airplane. Bonnie Bramlett, Tina Turner, and Suzi Quatro stay close to the rhythms of rock.

Women had to be larger than life, transcend their human limits to win the rock audience. They could not limit themselves to the Doris Day girl-next-door ideal, nor hope to get by with the outdated elegance of Marlene Dietrich, which would have seemed effete in a rock setting. To put themselves at the disposal of a political cause would have meant being eaten alive. The rock 'n' roll women appropriated a character drawn from female myths, part Texas Guinan, Boxcar Bertha, Mae West, and Medusa.

They were intense. Basic emotions were their repertoire: fierce joy or pain. Whatever else they were, they were at all times loud, emphatic, and emotional, from the pained sensitivity of Linda Ronstadt to the righteousness of Tina Turner, women of reckless abandon all.

Blues was a tradition the rock 'n' roll women found most amenable, since in its declamatory style the band kept in the background holding a steady pulse while the singer told her story. For the band's ego, the blues includes an instrumental break, then the singer returns to the narration.

Another factor that made the blues an accessible form to the rock 'n' roll women was that blues was a woman's domain where Bessie Smith, Ma Rainey, and the blues mamas of the twenties reigned in all their vitality. From the later rock 'n' roll era, they took the cantankerous provocations of Etta James, LaVerne Baker's suggestiveness, and all the sleazy whorehouse wails up through the century, sung with a new hardness that matched the potency of electric instruments.

Costumed in hooker finery, they benefited from the fantasy of the prostitute with a heart of gold, even though much of the glamour and style that formerly belonged to female divas was appropriated by male lead singers such as Mick Jagger, who with pouting, flirtatious airs had a certain transvestite flash. The female rock singer was a travesty of a travesty, when defined by rock terms, a double twist on the image, so that a rock writer did not realize the contradiction in calling Tina Turner a female Mick Jagger.

The rock 'n' roll woman was the opposite of a "nice" girl. Carnal knowledge is hers, she curses, drinks, and may wear a tattoo, an ornament usually reserved for male vanity that was taken over when women penetrated the male stronghold of the rock band.

A number of American rock 'n' roll women wear tattoos, but the British rock singers, who are closer to the niceties of femalehood, do not. The tattoo is significant to the Americans, it is symbolic of heroism of a sort, since it takes guts to bare one's flesh to the needle, risking hepatitis in the bargain. It symbolizes the courage to break forever with the "nice" values, and the commitment to the idea of the tattoo, an idea that would be valid for an entire short but preferably full life filled with passion and coquetterie.

Janis Joplin had a filigree style bracelet she designed tattooed on her wrist, and a tattoo over her heart. Bonnie Bramlett's tattoo is a small green frog on her hip. Several members of the all-female rock group Isis wear tattoos on their wrists or arms. Suzi Quatro's hand is tattooed with a star, and a rose is tattooed on her shoulder. Ruby Starr's rose is tattooed on her breast. The tattoos are finery as much as Dolly Parton's wigs, Patti Page's white gowns, and Eartha Kitt's minks, but they are carried closer to the heart; only a rock 'n' roll woman living out the myth would have herself tattooed.

Supposedly living out the hopes of the Teen Angels, the rock 'n' roll woman was considered "ballsy," a high value in the genre that prizes male anatomy. Tough as nails, she secretly wanted to be loved, and she was vulnerable but not to be crossed, since like Bessie and Billie before her, she would not flee a fistfight.

Reaching to become a part of the male rock world, Janis Joplin took on a swagger, her spirit rising to the challenge that she saw there. With "Piece of My Heart," "Ball and Chain," "Turtle Blues" she gave her message; she was tough, she was going to stand and fight "like a man," not sidle meekly off, since she was fighting for love and the struggle even unto oblivion was worthwhile for that cause.

Men there are who would not make such harsh demands on themselves, but Janis took the macho garb without receiving its privileges, saddling herself with the onerous burden of male strength and the draining chore of female nurturing in an effort to please everyone. There are guidelines for men to prove their toughness, but none to show the way for women, and to be part of a rock 'n' roll band she had to outdo everyone on the stage.

The rock press hyperbolized in ever increasing spirals of sexual fantasy on Janis' account. She responded to their direction, an accomplice in the illusion which became a relatively narrow discipline to do what she believed was expected of her, working like a typical driven executive sans cultural approbation from traditional sources. Many women's aspirations also rode on her shoulders, since in her struggle, she was following the carrot, not avoiding the stick. She offered women an alternative and showed how far it was possible to go, which made her death even more poignant because she blew it all.

Focusing a passion that had not previously been expressed by a woman in the rock genre, Janis inspired books and songs. David Dalton's *Janis!* was a sad tribute weighed down by quotations from Kierkegaard, Rabelais, and Ruskin. Peggy Caserta's remembrances as told to Dan Knapp, *Going Down with Janis* produced a book that was one long pant leavened with a smattering of facts on Janis' career that might have been written from anyone's sexual fantasies with characters named for members of the Janis Joplin entourage. Myra Friedman's book, *Buried Alive,* was edged with the tone of a harried functionary forced to deal with a client's caprices.

Songwriters, with poetry and emotion, came close with their summations after her death, creating visions based on hers. John Phillips wrote "Pearl," Mimi Fariña wrote "In the Quiet Morning," which Joan Baez recorded, Dory Previn wrote "A Stone for Bessie Smith." Nona Hendryx wrote a tribute with a warm, lush lyric, "Nightbird":

> *Nightbird fly by the light of the moon*
> *Makes no difference if it's only a game*
> *Released, relieved just for the day*
> *It's a nightbird's way*
> *She sees, she scores, she stores nothing away*
> *And tomorrow's a dream . . .*
> *Leaving bits and pieces in her way*
> *She lives the day before day . . .*

She lives, she dies, she buys
What life gives away
And yesterday's a thought unwillingly caught
In a mind where time has nothing to gain
She feeds the fire for the flame

Fly on nightbird, fly on
Why not let heaven be your home?
. . . You're flying high and all alone
*Nightbird fly on . . .**

Bravado, vulnerability, an overwhelming desire to please were endearing traits that blotted out her shortcomings: delusions of grandeur coupled with an inferiority complex that alternated in rapid succession, rancorousness, egotism. At worst, she was considered a flawed personality crippled by a drug habit, but difficult to dislike; those who came in contact with her were either indifferent or warmly concerned about her.

She was regarded by her audience with the same admiring awe that would have greeted someone who walked barefoot across red-hot coals. Her efforts when she flailed herself against music and lyrics were heroic, because she was not inured to the emotions she touched when she sang.

An argument arose during the time when "soul" was fashionable in the backlash reaction to her popularity. Since she was white, middle class, and educated, her right to sing the blues was questioned.

Blues never tied itself to ephemeral issues popular in the late sixties, the problems of racial discrimination, poverty, and war. Blues express the loneliness of a drifting life, the feeling that there is no niche in this world, which is at the core of any social or political issue. The blues is based on a more constant human need, which assured its survival from the early part of the twentieth century into the rock era. The spirit of the blues existed in laments of the sad canzonas sung at the courts in the Middle Ages while the knights were off at war. They were love complaints: "Lasciatemi morire," "Lasso

* "Nightbird" by Nona Hendryx © 1974 Gospel Birds, Inc. (BMI). Used by permission.

di donna." They bewail loss of love, the coldness of a haughty lover. Sappho sang the blues, and before her, Ruth, standing in tears among the alien corn.

Part of the idea that "soul" was lacking in Janis Joplin among those who believed in the concept of "soul," led to the thought that it was plentiful in Tina Turner. The comparison was unfair, since to slight Janis Joplin in favor of Tina Turner, whose every movement onstage is choreographed, is missing the point of each woman's talent. Janis Joplin was a singer who approached her craft as an amateur, emotionally. Tina Turner plans every motion as precisely as a cabaret entertainer. Tina Turner was the top rhythm singer in rock, but she is not a blues singer, since her roots are in gospel, nor does she have as melodious a voice as Janis Joplin had.

The emotionalism Janis Joplin cultivated, her improvidence, her disregard for her own safety or anyone else's, incidents such as her fistfight with a Hell's Angel over a bottle of bourbon, hurling an empty bottle of Southern Comfort into the audience, were part of her mystique; one does not move great numbers of people by being restrained and reasonable. To make an impact, gestures must be larger than life.

Janis Joplin made everyone aware of what she was "supposed" to be. Her role was clear, and she was doomed to castigate herself for not playing it fully. Her hot mama status was undermined by what she thought to be a lapse: she liked to read books. The toughie was subverted by her vulnerability and need for love. Down to her purported shortcomings she played the role. She tried to conform to her own standards, a set of high values that she invented, and above all else she wanted to do what was supposedly expected of her.

What ultimately captured the imagination of her audience was the force that drove her. Probably any image projected with the same conviction would have drawn the same respect, because rock music, with its volume, heroic imagery, search for greater knowledge beyond human intelligence, with its drugs, was based on an attempt to transcend human limits. It was a pursuit of happiness, a rejection of the futility of daily existence.

A professional performer learns to dole out her energy in measured doses for each show, but Janis Joplin did not pace herself. She was left with little energy to spare for off nights—those nights her shows were banal. Sometimes, she would exceed herself.

She tensed toward the crowd, stamped her feet, danced, broke her love beads, tipped the mike stand in a passionate tango, shrieked and testified. An orgasmic smile on her pimply, puffy face, she clutched and beat the air with her fists, kicked, shook her ass, scratched her frizzy hair, mouthed the microphone with a whispered groan, wailed and shouted, then danced away, clattering her plastic bracelets. She bent double with the effort of a scream that cracked into two or three harmonic tones, or delicately touched her breast during a tender passage. At that time, women were shedding brassieres and wearing transparent blouses. Janis was among the first female performers whose nipples could be seen through the filmy material, an irresistible draw for the front line crowds.

She was cathartic, exhausting, cleansing for the audience, not because they uttered a sound, though they did cheer, but because they roared and wept through her emotions. Like Judy Garland, she could not be copied effectively, because her appeal was in her own emotional force, that puts an artist beyond the rest.

To introduce her songs, she invented punchy raps that allowed the audience a closer acquaintance with her person of Janis the bacchante, the eater of men, the street girl who slept all day and always had her eye out for a good piece of aaa-ction.

She began to sing by imitating Odetta, then delivered a none too steady version of Bessie Smith, a wailing shout of the rock sensibility that lacked the sly elegance of the twenties. She hit her stride in 1967 with Big Brother & the Holding Company. She was influenced by the country singer Rose Maddox, and the black bluesmen Otis Redding, B. B. King, Leadbelly, and Blind Willie Johnson.

Janis was a diseuse, an actress who created a character for each song. Songs became an extension of herself in "Little Girl Blue," "Women Is Losers," and "A Woman Left Lonely." To Willie Mae Thornton's "Ball and Chain," she brought force and drama that Willie Mae's own version lacked.

Janis Joplin's death by an accidental overdose of heroin chilled the enthusiasm for "ballsy chicks" and revealed it to be a dangerous pose. The sorrow at her passing included mourning at the death of a dream, for aspirations failed. Her death was a coup for conventional mentality; Janis was greased by playing with forbidden drugs; score for the squares.

Drugs were a matter of course in the life and the songs of rock performers in the late sixties. Heroin remained underground, but marijuana and the newly discovered LSD were a popular idea. Grace Slick, while still with the Great Society, wrote and sang the song that brought the drug culture of San Francisco national prominence, "White Rabbit."

It was built on the strong imaginative foundation of Lewis Carroll's "Alice in Wonderland," which put the drug experience in a familiar setting, linking it to the classic children's story. In the latter-day version, Alice's adventures in wonderland were the fantasies of her stoned mind.

But even for Grace Slick the experience is no longer the same as it was during the late sixties with hallucinogenics:

> I get one biggie on about once a week, and that's it. I used to be able to tear through a couple of months, plowing through a bunch of stuff, but I can't do that any more . . . If you have a child, you can't be so crazy that you're sitting there staring at a wall for four hours, saying, "My, isn't the green and the wood beautiful?" because then the kid's drowning in the bathtub.

Grace Slick's lyrics are whimsical and witty, occasionally sardonic. She sings them in a hypnotic voice as if they are a set of incantations, with intense concentration. An occasional folk ornament gives her piercing style delicacy.

For the rock 'n' roll women who write their own songs, there is little reflection involved in the creative process. Janis Joplin claimed she never wrote songs, she made them up. Suzi Quatro describes writing with her guitarist and partner Len Tuckey as throwing an idea back and forth till it turns into a song. For Grace Slick, her writing is nothing more than ". . . glots of thought, slams of insanity." The bravura style of a rock 'n' roll woman leaves little room for sentimentality:

> I've never been able to write a ballad . . . I like to see other peo-

ple do it, like Tony Bennett—he's a good singer . . . I've tried it. I'll even do it by myself, sit down and start singing a love song, and it always sort of cracks me up, because I really don't feel that way. I'll love people or a certain man, but I don't have that "Gee-my-man's-left-me-I-think-I'm-gonna-fall-apart" feeling.

The vehemence of rock music is a special mode of expression for a certain type of person with special needs. With a bit of sardonic humor, she considers rock as being, possibly, primal scream therapy:

There might be a possibility that rock 'n' roll is primal therapy. If you have to yell at 100dB, you have to take out some of your stuff.

If the burden of being a rock 'n' roll woman is a heavy one, she does not feel the weight as a member of the musicians' community, as part of the Jefferson Airplane and later the Jefferson Starship.

But having a certain amount of aggressiveness in her personality and choosing rock music as a form of expression are part of the same impulse. It is also no surprise to her that her caustic remarks in the rock milieu have involved her in fights, or that violence occurs at the large rock concerts. Rock music is an expression of emotion. To dissect Grace Slick's music as if it were a technically sound genre with clear rules is wasting time. Perhaps the only trait a rock singer must have is that she be dauntless:

If I was cool, I wouldn't be in this business, I'd be in real estate, or in—oil? If I was intellectual this would be very boring. I'd have to be creating a new medicine for cancer.

I'm nothing except possibly more aggressive than most females my age; not younger, because they've been told to be aggressive—"Oh, now you can come out of the closet, it's okay, it's cool now!"—and than most men.

She claims no vocal techniques, since as a rock singer she is not noted for well-shaped tones. Even though the distinctive wows and flutters that mark her vocal style are unmistakably hers, she disclaims any amount of range or control. Whether or not she will sing well when she arrives on stage is a matter of chance:

An opera singer has a fairly good idea that she's not gonna blow the shit out of it. I don't. I never really ever know.

At concerts with the Airplane or Starship, she ambles along the apron casually, trades cracks with the audience, sings with her back to them, and acts as a member of the group, weaving vocals with Paul Kantner or Marty Balin.

The rock rap, related to the recitations in the teen and country songs, offset the lack of meaning in some rock songs that are constructed around the heavy dancing beat, and lend some concepts to the concert experience, since the lyrics of a rock song are often lost in the distortion. The rap is a sermon on rock attitudes, and more potent than the pop singer's patter between songs. It brings the audience closer to the singers, involves them with the parables they describe, gives them understanding and allows the audience to participate. As in a revivalist meeting or a gospel church, the rap is a revealing gesture.

The involvement of an audience with Suzi Quatro is enhanced by her raps that border on demagoguery. They are punctured by cheers and applause that gain volume as she continues to appeal to them:

Are you ready to rock 'n' roll!
. . . you know they told me, they told me cuz I'm originally from Detroit—you know where Detroit is, don't you—it's the other side of the moon.
They told me a lot of things about you people out here and I don't know if it's true or not. One of the things they told me is that all you people right here in L.A. could make a lot of noise when you wanted to . . . I think they was bullshittin' me—
Are you ready to rock 'n' roll!

When the crowd cheers loudly enough after more prodding, she sings. Part of a rock concert is the movement of the audience, clapping, dancing, and singing, which is one of the reasons Janis Joplin invited her audience to dance in the aisles, defending them against security guards like a big sister, urging them to defy fire regulations. A pop audience in an intimate setting might be intimidated by the lights, but a rock audience, realizing how large it is, will respond with cheers when lights are cast on them. They like to be part of the show. The klieg lights make them feel stoned.

Suzi Quatro provokes her audience, "insults" them, dares them to join her. While pacing herself by the band's rhythmic vamp, she asks the people gathered in the arena if they are midgets. No, it seems that they are small because they are seated. She commands them to stand:

> I mean you people up there in the cheap seats too—everybody! First of all I want you people up there on the lights to show me what Los Angeles looks like. Show me the people—I want to see the people!

Cheers greet the houselights. The audience responds to her populist sentiments. She urges them to their feet to sing along with her, she repeats the words of a song, then asks again:

> Now listen L.A.—Will you do that one time for Suzi! . . . I can't hear you! Come on! I want to see everybody singing: a-one, two, a-one two three . . .

Spotlights play over the audience as they sing. The song over, lights go out and the arena is plunged into darkness. The crowd stamps in rhythm, claps and cheers, matches light the arena like a birthday cake as people hold them overhead. It is ten degrees warmer when she returns for an encore.

Suzi Quatro's stage style is more aggressive than any of the women who began in 1967. She benefits from their strides and takes them even further. Where Janis wore feathers and beads, Suzi wore a leather jumpsuit. Janis danced teasingly, Suzi struts and kicks as if she were involved in a brawl. The prolonged wails of a victimized woman that Janis opened the field with give way at Suzi's hands to the victorious shouts of street kids playing stickball in the gutter, a throwback to the teen style. Janis was vulnerable, standing alone in front of the mike; Suzi straddles a blasting bass guitar. Their influences are different, since Janis was inspired by Bessie Smith and the softer blues singers. Suzi, for her part, took her attack from Elvis Presley, Little Richard, and Detroit's Iggy and the Stooges.

Rock music developed into a mass ritual bearing a hedonistic message in festive form. The performers subscribe to this philosophy and Suzi Quatro is no exception:

> I hope to make a lot of people happy, first of all . . . I want to leave this world with something—because I have an ego like everybody else—and make it a little bit easier for women and for men—but mostly for people that are having a hard time. If it helps in any way, I'm glad.

She appeals to both men and women in her audience, addressing love songs to either. It is not through a lack of discrimination, but a part of "attitude" music, a form popular with the young audience.

The main attitude in attitude music is "bad," the same rebellious, headstrong, and disobedient badness that was evident in teen. Suzi Quatro is the first "bad" female of her style. The other rock 'n' roll women were bad in their way, identified with a favorite vice, but Suzi takes her place alongside the Leader of the Pack, not as his moll riding behind.

She musters an insinuating voice for slower songs, but most of her material is upbeat rockers. Her virtue as a singer is neither melodious nor dramatic. Like Tina Turner, she is a rhythm singer. Her timing is her greatest asset. As she develops, her ballads become more and more appealing.

Rock singers took from folk a casual attitude toward both music and audience. They were populists who asserted the democratic right of the audience to dance in the aisles, and were of the people by being at one time the same age as their audience, and not professionals who kept their distance from them.

Bearing the influence of both folk and progressive country, Linda Ronstadt stands among rock singers for her bursts of power and her distressed stage manner. She revealed an anguished emotionalism at the start of her career with the Stone Poneys that was a characteristic of rock performers as set by Janis Joplin's openheartedness.

The folk singer does not question her audience enough to reveal such inquietude, and the country singer does not question herself enough to portray so wildly an embarrassed attitude, and no pop singer would leave herself open to the amusement such an attitude could bring upon her.

Linda Ronstadt gained confidence as she gained stature and technique since her beginnings with Bobby Kimmel and Ken Edwards in the Stone Poneys, a West Coast version of the Weavers or Peter, Paul and Mary, with Linda fronting, the others on acoustic guitars. They began during a transitional period in pop music, as the last of the folk softies at the time that Cass Elliot still sang with the Mamas and Papas. One of the blocks to Linda Ronstadt's self-confidence was the same factor that hindered Bonnie Bramlett: she was used to singing harmony in a group situation.

Linda had an arresting cry in her voice. She was a heart singer like her influences, George Jones, Ray Charles, and Dolly Parton. Linda had a powerful voice like Skeeter Davis, and a capacity to handle adult themes. Since her choice of songs depends on their lyric content, she suits her material to her personality, which made it impossible for her to reconcile with "You've Got a Friend," which was greatly successful for Carole King herself, or "I Don't Know How to Love Him," which launched Helen Reddy's career. Linda's womanly appeal would have been lost in the early Carole King and teen material that suited Skeeter Davis' limpid style.

Another side of Linda Ronstadt's stage jitters were guilt-ridden forays into petty obscenities. An occasional shit or fuck pronounced as if hell would crack open to swallow her reduced her audience to laughter. In Linda Ronstadt's mouth, surrounded with an aura of naughtiness, they seemed more gross than the same expressions pronounced by Janis Joplin or Grace Slick, to whom they are a natural ejaculation with no extra weight for their venial sinfulness.

Compared to the gutsiness of the other rock 'n' roll women, Linda's humble, old-fashioned sexy lady appeal made her seem vulnerable, touching.

While the mainstream of rock music became countrified in the early seventies, she drew on her country background and benefited from the softness that held her back during hard rock times. Her small obscenities, which would have repelled the family-oriented country loyalists, made the younger progressive country and country-rock audience hers.

There are few remnants of her former awkwardness in her stage manner. Her recordings bested the efforts of the women of her class, which includes blues picker Bonnie Raitt, jazzy pop singer with jugband folk roots Maria Muldaur, folk-rooted country singer Emmylou Harris, and West Coast singer-songwriter Wendy Waldman. Linda Ronstadt sings country material rock style, without a recitation in the midst of a song. In the seventies, she was the top female vocalist.

Another soft-core rock singer from the early period is Elaine "Spanky" McFarlane, who plied the same folk-pop route as Linda Ronstadt and Cass Elliot in 1967, in a group called Spanky and Our Gang, noted for mushy soft, goodtime sounds. A later transformation led her toward country swing material.

She resembles Cass Elliot superficially, with a smaller scaled convexity. Stage movements are conditioned by girth, and the similarity to Cass ends when she exploits a raunchy belly roll that Cass, who moved with the grace of a tethered blimp in a light breeze, would never manage.

Spanky has a limited pop voice in the low range, with simple phrasing and style that led her to middle-of-the-road singing, easy listening but insubstantial.

Bonnie Bramlett's career was tied to her marriage with Delaney Bramlett, whose mellowness was balanced by Bonnie's steamroller style. They both gained a larger audience while together than after their split.

In bands formed with their duo as core, Delaney and Bonnie and Friends, as the aggregations were usually known, formed an extended musical family from the time of their marriage in 1967 till their breakup in 1972. The friends were Eric Clapton, Leon Russell, Gram Parsons, Duane Allman, and others, who soon had heavy followings of their own.

Bonnie is a blues and gospel-based rock singer from East St. Louis who served her apprenticeship as a backup singer in the Ike and Tina Turner Revue as the first white Ikette.

Tina Turner's influence is strong in Bonnie Bramlett's energetic style. The main difference in Bonnie's rock style that sets her apart from the other rock singers is caused by influences from rhythm & blues. Her material is from the repertory of Etta James, LaVerne Baker, Aretha Franklin, Doris Troy, and Ketty Lester. Not having seen her, a Memphis recording company hired her on the assumption that she was black, since her style reflected her influences: Chuck Berry, Fontella Bass, and Albert King.

Her greatest songwriting success was her collaboration with Leon Russell on "Superstar," which became one of Karen Carpenter's best known songs. Bonnie's "Never Ending Song of Love" became the theme song of the Delaney and Bonnie team.

Her blues style is lightened with religious fervor from gospel influences, her blues are mellow, sweet, or with a growl. She was questioned about the authenticity of a white woman singing the blues. Janis Joplin had sincerely defended herself on that matter in her time. For Bonnie, the question arouses no guilt, blues are a part of life:

> Blues, you've got to go through it to get to it, and have the nerve to talk about it. It's not necessarily your own personal thing. You're not the only one who had this happen to you, so don't let it get you down. You're not the only one that's ever hurt that way.

She shares the rock 'n' roll woman's attitude toward violence: no fear. To friends, strangers, audience, and colleagues she is usually charming, affectionate, even beguiling. She speaks in honeyed tones with the ancestral Irish blarney that christened her Bonnie Lynn O'Farrell, but anyone trifling with her is asking for a punch in the face, and a knockout punch, it is rumored, she can deliver. She is volatile and, once aroused, gives no thought to the odds:

> Bonnie is bad—I'm from East St. Louis, honey, there ain't a bitch walkin' that I'm afraid of.

But the quasi-macho hardness that was the lot of Janis Joplin was unacceptable for Bonnie Bramlett:

> I just didn't like the lifestyle she patterned for women in this busi-
> ness 'cause I don't like to be slapped on the back like I'm a
> truckdriver and be handed a big fifth of Southern Comfort . . . It's

made on the banks of the Mississippi River beside St. Louis, so I cut my teeth on Southern Comfort. Weren't nothing new to me!

While Janis and Grace were beginning to attract notice in San Francisco and Linda Ronstadt left Arizona to join the Stone Poneys in Los Angeles, and Bonnie and Delaney toured from a home base in the same city, New York had its own rock culture, a darker style.

Andy Warhol brought together a mixed media troupe, the Exploding Plastic Inevitable, which included a rock group called the Velvet Underground, named for the sadomasochist novel classic. Nico, a German model in his film stable who was also a songwriter, became lead singer.

Nico's physique suited the role; she was a handsome, dark-haired goddess type with a demeanor that hinted at a certain postwar ennui. Her voice droned like a Luftwaffe squadron, and she unleashed it on purposefully murky, discordant songs. Nico sings with a flat lugubrious alto, a specialty perfected by Cher, probably while under the same illusion that it lent dramatic effect to the songs.

Nico plays the harmonium, a keyboard instrument with a nasty, sour sound that creates a mood of gloom, lending great Weltschmerz to her vocal expeditions.

The women who suffered the most intense scrutiny and came up against standards high enough for few groups to pass were the women in all-female rock groups. They were ambitious women who, in addition to singing, played electric instruments, wrote and sang their own material.

In itself, that was not exceptional, since Janis Joplin, Grace Slick, Bonnie Bramlett, Tina Turner, Suzi Quatro, and many of the rest write songs, and can play instruments, though they usually don't on-stage. The special problems the all-women bands came up against were caused by their being a group of women.

An obstacle the male groups were not forced to confront was the prejudice against women in the male-run music industry. The women in groups faced a wall of ice. Some of the comments typically used against Fanny came from prospective backers:

All chick rock group? Not interested. Too temperamental. You can't put any money on it. If they break up, who do you replace them with?

The idea of women's temperament being less stable than any male musician's was pure prejudice, but the deciding factor was the scarcity of women rock instrumentalists. They were few in number, and rarely competent, for the same reasons that women usually are not trained technically in any field. Since so few women made the attempt, the failure of any woman fed the myth that women were incapable of holding their own in the male rock world.

Women rock instrumentalists are not as numerous as their male counterparts, and they are usually encouraged to isolate themselves as solo vocalists. Goldie Zelkowitz, of Goldie and the Gingerbreads, became a solo singer and later a producer. Bassist Terry Garthwaite and keyboardist Toni Brown of the Joy of Cooking, went solo. Where close ties such as marriage in a mixed group held together, women like Bonnie Jean Foster of the Canadian Skylark group and Christine McVie of Fleetwood Mac stayed in the group while it remained an entity. But the pressure against a female instrumentalist is great. Even an excellent guitarist like Bonnie Raitt was convinced to forego playing guitar tracks on her own album.

Fanny, a group built around the core of sisters June and Jean Millington, guitarist and bassist respectively, broke up and reformed several times with different musicians. The group included at different times drummers Alice DeBuhr, Bria Brandt, and Cam Davis, lead guitarist Patti Quatro (Suzi Quatro's sister), keyboardists Nicoel Barclay and Wendy Haas.

Birtha, who might have stayed together longest, since they grew up together in the Los Angeles area and had played together since high school, also broke up. They were lead guitarist Shele Pinizzotto, drummer Olivia ("Liver") Favela, keyboardist Sherry Hagler, and bassist Rosemary Butler. All members of Birtha wrote songs, while most of Fanny's material was written by Nicoel Barclay.

The all-women bands considered themselves musicians, yet they bowed to conventional demands made by managers and record labels. In show business, the rationale went, competition is high and every possible angle should be exploited to gain the public eye. Once that task is accomplished, the rest can be seen to. Costumes and makeup for the all-female groups edged toward the usual female imagery, and compromised their music behind frills. That in itself would not have caused the demise of any group; it was the combination of pressures that created a special atmosphere for failure.

The earliest all-female rock group signed to a major recording label was the New York-based Goldie and the Gingerbreads: Goldie Zelkowitz, guitarist Carol MacDonald, keyboardist Margo Lewis, and drummer Ginger Bianco. They were better known in Britain than in the United States, since they appeared with the Rolling Stones, the Yardbirds, the Hollies, and the Kinks there. After a few single releases on the Atlantic label, they broke up and found themselves stranded in England.

They went separate directions at the end of the sixties, then gravitated together again in the early seventies when the pendulum swung their way again.

By then, rock had become so exclusively male that it was autoerotic. The lack of women in the genre caused a substitution of an androgynous style in some male groups, the most extreme of whom were the New York Dolls who created a subcategory of rock that was called lipstick rock by the press wags. The spiritual predecessors they claimed were the Shangri-Las, and their costumes were patterned after Goldie and the Gingerbreads—silver lamé stretch pants and high heels.

Two years later the core of Goldie and the Gingerbreads reformed as a group, with added congas and a horn section, under the name of Isis. They recorded their first album with Shadow Morton, who had formerly produced the Shangri-Las, Janis Ian, and the New York Dolls.

There is no musical comparison between the basic soft rock grouping of Fanny, the harder rock of Birtha, and the Latin-tinged sounds of Isis. The only vocal similarity is that, being women, their harmonies are concentrated on the upper end of the scale.

Singing and playing in a rock band with a group of other women is a different experience from being the only woman on a stage backed by a male band. Women instrumentalists are under less pressure to compete with each other than men are, since women have not been trained to compete. This lack of pressure can have a negative effect, since the competitive urge is often the spur that drives musicians to excellence.

Since the sexual aspects of rock music are basic to the genre, the women also have a point of view on the issue of sex and rock. There are comments about the sexual nature of rock music from Liver Favela of Birtha:

> It's like sex with somebody, but it's music doing the whole thing. I feel the most total physical contact with an audience when it's all happening right. I have orgasms, I climax, I laugh, and I'm sweating. I feel like I'm having total sex, we're all feeling it. The music is really taking it up, the lights, the mood. A lot of times it's very spiritual. Sex is a very spiritual feeling.

Birtha, a group that played hard, loud rock in its time, was a problem on the rock scene, since there was no female precedent for its sound. They could only be promoted on a male value system; "Birtha," the record company's promotion material stated, "has balls."

The rock press had sexual notions about female rock groups, so that a *Rolling Stone* writer who reviewed Isis at an early gig in New York's Trude Heller's reported on Carol MacDonald's guitar technique by suggesting masturbation and fellatio.

One group was a collection of fantasy women gathered by John Cale of the Velvet Underground from the ranks of girlfriends and wives of rock musicians, and dubbed the G.T.O.'s—Girls Together Occasionally—who periodically regroup for special occasions, parties, or affairs like the New York Dolls Trash Ball at the Hollywood Palladium. There they may be found singing a Chordettes harmony or backup to a male lead singer, sounding like Betty Boop overdubs. Never taken seriously to begin with, they were a freak value at the special functions.

An early member of the group, Christine Vrka, committed suicide in 1972, and others left, but the concept persists. They are fantasy women, not necessarily male fantasies, but unreal by any standards. A typical lineup includes: Cynderella, the airforce trip with the bowler hat, aviator jacket, and jodhpurs; Miss Mercy, the forties hooker effect with patent leather corset; Miss Pamela, who wears shorts with spangles; Miss Sparky, costumed in pink lamé with pompoms in her hair; and Geraldine, who flaunts a scarf-dress. They are a fashion show.

An all-female rock group wastes its energy making a political point, energy in being accepted as women musicians instead of musicians who are women. For all they may insist that they are musicians first, then women, the fact that they have formed a band of female musicians reveals a conscious choice of femaleness placed before musicianship, since women players are rare. The point is made neither musically nor politically, since the effort is drawn in two directions. Ideally, a female musician could be integrated into a band for whatever creativity she might add to the group effort.

Tina Turner is another fantasy woman, an excellent idea created by her husband, Ike, who conceived an image of her from the character of Sheena, Queen of the Jungle, one of the few strong comic book and TV heroines of the fifties. Sheena usually swings on lianas through jungle trees like Tarzan, and dresses in revealing tatters. Being a wild woman, she has long unkempt hair and strength enough to beat off any attacker.

Tina's thrashing wigs, her high-stepping dances, her forceful style are the keystone of a rock 'n' roll woman. Backed by Ike and his band, a trio of Ikettes, she trades innuendos with Ike, punctuates her songs with low grunts, struts, wriggles, points at the audience like a preacher, and twists the microphone cord.

Tina's live act is always exciting, since she is the most professional of rock singers who works in tested techniques and never trusts the emotion of the moment to get her by. Her vivid stage show is planned from the dresses that are usually short and plunge at the neckline, to her growls and well-directed glares. She practices like an athlete, as if each show were a race. The Ikettes are fined if they step in front of her, or if their dresses are not neat, or if a breast escapes the low-cut tunic.

Her apprenticeship in the music scene was a long one that began in 1956 when she joined Ike Turner and was transformed from

Annie Mae Bullock to Tina Turner. They played to rhythm & blues audiences on what was affectionately known as the "chitlin" circuit long before they found the wider rock audience.

Their first major success came a decade later in 1966 when Phil Spector, who just a few years earlier had been a top teen genre mogul, produced "River Deep Mountain High" only to have it ignored by the American music establishment. It was successful in Britain, which caused Spector to harbor a grudge against the U.S. industry, take out an ad in a trade paper in praise of Benedict Arnold, and temporarily give up his career as a record producer.

The rejection of "River Deep Mountain High" has been ascribed to racial prejudice in the United States, but certainly stylistic factors were also at work, since the Supremes were doing well, Stevie Wonder and Percy Sledge were on the top charts. The genre loyalties were strong, and few women were being heard. Tina was one year too early to cash in on the 1967 jackpot for the rock 'n' roll women from San Francisco, and in 1966 no one was interested in a new female vocalist of any sort, the only exceptions being the Mamas and Papas, Cher, and Nancy Sinatra.

The Turners left for Britain, where they opened for the Rolling Stones and built a larger reputation than in their own country.

The association with the Stones brought Tina before an audience that was receptive to her punchy style. Perhaps with their colonialist tradition the Kingdom was better prepared for the Queen of the Jungle than the Americans, to whom she was an exotic curiosity. When the rock attitude took over the audience's imagination, Tina was in her element, a rhythm singer, an incarnation of Mick Jagger and Keith Richard's fantasy, "Honky Tonk Women."

Unusual for any black female singer, Chaka Khan does not have a gospel background, since she is a Catholic. As a member of a church choir in her native Chicago, she sang "Ave Maria," not the free-flowing Baptist or Methodist hymns most of the black singers count in their early experience. Soul and R&B influences are further removed from her background by her choice of jazz and Billie Holiday as influences.

Arriving on the rock scene in the early seventies, she benefited from the efforts of not only the individualistic rock 'n' roll women before her, but also the effects of the women's movement on contemporary thinking.

Chaka began as the lead singer of a rock band, Rufus, which eventually became centered around her singing. Her voice is one of the most powerful and wide-ranging on the rock scene, with no trace of the roughness that came to be an affectation in many lesser singers after the success of Janis Joplin and Tina Turner. Chaka's style can be compared to Stevie Wonder's, for capably recording definitive versions of his songs, but that is as close to Motown as she comes. Fortunately, she does not have the punk sweetness that mars the style of many of the Motown-produced lady singers, who in the early period sang "ooooweeeee baby" ad nauseam.

Chaka Khan had a perplexing amount of female righteousness, or so it seemed to some members of the all-male Rufus, even when compared to the usually outrageous rock 'n' roll women. She was the only lead singer to tour with a rock band up to the last weeks of her pregnancy. She appeared onstage with an imposing belly, and after the initial shock the audience accepted her as they had every other apparition that the rock genre had presented to them. To reject Chaka would have been to deny sex, which a rock 'n' roller would never do, even though pregnancy was a more adult phenomenon than the rock audience was accustomed to.

With Chaka Khan, who is one of the most innovative and promising rock singers, the mold of the rock 'n' roll woman is broken, and new elements are introduced into a decaying genre, its music and its imagery. She brings long, complex vocal lines, a style of dipping into her lower register reminiscent of Billie Holiday's trumpet sound, a powerfully clear and flexible voice she never allows to be buried behind the amplified instruments.

Another energetic performer with an excellent voice is Ruby Starr, who couples a strong blues voice with stage movements like a rachitic stork, and focuses with an intensity like Grace Slick's. She is of the whisky and wild, wild women school of female rock performers, costumed usually in a halter to reveal the rose tattoo on her breast, a bare midriff to highlight a scar under her ribs, shorts, and barbarian furred boots. This crowned with a mane of fuzzy reddish hair gives her one of the most arresting images in rock.

Deborah Harry, Annie Golden, and Martha Davis are newer figures on the changing rock scene.

The British rock 'n' roll women arrive late on the scene in America, and reflect different social, political, cultural, and musical traditions. Coming from a different social structure, and a country whose protest movements were based on different issues and used different tactics, their attitude is different, and that attitude is reflected in their stage personalities.

The onerous rites of passage for teenagers in the fifties, resentment of adult authority that flared in the teen genre, rock and folk differed in Britain and America.

Female upbringing in Britain, conditioned by the presence of an ornamental queen, a passive, ultimately debilitating figure of power, was kept closer to conventional standards which made most British women who sang opt for the pop genre rather than rock. Usually the British follow the American trends rather than set their own.

The British lady singers have a lingering decorousness which sets them at a disadvantage in the rude rock genre. Their reserve is easily interpreted by American audiences as hauteur, rather than timidity. They have not developed contact with the U.S. rock audience by talking to them directly, partially because their accent makes them difficult to understand, although when they sing blues, it's with the open vowels of the American South. Since their dancing traditions are not the same as those of the United States, they do not cut a familiar figure. Their steps never amount to more than a smooth shuffle, unlike the grind popular among American rock singers.

Maddy Prior and the late Sandy Denny are singers in a British folk-rock tradition, Maddy with Steeleye Span and Sandy with Fairport Convention. British folk-rock differs from American folk-rock since the Americans drew from their folk roots, the later Appalachian folk and Child ballads, while the British went to Scotch and British material once they were out from under the spell of the U.S. folk movement. Maddy Prior, Sandy Denny, and the Scotch rock singer Maggie Bell ornament their vocals with graceful folk turns.

Maddy Prior has a strong, supple voice that soars above the harmonies of the male singers in Steeleye Span, a group she co-founded in 1969. She also entertains with clog dancing and plays the spoons.

Sandy Denny's voice was more delicate, requiring the musicians to hold back for her solos, usually on the fragile, pretty songs she herself wrote. In the United States she was best known as the writer of Judy Collins' "Who Knows Where the Time Goes" and was usually shy and withdrawn at concerts.

Maggie Bell, the Glaswegian former lead singer for Stone the Crows can also turn a phrase in the Scotch folk tradition, but usually sings a hybrid British style blues, despite having been influenced by the same sources as the American blues-rock singers, notably Bessie Smith. Her blues is affected by music hall influences and by the cadence of her Scottish brogue, which distinguishes them from the drawling southern blues of Janis Joplin or Bonnie Bramlett.

Although she is well-considered in Britain, Maggie Bell has not taken the American audience, since she arrives with an unusual mixture of styles that gives her more pity than pain in her blues, more warmth than rage in her rock, and an overriding sweetness that will not penetrate the American audience's sensibility.

Rock itself was being undermined by the softness of mainstream pop music in the seventies, so that rock genre loyalists closed ranks and rapidly reduced their number to a cult size. Stevie Nicks of Fleetwood Mac, Ann and Nancy Wilson of Heart are sweet pop singers. The spirit of rock passed into disco, new wave, and punk.

The rock audience in America is still sulking from the blow of Janis Joplin's death. Since she did not have as devoted a following in Britain, the rock 'n' roll woman is still an attractive concept there. But the rock 'n' roll woman in the United States is regarded with suspicion; she might destroy herself as Janis Joplin did, taking her audience's aspirations with her.

Joplin, Slick, Turner, Quatro, Bonnie Bramlett, Chaka Khan are bred from American revolutionary consciousness, a hope for the possibility of a new order that faded with the coming of the seventies. The idea of the rock 'n' roll woman, who is hard-living, hard-drinking, and ever-loving, seems a dream, with the casualties on the rock scene and the loss of hope for radical change that nobody's buying.

As for Janis, no one has stooped to take her place. The Red Shoes are still waiting.

VII
CHIRPS, THRUSHES, AND NIGHTINGALES

THE ennui of American pop music in the early sixties was broken by the British invasion. Britain then ceased to be the land of steak and kidney pie, and acquired a chic it hadn't possessed in America since the American Revolution. The Beatles, the Rolling Stones, the Animals, and other rock groups arrived in the United States as the revenge of a nation so long dominated by American musical tastes that it had developed little popular music of its own.

Pickings were easy, since a majority of the American audience was fragmented into folk, rhythm & blues, country-western and teen rock 'n' roll camps. Only the bastard form of British rock had enough elements of each to cut across genre loyalties and create a new mass audience.

Culturally, the British invasion was part of a reciprocal colonization between the United States and Great Britain. Influences flow easily between the two nations, carried by a common language. Song styles preserved in the mountains of Appalachia reflect British roots, and British singers influenced by American singers pick up American pronunciation.

Rock-A-Bye, Baby

Around 1963 there was little excitement on the American pop music scene. The genres which might have taken over the music audience had been reduced to formulas by their own success; they still reflected the conservatism of the fifties. Teen rock 'n' roll was pitched to a young age group. Much as its younger performers may have been sincere, there was a corps of profiteering adult Svengalis behind them. Folk-protest belonged to the next age group, a coterie of middle-class college students whose taste ran to elaborate lyrics that left many people behind. A current of liberalism that was amenable enough to folk music ruled out the conservatism of the country-western genre. Of all the American genres, the music of the black community was most active. The black liberation movement was in flower; the Motown girl groups with a more mature approach took over what remained of the white and teen girl groups' territory after they were pushed aside by the male groups, who had greater professional aggressiveness.

The British invasion might never have occurred and U.S. popular music might have developed differently if one event had not altered American consciousness to its core. Hopes for reform, the possibility of social change evaporated when President John Kennedy was assassinated. Gloom, despair, and Schadenfreude, the clown who follows disaster, took over the American spirit.

In the funeral atmosphere the melodrama of the teen genre, the narcissistic silliness of American pop, the down-home realities of country, and the effete ironies of folk-protest songs could not satisfy the shocked imaginations of the Americans, revealing them to themselves as victims of coy self-deception. They escaped to the sunnier climes of disinvolved British sensibility.

Streisand and Warwick held fast, but few other new American pop singers arrived between '63 and '66. The exceptions were Nancy Sinatra, Cher, Cass Elliot of the Mamas and Papas, Vikki Carr, and Merilee Rush, who sang "Angel of the Morning" and disappeared. Even so, they did not appear as independents; Nancy Sinatra was ushered in under her father Frank's parasol, Cher had Sonny Bono mugging at the camera over her shoulder, and Cass was attended by three members of the Mamas and Papas: Michelle Gilliam, John Phillips, and Denny Doherty. Whatever their value as singers, the women who emerged during these times found little interest in the solo female stage personality. Americans listened to sweet soul music, but most of all to British imports.

While the ears of the anglophile pop audience were closed to American pop singers, into the breach rode Dusty Springfield, Petula Clark, and Shirley Bassey. The British female vocalists had not broken with pop music traditions as had their American contemporaries, who were closeted with the U.S. genre cults. The British women were closer to the conventions of the fifties. They embodied a niceness that had fled from America with Hollywood musicals and Doris Day. Along with their sequined gowns, the pop singer's uniform, the British ladies donned the garb of long-gone illusions.

British singers were raised on American pop music, due to the World War II alliance. (The real popular genre of Europe is classical music, a style that has lost touch with modern society and technology.) Influences on the British "gel" singers' style were American pop singers of the fifties and the emergent black music of the early sixties. United States styles such as teen, folk, and country had not traveled well abroad since they were tied to American social conditions.

Female singers who had what was in the midsixties the golden aura of Britishness could sing pop style and present old-time feminine virtues and vices that would have been yawned off had they been attempted by an unestablished American.

The material chosen by the British was usually American or pseudo-American. The most attractive swipes by the British ladies were the smooth pop ballads of Burt Bacharach and Hal David that had been popularized by Dionne Warwick. The British females copped that material so well that Dionne Warwick remarked of a British copycat:

> She was a great mimic—copied note for note. If I had sneezed, she would have sneezed, that's how closely she followed everything I did . . . Take my vocal out, put hers in. I was hoarse that day and I couldn't do any better, and that's the way she did it.

The imitations, slavish as they sometimes were, succeeded in Britain and in the United States. Even while reaching for the exotic, the popular music audience in America had enough narcissism to choose styles that reflected its own culture.

The audience doesn't adhere to standards of purity that resist change in popular music, and it found the British women's sensibility appealing. The pained intensity of Dusty Springfield, Petula Clark's optimism, Shirley Bassey's sauciness are human attributes that transcend nationality. They accordingly captured an audience whose emotional needs were served by them.

The British singers were also exceedingly good performers who might have done as well without the derivative material that gained them commercial success.

There had been British visitors to the U.S. pop scene before the invasion of the sixties, but they had not come to stay. Vera Lynn crossed the ocean in 1952 with "Auf Wiederseh'n, Sweetheart," a song that called up a vision of farewell to the Lili Marlene of World War II for good and all. It helped that she sang the song with a Dietrich Weltschmerz, although in fairness Lynn was a top British vocalist with a more tuneful, sweet voice than the Deutsche diseuse Marlene.

Child chirp Laurie London did well with the gospel-style "He's Got the Whole World in His Hands" while folk was still an underground phenomenon and negro spirituals all the rage in 1958, but she was not heard again.

The year 1963 was important for British vocalists. It marked a change in their orientation. Dusty Springfield had till then sung in a Weavers-style folk group, the Springfields, a trio that included her songwriter brother Tom. They were the most successful pre-Beatles group in Britain and were lively and upbeat, peaking in America with the country-folk standard "Golden Pins and Silver Needles." When Dusty went solo, she reflected the smooth pop influence of Peggy Lee, Dionne Warwick, Jo Stafford, Baby Washington, and other Americans.

British musicians in the early sixties were aware of being part of a phenomenon, and responded with a euphoria for which Dusty ventures a deflating comment:

Suddenly England discovered enormous talent within its own

ranks. It was a kind of an ego trip for the British. Suddenly all the charts were British. Everything that counted was British, and that was the start of that great upswing in the sixties when it was fashionable. Music and fashion, everything that was important was British. We were feeling good then . . . We became sort of enraptured with our own charm—we discovered that we *did* have charm—and marketed it.

More than the enchantment of Britishness that made of any chirp a Circe, Dusty Springfield arrived Stateside with the regalia of the compleat pop singer: a beige beehive 'do, huge false eyelashes, a porcelain makeup job that was the result of four hours' labor, and beaded gowns. The female fantasy she embodied received the accolade of female impersonators, one of whom transvests regularly as Dusty Springfield: Wayne County.

The look of Dusty Springfield is a masque that would be missed by her audience if she should part with it:

That was a very calculated thing, it worked at the time. It was a strong image; people copied it, that kind of tacky glamour image, the beehive hairdos, the black eyes, it was the thing in those days.

I wanted to be tacky glamour. I didn't know it was tacky, I thought it was glamour, so it wasn't difficult . . . It wasn't calculated because it was eccentric, it was just slightly larger than life.

Creating this female image is not simple. The stage person of Dusty Springfield is carefully prepared, and the job robs some of the pleasure from the glory:

Female performers, I don't think they can enjoy their success as much as a man, because it involves so much more effort with the accessories, so much less gut-level enjoyment. A man very seldom has the same trappings to attend to; the face, the hair . . .

A woman's appearance, the image she presents, the vision, still requires in most cases more effort than a man's. Therefore the sheer drudgery of presenting that is so time-consuming that there is less time left for enjoying things on a gut level . . .

There are female performers who don't go through all that shit. I am not one of them.

Rock-A-Bye, Baby

Although she did her share of hoo-hoo-hoo's in the early sixties and allowed some "dumb" girl singer attributes to crystallize around her (abetted by a record label that released collections of songs such as an album entitled, significantly, *Oooeeeeee!*), Dusty Springfield's forte is the type of song that contains all the woe of a woman's heart: "Someone Who Cares," "Just One Smile," or the mea culpa of "You Don't Have to Say You Love Me."

The thrall of the singing ritual is a gilded cage for Dusty, an emperor's nightingale who sings so prettily not because of it, but in spite of it.

In the pop pantheon, Dusty would occupy the niche of St. Jude, to whom the faithful flock when hope is gone, in itself a gesture that implies continued hope. Dusty's audience wears out the grooves of their *Dusty in Memphis* albums and is moved to tears at her live performances.

> You know you've touched something in them that is special, even if it's painful. To smile after you've had a couple of drinks sitting in a nightclub is very easy because it's very superficial. We're trained to smile. We're not trained to cry . . .
>
> I think you've really reached somebody if you can get through the façade of all that politeness and pleasantry. I think it's an achievement; if it has to hurt, it's too bad . . . That gives me a sense of achievement, to see a flutter of white handkerchieves in the stalls, to feel that people are moved . . . it doesn't give me joy.

In the press of the British invasion, not all of Dusty Springfield's talent was discernible. The United States was also rooked by the "soul" conspiracy, an economic ploy to fuse an audience along racial lines. Dusty sounded "black," and had to be thrown in a category that would capitalize on the black cultural upsurge of the time. She was acceptably white, and she sang with passion, and some gospel turns, living proof that the white race possessed some semblance of that lucrative quality of soul. Publicity, pinning the tail on the donkey, claimed the Scotch-Irish singer with green eyes possessed blue-eyed soul.

Her distinctive voice was imitated by dozens of chirps on both sides of the Atlantic, and made of her a singer's singer, a superlative.

Most singers are either instrumental vocalists who try to sound like a horn, or diseuses, singing actresses who elevate lyrics as the main purpose of a song. Dusty creates a musical mood with the song structure, fathoming its cadence. Her main concern is how well a song expresses a musical emotion. In hindsight, her disregard for lyrics and their meaning dogs her.

> I was singing such sexist lyrics . . . But I never thought about the lyrics, they meant nothing to me! . . . voices are being heard, and I would now be more conscious of the lyrics that I sing . . . That consciousness thing is coming through in the lyrics . . . without the great yearning and beating of breasts because he gone away and left you . . .
>
> Half the time when I sing lyrics I haven't got a clue what the song is about . . . Why do you think I would have sung "Wishin' and Hopin'". Do you think I would have sung "Wishin' and Hopin'" if I'd listened to the lyric? No. Thank you for that, Hal David. Sorry 'bout that, Hal David.

The British woman with the greatest impact on the American music audience was Petula Clark, who had more exposure than all the others, and a better campaign to conquer the U.S. audience. Songs written for her by Tony Hatch seemed to be custom-made for the American market. "Downtown" is a New York City locution referring to the business and entertainment district. Since streets are numbered consecutively there and in many American cities the concept is familiar in the United States. British and European cities have name streets. Petula Clark's great success in the United States was a song of that title written by Tony Hatch, who also wrote "Don't Sleep in the Subway," another reference to the United States, since the British transit system is more often referred to as the underground.

Petula Clark slipped easily into American pop. She was a natural. She could have been the prim cousin of Doris Day vacationing from London. She does not attempt glamour, but a warm, mildly innocent simplicity with humor enough to put on a pair of baggy pants and a top hat for a London music-hall number.

Her career started when as a child she played in dozens of films for the J. Arthur Rank organization, appeared on BBC radio shows, and entertained the troops during the second world war. In earlier days she followed popular trends, had long blond hair, sang negro spirituals.

She sings well, with a pure tone that occasionally resurrects the spirit that Edith Piaf projected in so many songs about getting through it all. The fresh, uplifting style is her value as a singer; angst can be found elsewhere. There is always a discrepancy between a performer's stage personality and private nature, otherwise he or she would be a mannikin instead of a person. Confiding to *Life* magazine writer Richard B. Stolley, Petula Clark explained:

> The Judy Garland business of letting it all come out—I'm not capable of that . . . I think the emotion you don't show, maybe only hint at, makes a song more interesting . . . I am haunted by all kinds of morbid things, but I can't see any point going through life being tortured by this.
>
> I think I'm a bit of a bore to some people . . . so cheerful, always smiling, never raising my voice. Actually, I'm the contrary. My mother was Welsh . . . I've had to train myself not to give in to gloom or pessimism. I fight my real character all the time.

British performers invaded the entire U.S. entertainment scene, appearing in theater, films, and television as well as in the concert circuit and recordings. Julie Andrews reigned over Broadway, Petula Clark appeared in the depressing British remake of *Goodbye, Mr. Chips,* Ed Sullivan capitulated to the Beatles. Nostalgia for what never was took hold of the popular imagination so well that all things British became desirable. The U.S. audience did exercise some discrimination, since the British artists were usually import quality; they had to be of a certain stature at home to leap the Atlantic chasm. Even so, it was surprising what the public chose to embrace and what to ignore.

The James Bond movie thrillers were a filmic part of the British invasion, and in 1965 Shirley Bassey sang the title song on the soundtrack of *Goldfinger* with such glossy flair that the song rose to the top ten on American music charts.

Her impression on the pop scene was brief but deep, though she didn't follow up the success of "Goldfinger." She became a cult figure with a following that enabled her to sell out Carnegie Hall for four consecutive nights, nine years after her greatest hit.

Promoting gowns and glitter, she is forceful onstage, singing in her distinctive hard and glassy voice, biting off each phrase as if it were so much sticky nougat that she wished to have done with.

Another import to the American scene was the young Scots singer Lulu, who was influenced by Connie Francis, Kay Starr, and Teresa Brewer. A British penchant for silly names caused her to be called Lulu when Marian Massey, her manager, remarked to a theater owner that she was "a lulu of a kid!" when she got Lulu her first job at age fourteen.

Lulu made her reputation in America with the title song of *To Sir with Love,* and was featured in the film, an attenuated British *Blackboard Jungle* of the sixties. The teen-flavored style of that song quickly faded from U.S. attention and Lulu with it, although she remains an excellent singer.

There were British singers who succeeded on their own turf with cover versions of American songs but never had any following on U.S. shores. They offered nothing distinctive to the United States at the time, lacked energy for the conquest of the huge American public, or were firmly tied to British genre styles.

Competent singers who never made good in the States were Ellen Maugham, who in 1962 covered the unfortunate "Bobby's Girl," popularized in the United States by Marcie Blane, who herself deservedly disappeared. Cilla Black, one of the prime swipers of Dionne Warwick's Bacharach-David material, is a charming singer with a sincere style whose voice is strident when compared to the gossamer tones of Warwick. "Barefoot" Sandie Shaw appeared briefly with "The Girl Don't Come" but made no important records to warrant a further incursion to the United States. The delicate folk-rock of Marianne Faithfull is missed by a cult following that awaits her return without reasonable hope. Julie Driscoll made an impression with Memphis stylings and is slightly known in the industry.

Mary Hopkin benefited from the backing of Paul McCartney, who produced "Those Were the Days" for her. The old Limelighters' chestnut was a great success, but Hopkin's dulcet voice could be capable of more.

In the later British rock camp, Elkie Brooks sang with Vinegar Joe and the Scots blues singer Maggie Bell was part of Stone the Crows. The eventual acceptance of Brooks, who has a powerful, big voice, is only a matter of exposure. Maggie Bell bears a totally superficial resemblance to Janis Joplin, a fact that works against her, since the U.S. audience is fiercely loyal to the late empress of rock.

Maddy Prior, one of the stronger voices in popular music, and the late Sandy Denny, one of the most fragile, are both part of a British folk-rock trend, electrical instruments and rock stylings on folk modalities, an eclectic pursuit in America without a large following.

The smallest minority of female singers are the writer-performers of Britain. If there is little living space for the woman singer in Britain, there is even less for the singer-songwriter. Women who do write songs write fewer of them. Sandy Denny, Kiki Dee, Lesley Duncan, Lynsey De Paul, Linda Lewis, and Joan Armatrading are writer-performers known in the United States. More arrive periodically, such as the greatly talented Claire Hamill and the classy decadent Dana Gillespie. Of them all, only Joan Armatrading has gained any important recognition. Justly so, since she has made the most original contribution.

Since the singer-songwriter trend rose out of folk, the writer-performer tradition is not very deep in Britain. England did not go toward the European continent during the latter part of the fifties to be inspired by the French chansonniers.

There seems to be little encouragement to write, for a female performer in Britain, although many of the popular British singers are capable of writing their own songs on occasion. Maggie Bell, Elkie Brooks, Petula Clark, and Dusty Springfield have.

For years Kiki Dee seemed to have a hex hanging over her, like the cloud that follows sorrowful Jones to rain on him wherever he goes. Her name was changed from Pauline Matthews to the handle she now bears. Though she balked at it, she accepted it in preference to the doubly damned alternative of Kinky Dee that was offered her. Beginning in the early sixties as a backup singer, she spent a decade on the U.K. cabaret circuit. When Tamla-Motown signed her as its first white artist, she arrived in Detroit in time to be caught in the backwash of Berry Gordy's departure for film moguldom in Hollywood.

The change in her career when she joined Elton John and Bernie Taupin was so radical that it was as if the ten years spent singing in cabaret never happened. To the United States she was a newcomer, even though she had a BBC-2 television series at home.

Before a U.S. audience, which is usually large and seemingly rough, Kiki Dee displays a decorum that is diffident, timid, detached. It is all the more exasperating since she has a very fine natural voice.

Another former backup singer who possesses a disarming amount of charm when she sings is Lesley Duncan, who more often writes than performs. Her lack of stage savvy limits her allure, but her dusky mezzo is interesting as a pop voice.

The West Indian Joan Armatrading is an exciting guitarist as well as the mistress of a large, boomy voice. Her melodies are touching, though set to lyrics that are mystifying at best. They may mean nothing at all, simply groupings of interesting words that could obliquely suggest some meaning if one is driven to fathom it.

Linda Lewis considers herself more a singer than a songwriter, and frankly attributes the success of one song ("Rock a Doodle") to the use of a formula.

> I was fed up about my records not selling. So I thought, awr, I think I'll just sit down here, and I got all the catch phrases from my little sister, who's thirteen. I just put them in a song. I had a very instant melody . . . It got through. It was nice, because I got on "Top of the Pops" and my mum thought I was a big pop star for a week.

One of the youngest British singers and songwriters, Claire Hamill is one of the most promising performers. Her effervescence and her supple voice brought her fast rapport with live audiences, although her records are not readily available. Performing is hardly the chore for her that it is for most writers:

> I'll do it at a bus stop, you know—so long as it's my stage, I'll do it!

Biding her time for a late arrival on the American pop scene, Cleo

Laine was aware of a current of distaste for female vocalists on the U.S. pop scene, and did not rush to arrive:

> I decided for a long time America had enough of female singers and could well do without me.

Her career began in 1952, but she was not seen in the States till 1972. She came equipped with a vocal range better than three octaves, a facility with pop, jazz, and classical styles, a repertory that included Brecht-Weill, Jerome Kern, Lieder, modern classical music of Ives and Schoenberg, and a background in the legitimate theater. She is a singer of taste and craft who approaches every song as her personal message.

> Each song that I sing I have to approach in the very same way. If I don't understand that lyric, then something goes wrong. There are a lot of songs that are rubbish, that lines pop out and you think, well, what the bloody hell does that mean? Unless in the end I can get myself a meaning . . .
>
> "Tea for Two," which on the face of it isn't a particularly strong lyric, the way I approached it was that in this day and age most young people when they get together and get married . . . there's probably little chance of their marriage or relationship ever surviving. This would be something that maybe a girl, if she were a poet, might want to say to the bloke she was going out with. If this could happen, I think we might survive together.
>
> When I sing it, if I have this thought in my head, then those words mean something somehow to the audience.

She was given rave reviews by the U.S. press, classed among the best singers in the world, called the best pop singer, the best all-around singer. England at last had sent a woman singer, a poised, mature vocalist who was an uncompromising artist. The key to her loyal following, beyond her musical ability, was that she possessed one quality that is rare among popular singers: Cleo Laine is an adult.

That attribute does not rule out the vulnerability needed to touch an audience, or the humor to deliver a song with good timing. It does mean that she chooses themes that are adult, not pretending girlishness:

> . . . the baby talk type lyrics—me singing lots of "ooo ooo ooo's" and "aaa aaa aaa's," "ooee ooee ooee's" and up your flooees.

Not every singer adopts adult themes or is able to transmit all levels of language gracefully. She handles the most unusual material with intelligence. A composer brought her the lyrics for a work commissioned for one of London's Promenade Concerts, and considered too advanced for that institution:

> As I read through I saw a couple of bums, then I saw an ass, then I saw shit, and a fuck. It was an opera, and as I was reading through, the whole thing had some point because it was about Adam and Eve in the Garden . . . There were a hell of a lot of I suppose some people would call them—obscenities—but today, what's a fuck between friends?

The flow of British singers had hardly slowed when a number of Australians began to appear on the American music scene. The Australians were eminently palatable to Americans; they had less of a cultural tie to their mother country than even the British.

Australians sound like Everysinger; very good, but every regionalism is trained out of them. They are so easily ingested into the American system that it is debatable if an Australian singing style exists at all. Diana Trask and Olivia Newton-John easily sing country style material, and Helen Reddy rose to be the top pop singer in the United States. The lesser-known Lana Cantrell and Judith Durham of the Seekers singing group might have been anybody's neighbor in Poughkeepsie.

After the peak of rock popularity was past in 1970 and laid to rest with the death of Janis Joplin, many of the press who had come up during the late sixties remained as established writers.

Their expertise was built up during the rock period, and that genre was steadily slipping from its leading role. They applied old rock standards to the new softer form of popular music. Some of their reactions to women, to pop singers, to foreigners were more vitriolic than necessary.

Their annoyance was intensified by an assumption that the out-landers were on the take, that women singers lacked vitality, that pop singers were exploiting what should not be sold, pandering to tastes that should not be acknowledged.

They objected to the new pop softness on principle, because they were rock genre loyalists. They fumed at Olivia Newton-John because she was a softie, against Helen Reddy because she in no way could be fitted to the role of the victim rendered incompetent by her wild affections that was the female legacy of the blues.

The press was most unchivalrous on the subject of Helen Reddy. They did not like her looks, and took particular glee in describing her performances with vivid disparagement. Something there was in Helen Reddy that annoyed them. One critic claimed that she was plain even in a sequined gown, "as though she could sneak an over-due book back to the library unnoticed." Another considered her "beneath contempt." Another sputtered like a priest raining down anathema from the pulpit: "Helen Reddy, that symbol of kitchen freedom and fashionable liberation; that heroine of the suburbs and purveyor of all that is silly in the women's lib movement . . ." Still another: ". . . her screams and get-down histrionics were about as effective as a one-legged man in an ass-kicking contest." Her dancing was compared to an ostrich or, more kindly, described as a cross be-tween a drugged chicken and a very hip Chaplin. Positive facts could be given backhanded, as in the review which stated: "Helen Reddy has broad audience appeal—no pun intended."

She offers a large target, since her performances are important enough to warrant side-by-side review with Joni Mitchell's concerts. But the result:

> "Helen Reddy got the usual standing ovation." "Joni Mitchell brought the audience to their feet." Or if I put on a sequined dress or sing a jazzy song he says, "Well, she sold out to the commercial Las Vegas interests." If Joni does it, "she is experimenting with a new form of self-expression . . ."
>
> I go up to him when there's a group and say, "Oh, what did you think of the trumpet player?" (and there was no trumpet player, it was a sax) and he'll say, "Oh, he wasn't bad."

HELEN REDDY   OLIVIA NEWTON-JOHN

Courtesy of Capitol Records

NATALIE COLE

ANNE MURRAY

ROBERTA FLACK

FREDA PAYNE

DOLLY PARTON

TANYA TUCKER

LORETTA LYNN

KITTY WELLS

LINDA HARGROVE

Without a boost from the media, bereft of magazine covers and critical brouhaha, she has captured the imagination of a great number of people and had a good deal of success:

I just go quietly plodding along, probably making more money than anybody.

If writers sharpened their claws on her, part of the reason for their hostility was her support of the feminist movement. This draws criticism from the group opposed to the women's rights movement, and from some feminists who feel that she has sold out the sisters in attaching the cause to her career.

Part of her identification with the movement came from her success with "I Am Woman," a song she first wrote and recorded in 1970 above the objections of her producer, who considered the song too "butch."

It had no closing verse on the first album version. When she added the last verse (which managed to rhyme "go" with "embry-o") in a later version, it held an offer of reconciliation between the sexes.

With lyrics set to a peg-legged march tune, the song hit the feminist idea broadside. No doctrinaire nuance, gray areas to shelter ambiguities, subtleties to beguile the armchair revolutionary.

". . . Not effective either as propaganda or as schlock" a critic thundered, though pop is home for all, with nothing human foreign to it, where one's schlock is another's chic.

But "I Am Woman" was effective. In December 1972 it hit *Billboard*'s number one spot. It was selling twenty-five thousand copies a week, seven out of ten of them to women. Within a few months Helen Reddy received a Grammy award as Best Female Vocalist for "I Am Woman" over Barbra Streisand, Aretha Franklin, and Roberta Flack. Accepting the award, she thanked her record label, her husband-manager Jeff Wald,

. . . and God—she makes everything possible.

"I Am Woman" did appeal to women and, like effective propaganda, did not woo the vanity of the already convinced but caught the minds of the indifferent, the hostile, the isolated:

So many women who wouldn't have a copy of *Ms*. magazine in their house, or if Gloria Steinem came on the tube they'd turn her off—they'd be driving their cars home from the supermarket and the song comes on the radio: "I am strong, I am invincible," and it's seeping in whether they know it or not.

I was speaking in personal terms. You can be knocked down a hundred times. As long as you get up again a hundred times, it doesn't matter. It's just a way of saying snatch victory from the jaws of defeat, don't give up, keep going. Don't allow yourself to be put down. Know that inside there's a core of strength that you can rely on.

Helen Reddy appeals to women. They are her audience. Her appeal goes beyond support for feminist ideas to a simpatico for women's sensibility:

Women write to me and say, "I'm going through a divorce, and I put your album on every morning, because it helps me face the day." . . . You've had an experience which you've survived, and in sharing it with others, you've managed to make it a little easier for them.

Not everyone cottons to the glamorous ideal of the pop singer; the natural woman is not necessarily ignored. There's a place for a female performer with a minimum of artifice which Helen Reddy has occupied. But she was not always the plain Jane of pop. She began her career with the customary modish appurtenances of a pop singer, wigs, makeup, and gowns:

Here I was living in a communal type situation. At night I would put on the wigs and the eyelashes and the padded bra and the whole bit. Somebody who met me in both situations wouldn't recognize me, the change was so drastic. I used to feel like a female impersonator coming home and taking all this crap off.

I already looked like a woman, and when the consciousness finally raised far enough for me to realize that, I said, well fuck it.

It was gradual. I stopped wearing a bra, I let the dye grow out of my hair . . .

The brassiere became a point in contract negotiations with NBC-TV executives. The problem of her female image was resolved when the network granted that she would not be required to wear a bra, but she would indeed be expected to shave her armpits. Ridiculous. Later there was a fuss when she tried to dress up.

Her feminist ideas did not necessarily win her welcome in all circles of the women's movement. Elements in the movement can be particularly critical of a successful woman with feminist ideas, casting suspicion on her motives. Success in the world at large does not entitle a woman to leadership in the movement. Some attacks on a woman's professional success take on invidious overtones, and as is true of any movement that quits moving, there is not enough a person can do to satisfy these critics; the oppressive mentality is not limited to either sex.

Recording industry businessmen at first criticized Helen Reddy's voice as a sound that was too unusual to sell. Sell she did, and her unique horn-like tone cannot be mistaken for anyone else's. She's a jazz styled crooner careful of phrase and delivery at her best with songs like Leon Russell's "Masquerade" and Ron Davies' "Long Hard Climb."

Her pure tone makes her the interpreter par excellence of a type of song few singers can carry: the freak song. Freak songs are about isolation, loneliness, about individuals without a place in this world who live a life of illusion.

"Georgy Girl," "Ruby Tuesday," "Suzanne," and "Eleanor Rigby," other outcasts, found their place in popular music, and Helen Reddy has introduced a greater number of them to popular imagination.

Freak songs are stories of loneliness where the character has made an adjustment to a less than full life, carrying on regardless, although in the eyes of the world their lives are strange ones. Helen Reddy's people are "Angie Baby," a young girl who only relates to the radio (she's "a little teched in the head"), and forty-one-year-old "Delta Dawn," who still waits for her lover to return (folks say she's crazy), and poor Ruby Red Dress, whom people laugh at when they see her talking to herself.

These are the crushed roses of a harsh world. They are the freaks, the inconsolable Delta Dawn, the wary Ruby Red Dress, and the bizarre Angie. Freaks, who have as little voice in pop music as they do in the world it reflects. What appeals to a multitude is that everyone suspects that the freak probably exists inside themselves.

Olivia Newton-John sings from a place in American popular music where folk and country come together, a bridge between sixties and seventies pop styles. Her voice is old-line folk, but her phrasing is country. Bob Dylan's "If Not for You" became a lovesong in her version, without the darker connotations that Dylan himself imparts.

Later she sang "Banks of the Ohio," the tale of passionate crime, in an innocent voice which obscured the fact that the heroine of the song was murdering her lover.

The wistful sigh of her voice, a certain unassuming modesty were seen as evidence that she was another damned girl singer, a wimp. It was another opportunity for press to pounce and patronize: "no guts . . . cotton candy . . . a singing bunny rabbit sugar plum"; she had "the face that launched a thousand albums."

Some invective hurled at her was remarkable. Accusations: She's a record-selling machine made in Australia, bearing to country music the same relationship that astroturf does to grass; she mocks the music, mugging as if to tell the audience she considers the music silly.

She ruffled the sensibilities of country loyalists by making off with the country vocalist Grammy and awards from the Academy of Country and Western Music and the American Music Awards, and came up against their ultimate chauvinism: you ain't country.

When the invasion reached the country genre in the midseventies, the result was a down-home hornet's nest. Olivia Newton-John had not only not cast her lot with the country folk and played their circuit, as Diana Trask had done, she had songs written country style by an Australian, John Rostill, "If You Love Me (Let Me Know)," "Let Me Be There," and "Please Mr. Please," and before ever seeing Nashville, she had become popular in the country field.

Soft country style was moving into the pop middle of the road when Olivia Newton-John arrived, a position it had not occupied for twenty years.

Singers from Britain and the Commonwealth arrived in America through the sixties and midseventies. They had varying degrees of commercial success, but the important change was that cultural resistance no longer blocked their acceptance.

There is a cleavage in the pop genre at the time of the British invasion. The arrival of the Beatles, the Stones, and other male rock groups from Britain distracted the U.S. audience from American pop music everywhere but in the R&B/soul genre. The consequences for the solo female singer were grim.

The worst year was 1966. The veriest nightingale had as much chance of being heard as a butterfly in a hurricane; it was the nadir. Putdowns of the entire sex were in the air, the voice of a female was sissy stuff. That year the Rolling Stones released "Stupid Girl" and "Under My Thumb," putdowns not so much of femininity itself but on the suspected duplicity it may contain in its treacherous submission. The problem was developmental.

There's potential profit in every movement of the human sensibility, and so the ephemeral career of Mrs. Elva Miller was launched to capitalize on the unpopularity of the female voice. She became a satirical incarnation of the feminine principle in song. The pop standards she gave the Geschrei to, with an operatic hoot 'n' holler, took her to the stage of Carnegie Hall. When the joke wore thin, she disappeared.

In that deplorable year, women were not wanted in pop music. The few who did appear were associated with a male partner or a group.

Established pop singers were acceptable, British singers were welcome, and the genres maintained their own. Among the Americans, Nancy Sinatra, Vikki Carr, Cass Elliot, and Cher appeared. Cher got by in tandem with Sonny Bono, Cass came out under the banner of the Mamas and Papas, Vikki Carr benefited from the services of a husband-manager, and Nancy Sinatra has the name that means magic to any listener of pop music. These are immensely talented women, but between 1966 and 1970 America might not have listened to them, as she did not hear many another female vocalist who went begging.

In 1966, Helen Reddy was playing weddings and bars around New York City. The world was not ready for her nor for the soft sound of the Carpenters, who, even though they won the Hollywood Bowl Battle of the Bands that year, were ignored by promoters.

The British were so well regarded that when Sonny and Cher arrived for their New York debut in 1965, they were promoted as a dynamic new British duo.

Diminutive, exotic, modish Cher, or Cherilyn Sarkisian, more Armenian than Cherokee, then seemed like a leftover from folk days, safely apolitical, and with the same heavy straight hair that flowed over her high cheekbones as Buffy's. Cher's almond eyes were the better to take a dim view of Sonny with, for the years they were the Punch and Judy of prime time.

As part of the California resurgence that never really materialized against the British invasion, Cher had some of the appealing toughness of a teen singer, maybe an attitude she'd picked up in the old days when she sang backups on Phil Spector's Philles records.

Whatever shallow roots she may have had in the teen style, they were vitiated by the deep somber voice and wry humor of her phrasing. Cher does not do the "dumb" sound with the conviction of a teen singer, for a trace of irony in her delivery blows the "dumb" sound away.

In 1965, Sonny Bono wrote the Dylanesque "I Got You Babe," and launched Cher on a winning style that she still sings, ever with sleek melancholy, occasional grimness, songs that wend their way neatly between folk broodings and teen wails.

Cher is Cher, a unique character on the pop scene, whether by choice or by chance, surprisingly hitting the charts with "Bang Bang," a silly song with an Oriental style melody, a tune in the same mode as "Those Were the Days," a Slavic tune, something Melanie might have done to perfection although she probably would not have touched the lyrics to "Bang Bang."

When she gained more exposure on television, Cher lost singing technique instead of developing it, although in 1971 the *Gypsies, Tramps and Thieves* album had her at her height of strength and drama. But the rigors of television schedules can simplify a singer's technique, sap her energy, and make her singing emotionally thinner instead of richer.

She is still modish, having gone from the bizarre defiance of hippie chic in bowdlerized frilly bell-bottom trousers to the television vogue of sequined backless strapless jobs worn with attitude that says, "Hey, look at me—I'm dressed like some kind of big lady, huh!" Cher is the eternal arriviste. If she can do it, so can you: u 2 cn gt a gd jb w/mo pa.

There were other American replies to the British invasion. The most typical voice of 1966, the sound that captured the feeling of the year, was the gentle voice of Cass Elliot in the Mamas and Papas.

The group began in the Greenwich Village folk houses, where Cass Elliot, Michelle Gilliam, Denny Doherty, and John Phillips met. Just as Cher supplied an acceptable native American, the arrival of the Mamas and Papas met the need for a slick version of folk music. Their blend of Beach Boys chorals with a Washington Square kick was a prime combination.

Cass herself (Naomi Cohen) was an appealing hippopotamus of a woman, by modern standards an androgyne, although in a more ancient civilization she might have had the following of a fertility goddess. In the pop scene of 1966, not to irritate that sore spot with feminine attributes was an advantage. There were no rivals of either sex for her standing in the music scene, and Grace Slick said of her:

> This doesn't sound like the right thing to say, but . . . people are used to male-female roles, and since she was so big, she was neutral. You could go over to her house, either sex, without feeling you had to appear a certain way or come on a certain way.
>
> She was a warm person to be around, and damn near everybody in the world knew that chick . . . she wouldn't hassle you for any reason, because of her size, and she was genuinely warm and friendly.

Nor was there any hassle in the open, childlike lilt of her singing. It was as if every song were a lullaby, the driving "Words of Love" or the flowing "Monday, Monday" or the gentle "Dream a Little Dream of Me."

Her easy style was best in a group, where a pleasant tone blends well. The same transparent lightness was out of place when she took on Broadway tunes that need theatricality to put them across, and Cass never learned to sell her material with the desperation of a pop singer.

Cass went solo toward the end of the sixties, losing the feeling she had as a fronter for the Mamas and Papas. To forge a pop audience of her own, she embarked for Las Vegas, only to flop there like a dropped soufflé.

To Vegas she had gone unprepared for the crowd that demands polished entertainment. Cass' audience, the rock and folk people, are younger than the pop crowd. They become part of the show, they share the ritual. Las Vegas entertainment is show business; professional, groomed, slick. Cass the amateur, at heart a folkie, gained no friends there.

She always had a touch of bitter self-deprecation, a schtick that did not sit as well on her as it did on Streisand before her or Bette Midler after her. Cass, though she subverted her own wish to be taken seriously, did not want to be considered a clown.

When Cass died, even though it was common knowledge that she had weakened her body with heroin as well as the usual run of a performer's uppers, downers, and fatigue, the story went that she had choked to death on a ham sandwich. It was grotesque, to be done in by the humblest staple of the workingman's diet, for a woman whose gastronomic excesses were legendary. The reports of Cass' death were factual but had an undercurrent of black humor; leave 'em laughing. The truth was that she had died from having placed too much stress on her heart which was already overburdened by her weight with a two-week run at the London Palladium and the inevitable series of parties.

The image that will remain of her when the others fade is as she appeared on the stage, a tethered blimp swaying in a light breeze, floating, buoyant, smiling, wagging a finger at the crowd: "California Dreamin'," "I Call Your Name," "Monday, Monday."

When Nancy Sinatra reappeared from nowhere in the dreary year of 1966 with "These Boots Are Made for Walking," she struck a welcome attitude in the run of the pop charts. By then, the constant breast-beating by the women pop singers had earned them some of the oblivion they were faced with. Against Cher's "Bang Bang," Dusty Springfield's "You Don't Have to Say You Love Me," and the Supremes' "You Keep Me Hangin' On" and "My World Is Empty Without You," the women were putting up this howling jeremiad that was not appreciably balanced by the ever brave Petula Clark, who was singing "My Love," or by the airy sound of Cass Elliot. Nancy Sinatra's was the only voice raised in protest, carrying a different message; she was like Calamity Jane come to liven up a boring party.

"Boots" and a few other songs had a distinctive lady pirate roll to them; some of the feeling arose from the creative combination she had found with Lee Hazelwood. While the combination lasted, they made "Boots," "How Does That Grab You Darlin'," "Sugar Town," and more songs. A duet with her father, "Something Stupid," was also an inspired idea. That sudden success in 1966 would not have been possible without the considerable experience she had had singing since 1959, or the years of vocal training with Gian-Carlo Menotti, and the pure, full voice that she was naturally endowed with.

In the 1966–67 doldrums, another exception was Vikki Carr. "It Must Be Him" brought her to public view in 1967, while judicious management by her husband, Dan Moss, and backbreaking work on her own part kept her there.

Her talent for shedding tears on cue is stunning, even though the audience has witnessed the very same tears on the very same phrase of the very same song on her last concert tour. The very real tears give way to an upbeat straw-hat style number to end the show on an optimistic note.

Another highlight of her show as riveting as the tears is her a capella tour de force when she sets the microphone aside and fills the arena with her voice. Her hard-edged, brassy cabaret voice can stretch into a Judy Garland riff, but with more nuance and less neurosis.

Vikki Carr, Florencia Cardona por favor, seems to have cashed in on the chiquita charm that earlier swept the States with Carmen Miranda, offering fast, painless translations of the Spanish songs that dot her repertoire. She doesn't play Latin Bombshell or Sultry Señorita. She considers herself a representative of the Chicana of the

Southwest and must comport herself with the proper modesty as becomes a Latin woman. She doesn't shake her ass.

That quiet modesty does command respect, as do her restrained gowns, usually a modified mantilla draped over the sequins, one of those mantillas that make Latin women seem so sad, as if they were perpetually in mourning.

In 1968 only Merilee Rush was a fresh face on the scene. "Angel of the Morning" was not the type of song to build a career on, even though the poignancy of the melody more than the surprising lyrics accounted for its success. The song was for the single woman what Frank Sinatra's "Strangers in the Night" was for the gay community. "Angel of the Morning" was about that moment when the companion of a one-night love affair takes leave, but unlike all the other songs, *she* leaves. This was a revolutionary attitude; the woman was brave. There was no similar song to follow it. There were in fact very few songs of this sort ever written from a woman's point of view, since that attitude toward lovers by women has only recently become acceptable—possible—with the proliferation of contraceptive pills. And this passed in pop in 1968, though maybe only because Merilee Rush had tears in her voice.

The Carpenters, Freda Payne, and Anne Murray appeared during 1970. That was the year of the emergence of singer-songwriters, the great change in popular American music, the death of Janis Joplin. The strength of rock as the main influence on popular music had begun to ebb. Roberta Flack arrived in 1972, Bette Midler in the following year. By the middle of the decade there were great changes, and then came Minnie Riperton, one of the most unusual pop voices, and Toni Tennille, at the time one of the most banal, who later showed how fine a vocalist she is.

Karen Carpenter, the vocalist and sometime drummer of the brother-sister duo, had no independent musical identity. Soft California pop songs with her deep voice in a dozen overdubs might by 1970 have been passé, but instead a caprice of fate turned America away from genre music and toward the middle-of-the-road pop of Richard Carpenter, Paul Williams, and late-blooming hits of the now hoary team of Bacharach and David.

This, to the chagrin of rock loyalists who remained fixed in the delusion that their favorite style was still the core of popular music. At the same time, they were further irritated when Anne Murray's easygoing croon brought back a style that never entirely goes out of favor in pop music, from a blend of influences that an American from America might have blushed to acknowledge: Mahalia Jackson, the Mills Brothers, Perry Como.

Anne Murray was wholesome. But the Doris Day girl-next-door laurels sat on her stoop like unwanted occupant mail. Fresh good looks and flawless smile notwithstanding, the straight-thinking Nova Scotian had little taste for the show biz imposture that delights some of her sisters, and the corn-fed farm girl routine was as phony as the rest of the hypes.

Since she liked nothing better than to guzzle a quart of beer, she struggled to maintain her individuality while her audience, determined to beatify her, ignored it. "Hello, New York," she called out at a crowd on a chilly night in Central Park during the Schaefer Music Festival, "how's yer buns?" At Ottawa's National Arts Centre, she played the Opera house, and told the audience:

> My image has been the wholesome girl next door, apple-cheek Annie thing. But I want you people to know that under these clothes and behind this façade—this body—is a mass of hickeys!

That lumpish humor belongs more on a track queen than on a pop circuit thrush, and playing turnabout with the crowd by clicking cameras at them, and eyeing them through opera glasses she claimed to have gotten at a Swedish strip joint is mildly outrageous behavior for a performer who should be in the throes of the performing trance, weaving a spell over her audience. But the people are never quite sure exactly what they want from Anne Murray. They want her to look and to behave in a certain way, but most of what they demand is not in keeping with her personality.

> When I was in Chicago, during the lull between "Snowbird" and "Danny's Song," the guy who owned the club said, "Show some boob—if you show boob and use four-letter words onstage, everybody'll love you."

Not only the people who are in the business, but groups of unrelated individuals consider it their business to dictate to Anne Murray. One day she was fed up with her wavy blond hair and had it kinked into a barely successful Afro. The move was neither becoming nor popular with some members of her audience.

From a small town in Canada came a petition with two hundred signatures against her new hairdo and six for it, along with a threat to take action if she did not return her hair to its former state.

The presumed wholesomeness of Canada's Singing Sweetheart annoyed some as it enchanted others. Particularly for the rock genre audiences, there was not enough anguish in her singing, nor evidence of any suffering in her life. She had in fact been trained to sing, enjoyed it, and sang with ease. One night she faced the rock-oriented freebee studio audience of "The Midnight Special."

> I walked out, and I look healthy. I saw all these scruffy-looking folks on the floor. They weren't booing me, it was just—ho hum, bla bla. I was hosting the show and I had to spend the rest of the evening with them, so I just kicked ass and said, "Well, if you folks are so hip, how come you're sitting around on your asses for five hours, and I have three hit records, and I'm sitting up here?"
> . . . They all just came around.

Anne Murray was trained on her CBC-TV appearances. Her earliest moves were geared to a television camera. TV technique translates poorly to a live stage, so that she was often stiff and lacked visual projection for a large stage. That was the worst that could be said of her.

The reason for her popularity is that she does possess one of the most beautiful voices in popular music: smooth, mellow alto that never strains or falls short of a note.

Hers is a translucent, simple style that lends sincerity to the most arch material, such as Lennon-McCartney songs. In fact, when they are sung without irony, they seem like totally different songs. Her simplicity can renew a song.

That simplicity allows her to choose songs that would be ignored by most sophisticates, like the pretty homespun Canadian ballads of Gene McClellan, "Another Pot o' Tea" or domestic scenes such as Gordon Lightfoot's "Cotton Jenny," or the delicate "You Needed

Me." Simplicity is why she sings country so well, and receives country awards, and is considered a country artist by the Academy of Country and Western Music, Nashville's Country Music Hall of Fame, and the National Academy of Recording Arts and Sciences, to the chagrin of old line country performers.

Anne Murray was considered not only an outsider to the country music scene, but a foreigner, even though her native Canada has access to essentially the same popular music as the United States. Country is a regional genre jealously guarded by its purists, for their own economic purposes.

While the country genre tries to exclude artists with pressure from within, the "soul" genre is a repository for artists who are placed there by outside pressure, on a racial, not a regional or stylistic basis.

Because she is black, Freda Payne was pushed into the "soul" or rhythm & blues category, even though her background was pop-jazz, not gospel.

Real gospel is from the Baptist and the Pentecostal churches, you know, where they shout and everything. Our church was an African Methodist Episcopal church . . . They were not doing any real strong gospel music in our church. It was more—hymns, spirituals, the Hallelujah Chorus around Christmas and Easter—more classical type spiritual songs.

Freda Payne and Roberta Flack and other black female singers who emerged during the Black Power years were categorized "soul" singers for years, even though they lacked gospel background. The category had little to do with the women's singing styles. To consider Freda Payne's "Band of Gold" R&B or "soul" is nothing more than segregating the singer by color, but at the time if a black female did not sing "soul" style, she was suspect, perhaps of being a turncoat. It was a convenience that kept the black women out of the pop camp, but since the R&B market was lucrative, it would have been wasteful not to pump it.

In the 1972 Grammy awards, Freda Payne competed with Aretha Franklin, Roberta Flack, and Janis Joplin in the R&B category. Only Aretha was the true "soul" singer; Aretha *was* soul. Janis, long dead, might have qualified by having blues roots. Roberta Flack and Freda Payne were placed there as a convenience, for their blackness. None of their styles matched.

Freda Payne, at heart a pop singer with a preference for pop ballads, was propelled into the R&B market by being teamed with Holland-Dozier-Holland, songwriters who at the time set R&B cash registers a-ring. It was a commercial success, but an artistic cul-de-sac for the singer.

> I got to be intimidated by my own feeling that I was trying to impress the blacks. I got the feeling that I had to show them that I had soul—*their* kind, soul-soul—like gospel church, although that's not my favorite kind of singing. That's not my *love*.

She is more at home with Jacques Brel than with R&B material. In the future, she may not be so easily railroaded, not only because the "soul" conspiracy no longer has the force it once had, but also because the experience taught Freda Payne a lesson.

> I felt that as a black woman, I had to do it. But now I don't feel that way because those were my own insecurities. I was getting uptight about it because I felt that I may have pressure to do it, like they say, "Why don't you get down more?" Well, hey, what if I don't like that style? What if that's not my feeling? . . . It's too rough for me.

The other black singer whose "soul" was in question in the early seventies was Roberta Flack, who like Freda Payne possessed nary a whit of gospel background. She was not raised in the gospel tradition of the Baptist church, but in Washington, D.C.'s African Methodist Episcopal Zion Church. While she may probably have more in common musically with Judy Collins and Nina Simone than she does with Aretha, a lack of gospel background does not set her apart from loyalty to the black cause.

> It makes a difference. You have to reach back and help, particularly among black people. Most people in the commercial side of the business assume that black people can entertain very well, and they don't give you much credit for being able to think.

So it's up to black people to help each other and to be the strength we need for each other.

Roberta Flack studied classical music and voice. She does not improvise or execute vocal ornaments gospel style, but the training is no drawback for her:

What you hear has two major elements, the heart and the head as well. Classical training does require a kind of discipline that is not necessary to perform popular music but is certainly a great help. Billy Preston, Donny Hathaway, the baddest ones—Stevie—have studied. The most influential ones are the ones who prepared, who work at it. I would like this level of performance to be accepted as a real art form, not as some quirk.

Considering herself adequately prepared, she decided to produce her own album, *Hubris*. Producing a record is one job, singing the songs is a second, and doing two jobs at once is twice as difficult. Then there were other barriers:

Record companies and people in the business want your knowledge of the technical end of production to be rather limited, and I guess it is because it would be basically insulting to have a woman who sings a love song sitting there with her boobs over the sound board going like this . . .

Ro is a poised woman, an artist of great dignity, a mentor and teacher who brings protégés onto her stage to introduce them to her audience. Her voice is a marvel of warmth and precision, sometimes too rigorously exact. When she succeeds, as she did first with "The First Time Ever I Saw Your Face," she usually creates a new song from old elements. In this case she sang the words like an operatic aria gone folk and in doing so evoked the feeling that lay just underneath the stiff lyrics. She knows her strengths:

I consider myself basically a reader of words. In the business there are a few people who do that better than they do anything else . . . they're not fad entertainers, fad singers.

Minnie Riperton became widely known in 1975, although she had sung with Rotary Connection, a late sixties Chicago rock group. Neither a rock nor an R&B "soul" singer, she had one of the most unusual vocal styles in pop music, a five-octave range which was developed by operatic training. When she hit a high note, her voice was no longer human, but an instrument: a flute.

Her songs, her music, her identity were radically different from anything that had gone before.

> My writing is my life, that's what it is. It's my personal revolution. I can't pick up a gun and go out and fight, and I'm really not that great a speechmaker, but there are a lot of things I'd like to say to people, to children, to women, to men, just to all of us humans; that there are brighter sides to life, because I've seen them.

She stood for the affirmation of life and joy just as Piaf at one time represented the French Resistance. The sound of birds in her voice, the plants she decorated her stage with, the utter dignity of her bearing when she appeared before an audience were her statement.

> I think my music is very political. It's all about what everybody wants to do, and can never really find the time to really do it: to enjoy life, to give, to share . . . I don't want to sing anybody's blues. I have, but in a different way. I don't want it to be sad! To dwell on something that happened to me really heavy . . . it would reflect on my loved ones, on my friends. It's not healthy. It's not good for anybody. Why should you bring everybody down? . . .
> We all know that all these things are happening: droughts, famine, killing, raping, and robbing . . . Meanwhile, even in the midst of all these things, people find happiness in themselves.
> When you think about helping people, it's not only feeding them, but helping them learn to love.

Natalie Cole, the daughter of Nat "King" Cole, began performing in the midseventies. Surrounded by the best jazz and pop influences since childhood, she blended and assimilated these influences, as well as the "soul" style of Aretha, into her personal style, and transcended the categories. By then the thrall of the "soul" conspiracy on the black singers was broken.

In 1973, little stirred in popular music. It was still easier to break through the lassitude and the backlash to the women's liberation movement within a mixed group. Tony Orlando and Dawn became popular, a group that featured the teen scene veteran, Telma Hopkins and Joyce Vincent Wilson.

Maureen McGovern sang "The Morning After" and no more, while the pop scene maintained the status quo till the appearance of Bette Midler, an organ of calculated triteness, who sprang out of New York's Continental Baths.

"Tacky" was her clarion call, and blessed be they who are so chic they may embrace banality. "Am I Blue," "Drinking Again," "Leader of the Pack"—her show was a compendium of the female singers who had gone before. She was a young cabaret-style singer with enormous talent and, as the old pop tunes might have called them, great charms—the biggest knockers in show business, she called them.

She quickly gained a gay audience that it takes a regular pop singer a lifetime to earn, and the gay audience is the best that a performer can have, since gay men earn enough to support a family and don't, and entertain themselves and each other outside the home, rarely being coupled and housebound as are married men and women, or confined by tradition or lack of money as single women are.

Part of Bette's legend was her not demure but broad, camp, aggressive, and irrepressible humor. In 1973, she was presented with a Grammy award for best newcomer. Karen Carpenter handed her the award.

Wow—Karen Carpenter! After all I've said about her she should have thrown it at me!

A while later, Bette canceled several shows while recovering from appendicitis, then finally opened in Los Angeles. The curtain parted to reveal a screened hospital bed, the screens removed by the Harlettes, her backup singers, who were dressed as nurses and carried bedpans. Bette was in the bed, singing.

"How many of you did not believe it was appendicitis?" she asked the audience. "How many of you think it was a D and C? I'll tell you what it was—I had my tits removed!" She had, in a moment of charity, she claimed, donated them to Cher.

She digs and jabs at the audience, and if they disapprove of a remark, she greets their reaction with:

Oh—*Crowd Turns On Diva!* . . .

and provokes them with:

You all don't look so depressed—except for *you* darling, you look like shit! Oh, I didn't mean it, I didn't mean it. I figure, whoever can afford to sit in the front row . . .

The stageshow quack that was almost squelched by the British singers and undermined by the relaxed folk approach of the sixties was revived just for yocks by Bette Midler. As her stage persona, "The Divine Miss M," she went easily from one musical period to another, through a half century of female vocalists in every style from subway to sequins. Her facility was her downfall. In the push it was not clear that the fond parodies that Bette Midler sang lacked the technique of the Andrews Sisters, the "dumb" heart of the Dixie Cups, the worldliness of Lotte Lenya. Bette Midler's sweetness and energy carried, but the pity was that the real talents she had were ignored, overwhelmed by her talent for mimicry.

She was disadvantaged by a sudden rise to fame on an ephemerally faddish style. The brief surge of nostalgia in '72 left her stranded two years later when the hokey taste wore out. Her staples of the thirties, old Hollywood, the Depression blues were no go. Struts, shimmies, machine-gun versions of "Boogie Woogie Bugle Boy" and "Chattanooga Choo Choo" were passé. Her real métier is audible when she sheds her brashness and becomes a singer of poignancy, conviction, and tenderness, in John Prine's "Hello in There" or in Tom Waits' "Shiver Me Timbers." She can sing.

The fad that raised Bette Midler also brought out a mixed quartet called Manhattan Transfer: Janis Siegel, Laurel Masse, Tim Hauser, and Alan Paul. Janis Siegel had been a cog in the teen music machine when she was twelve years old, the Shangri-Las to her had been the big girls. Later she worked in a folk group, Laurel Canyon, which played a few folk clubs in New York before folding. The trend for revivals of old songs did not last, and so the quartet is still searching for a permanent status on the United States pop scene, though they are popular in Europe.

The pop vocalists new in the seventies are a new style of woman. They are more casual, reflecting the influence of folk. They are more outspoken, more vehement, reflecting the style of the rock singers, the awareness of soul, the protest and vigor of disco. With the exception of the schtick artists, they assert their own personalities and do not try to fit a pop singer mold.

The pop singer is now concerned with her meaning to the audience, which supports her because she represents a certain point of view.

The style of the seventies was a romantic one. The harsh attitudes of the sixties faded away, helped to their demise by the rise of the personal approach of the singer-songwriters. Romanticism has always been at the heart of popular music, but particularly in the seventies, sentiment became respectable once more. At the end of that decade, values were again called into question, and the pendulum swings. Pop music is attenuated rock, sweetened disco, tamed soul.

VIII
COUNTRY QUEENS

COUNTRY songs express every abuse that can be inflicted on a human being in the name of love. Every disaster, every bit of newsworthy and banal information found in the daily paper is a fit preoccupation for a country song, from triumph to trauma. Nothing human is unknown: adultery, revenge, larceny, faith, passion, innuendo, slander, murder, and divorce. There are songs about the seven deadly sins, the three cardinal virtues, the ten commandments, and all the justice, tyranny, loyalty, and moral righteousness that can be derived from them, as well as ditties like "Sad Movies Make Me Cry."

Country takes its strength from facts, or at least popular notions of facts. It is solid as earth, and asks to change nothing.

The themes may be trite, but they are values that people kill for. Human beings would probably not come to blows over a literary conceit.

It's God, country, mom and apple pie, treated with intimate emotions not often viewed publicly in American society, where the strong silent approach to feelings is accepted. Country songs blare them out openly, expressing what people would be embarrassed to say.

Anyone lacking sympathy for the country style is repelled by its ungirt emotions. The most bitter remarks about country music are made by loyalists from genres in decay, revealing parochialism, prejudice, ignorance of the place of country music in American thought. Their venomous attacks on country music make amusing controversy.

Stan Kenton in 1974 called country music a national disgrace. Drummer Buddy Rich claimed it appeals to "intellectuals with the minds of four-year-olds."

Country music is a narrative form of popular culture that hides its artifice. If country lyrics are simple, and melodies can be accompanied by three basic chords, it is because neither words nor music stand in the way of the story. The songs express basic human emotions, which are unchanging. No way of making emotions subject to any sort of sophistication has been found, and the emotional accuracy of country is its strength.

The ideal of woman in country music is conventional to the point of being bizarre. One of the first country songs recorded was from the old folk tradition by the Carter Family:

> *Single girl, single girl, she's goin' dressed so fine . . .*
> *Married girl . . . she wears most any kind*

The single girl is free to do as she pleases, the married girl rocks the cradle and cries. The idea that women might lead an unhappy life is not a new theme to the ballad tradition, where women are cudgeled, strangled, knifed, hanged, often by their own true lovers, even if they are inconveniently pregnant. It's news; the daily paper carries the same stories still.

Country has carried the mournful tales of women into the modern era. The women are less often killed, but they usually live unhappy lives and suffer a lot.

The belles of Nashville sing in tuneful reproach, wail in plaintive melody as steel guitars echo their poignant cries in the background.

Though the audience is made up of couples and families, country is women's music. Eighty per cent of country records are bought by women, the taste makers of the style, which makes country the real barometer of the status of women in America. The country audience long preferred male singers to females; the women vocalists could not gain the ear of that audience because they lacked status.

There is one type of country song where female vocalists excel: sad ballads, weepers. They are traditionally a women's form, since tears are considered a feminine weapon, protests couched in tearful complaints a style suited to women's helpless state.

Weepers are the soap operas of popular music. In theory, a housewife passes the dull hours doing dishes, cleaning house, the radio tuned to the country station to hear stories of other lives similar to her own, some sadder.

Supposedly faced with the conventional lot of a woman—never in her life doing what she wants to do, obeying the wishes of whatever man she answers to—the housewife may consider death the ultimate release, her only liberation in fantasies. Country songs, like teen material, portray excessively romantic stories because women, like young people, are trapped by the barriers in society. Country has a lot in common with teen, the only exception being that the stories and characters are adult.

That would be a simple explanation for the popularity and character of country weepers. But sympathy is wasted on this hypothetical belle: she cannot exist in reality, even though when weepers are looked at closely it's clear that the woman is a vast authority in a limited sphere.

All is not what it seems in the world we see in country songs. Florynce Kennedy once mentioned loving southern women because they are like cupcakes and razors. The southern woman has high status in her society; the country queen singer of the weepers is a performer of endurance and finesse to make these songs come across convincingly.

The woman in country ballads is more than a lil' darlin' done wrong by some man. At her most exaggerated ideal, she is womanhood's complement to the equally absurd male fantasy of the hulking macho of cock rock: cunt country.

A dopey broad she is, living a hell of a life. Cunt country values are either wishful thinking or simply false; the records sell like hotcakes at a weight watcher's picnic.

In one of the most popular of the cunt country songs, Tammy Wynette's "Stand by Your Man," the ideas are tricky, not flattering to the big man who goes off to have some fun while the lil' darlin' mopes around waiting for him at home. The guy ends up looking like a jerk. Lil' darlin' outclasses him. The point of songs like "Stand by Your Man," for all their apparent acquiescence to the values that be, is that, after all, a man is "just" a man. Fallible. He isn't even as good as a woman because a woman would "know better." She takes no part in the sordid business of man, since she is child and queen. An immaculate milk-white innocence prevents her from delving into the dross the man is involved with.

She grants him forgiveness from aloft: she, a woman, having learned right from wrong at her mother's knee, is a keeper of the fire, source of wisdom, herself mother to men, and his superior. He's just a little boy who never grew up, and must be taken in hand, gently chided for his transgressions. These elevated ideas about a woman date from the medieval ideals of courtly love and are relevant to today's world.

Country advocates with academic leanings bemoan the fact that their favorite music has not been taken seriously. At fault were the *aw, shucks* attitudes of the forties, when country was derisively called "hillbilly" music. A number of performers engaged audience sympathy by playing hayseed, as if they were one with the audience of uneducated farmers who knew nothing and liked it that way. On the other hand, they were supposedly gifted with some sort of native wit basically better than education. In political circles this is the "plain folk" appeal to the poor vote, and country was the music of the poor, the white trash, the agrarian South.

To counteract this trend, country scholars point out that country music is an authentic American traditional music that dates from the troubadours, unlike the rest of American popular music that takes ideas from anywhere.

Aw, shucks country belonged to male performers. If there was a woman sharing the stage, she was not the ideal of the lady. The stage was no place for a lady. A tomboy in boots and Stetson might get by, or a comedienne who is androgynous, but what lady could be one of the Skillet Lickers, and how would it look for her to join the Carolina Tar Heels? Could she make it in the Fruit Jar Drinkers, the Washboard Wonders, the Hoss Hair Pullers, or the Corn Shuckers?

Female country singers, the queens as we know them now, often were attached to popular male vocalists as duo partners. Loretta Lynn was paired with Conway Twitty, Dolly Parton with Porter Wagoner, Tammy Wynette with George Jones. There are husband-wife, brother-sister, father-daughter, and unrelated duos.

The worship of the country queens by ardent fans is suffused with both awe and proprietorship. They belong to their audience like a store-boughten object, as a woman once belonged to her family, as a statue of the resident deity of a house belongs by the hearth.

At every country music show, performers stay as long as needed to sign autographs and talk to people; they are approachable. The fans know about their marriages, divorces, and children; about their hobbies and the property they own. Everyone is aware of Loretta Lynn's tumors, Lynn Anderson's quarter horses, Tammy Wynette's domestic problems and her opinions about alcohol; they are stated in fanzines, stage raps, discussed backstage after the show, or appear in their autobiographical songs.

There is no lack of calculation used to maintain this easy rapport between performer and audience, not all of it in bad faith. Mystiques are carefully tended, even though they are antimystiques, "plain folk" public images. The country singer wouldn't want to appear snobbish or uppity to her people, who consider her one of them.

Many performers are diffident about their success, insisting in interviews on their love of home and family, the joys and fulfillments of domestic chores, the pleasure of wifely duties, the delight in children. Even with minimal success a country singer hardly has the time to grow bored with a daily routine that has driven many a woman out of her mind, and if they often make statements about women's roles, it is because the questions they are asked are loaded. They are considered spokeswomen for middle-American women. They are, in fact, performers.

The country queen carries the brunt of American nostalgia for convention, which is part of the conservative nature of the country music ethic. It is no accident that Patti Page, Brenda Lee, Teresa Brewer, and other pop oldies gravitated to country when their pop careers fizzled. Country looks backward, and moves more slowly than pop music.

Country singers have longer careers and more loyal audiences. Maybelle Carter performed from the late twenties to the seventies. Kitty Wells began in the forties and still sang in the seventies. Loretta Lynn, Dolly Parton, and Tammy Wynette have had long careers. Top singers in country remain at the top for years; they are not replaced in a matter of weeks as pop singers are. They score top ten hits on country charts year after year, and they maintain a loyal following by continuous tours and live performances that add up to a grueling amount of work.

Manifesting itself in all facets of country music, from song lyrics to business decisions, the conservative vein in country plays on the xenophobia of its audience.

Claims to homegrown virtues by country to the contrary, it is difficult to ignore the results of exaggerated conservatism in country; the paranoia that goes disguised as love of home and family, obscurantism, the mean whelp of cultural pride, isolationism, mere fear; religiosity that masks ignorance, malice, bigotry, and superstition.

Tent evangelists often attach a country singer to their show. The mixture of music and religion has always been a potent one, and not by chance are singers who involve themselves with religious movements so often country style.

Equating musical popularity with competence in real-life issues is the same mistake as assuming that a performer, for being in the public eye, is personally a representative of public opinion. The ability to hop from any celebrity status into leadership in religioso and political involvements is a dangerous one.

The worst are fanatics who abdicate personal responsibility for their statements by claiming authority from the Bible, or the Word of God.

A pleasant singer who had scored with "Paper Roses" years before, Anita Bryant, suddenly caught the spotlight again with publicity she got by spearheading a drive in Florida's Dade County to strip homosexuals of "alleged" human rights to jobs and housing.

Generalized fear and hatred focused on an object, and in San

Francisco a "queer" baiting incident ended in the death of a young homosexual man. "This one's for Anita," his attacker said.

The crime might have occurred even if she had not taken her well-publicized stand against homosexuals. The pity of it is that her campaign created a context that could lead to the rationalization of such a brutal act.

Moralization is an old tradition in country music, which must be geared for a family audience; poor folks don't hire babysitters or leave the old people at home. Early in the modern tradition, the Carter Family distributed handbills that advertised their show: "The Program Is Morally Good." Morality even much later was a source of arrogance in the country genre, among performers who resist not only the mood of the country but also changes in country music itself, when it followed its natural penchant to keep up with real-life concerns.

A lay minister and Grand Ole Opry member, Billy Grammer in 1975 focused attention on himself by denouncing country music: "slut and slanderous" it was.

His remarks before the Opry audience and carried on radio station WSM were:

In order for a country song to be popular these days, it has to have lyrics about laying in bed with someone and getting them pregnant before they get married . . . Country music is becoming a smutty world. It's a shame to think the pornographic business has hit country music and infiltrated the ranks. We don't need it. We are above it.

Trying to conform to a standard that would supposedly be acceptable to the great range of tastes in the audience means that the sensibility should be scaled to the simplest terms, with sexual innuendo veiled, albeit crudely. Grossness is no new trend in country music, although the manner of putting it has changed.

During the *aw, shucks* period the risqué jokes had a malodorous humor of poo-poo pee-pee puerility that stigmatized the entire country music field. A Maddox family schtick that survived to be told still in the seventies was a story about a revolting waitress who, when asked to warm up a couple of hamburgers, stuck one under each arm. Punchline? The customer didn't dare ask for a hot dawg.

The first recordings of what we know as country music were made for Victor in April 1927 by Ralph Peer, who paid Jimmy Rogers and the Carter Family to sing the songs they knew into a horn in a back room.

The Carter Family was Sara Dougherty, Maybelle Addington Carter, and A. P. Carter. They collected country ballads by learning them from other singers. Their innovation, which helped speed the adoption of country music by a music audience, was to adapt the medieval modes of the solo ballads, which had been handed down through generations since the British settlement, to a form that made them easy to accompany with tuned instruments and chord patterns.

The guitar was Maybelle Carter's contribution to country music. She helped popularize it with her style of playing melody on bass strings and chords on upper strings of the guitar. She was not credited with writing some of the Carter Family songs, since she deferred to A.P., the man of the family.

While country did not have many women in the performing groups of the thirties, Maybelle and Sara drew from the sacred and ballad traditions, traditionally a female stronghold.

At the same period Patsy Montana, the "Cowboy's Sweetheart" played county fairs with the Prairie Ramblers. She was a yodeler, a cowgirl in western duds, the first female country singer to sell over a million records with "I Want to Be a Cowboy's Sweetheart" in 1936. She had more songs along the same lines: "I Only Want a Buddy, Not a Sweetheart," "The She Buckaroo," "Sweetheart of the Saddle."

Country was not known widely till the forties, since only in 1939 did the NBC radio network begin airing the Grand Ole Opry a half hour on Saturday nights. Then country became an economic trend in the recording industry of enough magnitude to be listed on the *Billboard* record sales charts of the forties, though it was not certain whether it should be lumped with the foreign category, race records, American folk records, or placed side by side with Ella Fitzgerald.

The loutish *aw, shucks* style, "hillbilly" music, then began to change character. Capitol and Decca pressed the market, and by June 1949 a country music chart appeared in *Billboard*.

Commercial possibilities of country came to light when Patti Page
recorded the phenomenally successful "Tennessee Waltz," which had
been released in country circles two years earlier. As a "B" side in a
pop version in Patti Page's melting style, in 1950 it became the biggest seller till then in popular music.

Country music in the early fifties was still a male club till Kitty
Wells brought out a new consciousness with an answer song to Hank
Thompson's "Wild Side of Life." Thompson's song made the usual
accusation against women, the same made in the first pages of the
Bible. He sang that women are placed on earth to be the ruin of men.
Au contraire, "It Wasn't God Who Made Honky Tonk Angels"
Kitty's song replied, what a shame to put the blame on "us women"
when it's the men who actually drag us down; no, God didn't make
honky tonk angels, men did.

Honky tonk angels hadn't been looked at in that way before, al-
though it was allowed that a woman's lot was a miserable one. Kitty
Wells' career made a quantum leap, with the commercial success of
"Angels."

Women still had far to go before they sang their own songs, expressed their own visions, but attitudes toward female singers
changed. Kitty became the first queen of country music; a mere title,
but one of stature.

She was the greatest vocalist of her time in country, she set the
style for country female vocalists at her level, a clear, twangy sound,
country nasal, ornamented with deft, delicate turns. Her clear voice
bled through the aching "Back Street Affair," "Release Me," "I
Don't Claim to Be an Angel," "They're Stepping All Over My
Heart," "I Hope My Divorce Is Never Granted," "I Can't Stop Loving You," "Repenting," "A Wedding Ring Ago," "I Gave My Wedding Dress Away," and other classic country hurtin' songs, material
that helped earn country its reputation for misery.

Hurtin' songs are a professional role; dry as it may sound, Kitty
Wells says, "I sing songs that I think the public expects of me."

Kitty Wells reigned till a challenge came from Patsy Cline in '57.
With a sweeter sound, Patsy Cline arrived professionally via a new
route to popularity: television. She froze the applause meters on
"Arthur Godfrey's Talent Scouts" show with "Walkin' After Mid-

night." Her best known song came a few years later, "I Fall to Pieces."

Throughout its existence, country has been drawn closer to pop. Patsy Cline's style took it one more step toward formula pop à la Patti Page, Georgia Gibbs, Connie Francis; farther from yodeling Patsy Montana and the folksy Carter Family.

Patsy Cline might have moved closer to pop acceptance, bringing with her the entire country genre, but she died in a plane crash in 1963.

Popular music was being made aware of country by pop singers who took country material as their own. The most notable cover version was Ray Charles's "I Can't Stop Loving You," a D. Gibson country classic unveiled to the pop audience in 1962.

That year Loretta Lynn began to sing professionally. Dottie West wrote and sang "Country Sunshine." Melba Montgomery, Skeeter Davis, and Connie Smith were on the scene. Jody Miller switched to country for keeps with an answer song to Roger Miller's "King of the Road," called "Queen of the House." Pickings were slim, and country was being forced to retrench by a new political atmosphere in America.

Loretta Lynn was next in line as country queen after Patsy Cline. Loretta returned country to the harder Kitty Wells style. A rift developed between hard country and material that could cross over to pop.

Melba Montgomery, a singer with a smooth, tender way of singing conventional country was George Jones's duo partner before the advent of Tammy Wynette. Melba's style is a marvel of subtlety in songs about illicit love affairs, kids, hurtin' without complainin'. One of the most well-known songs she wrote was the duo standard, "We Must Have Been Out of Our Minds."

Before disappearing into the entourage of Billy Graham's religioso crusades, Connie Smith was one of the best country vocalists, particularly in '64 when she sang Bill Anderson's "Once a Day."

A delightful singer who also tends to the religioso, Skeeter Davis crossed into pop with "End of the World," an affecting love lament of mournful wistfulness. The only heiress to Patsy Montana of any note, Rose Maddox had "Sing a Little Song of Heartaches," a departure from the type of her earlier success with songs like "Why Don't You Haul Off and Love Me," "I Wish I Was Single Again," and "Wild, Wild Young Men."

Planing bravely above the rest, Loretta Lynn; sassy, witty, brilliant, with a formula rags-to-riches story that a Hollywood hack would blush to write. Daughter of a Kentucky coal miner, she lived poor as one of twelve children till she went from home, a child bride at age fourteen.

She was a mother the same year, and drudged with her husband Mooney Lynn to survive till he hit on the idea of having her sing country music. In '62 she recorded the first song she wrote, "I'm a Honky Tonk Girl."

To promote the record, they packed off the children and drove through the country from one radio station to another, living on baloney and cheese sandwiches, sleeping in an old car. Loretta hand-carried "Honky Tonk Girl" to disc jockeys and won air time for her song.

Her songs and writing style have a triumphant flair for straight talk: "You Ain't Woman Enough to Take My Man," "Don't Come Home A-Drinkin' with Lovin' on Your Mind," and her affectionate autobiographical statement, "Coal Miner's Daughter." One of the most valuable assets of Loretta as a songwriter who makes statements about herself, as a woman in regard to her own life, is her upstanding pride. She does not believe her themes are limited to a country audience; country or city, life is the same:

> They live and they die. They all get married, have children, get divorces. When a country song is wrote it's about life—a country song don't pull punches . . . that's where we're all going to get to—down to earth.

Running against country righteous, she falls in and out of trouble with religiosos ever on the lookout for sin and smut-checking disc jockeys. "Wings on Your Horns," "Don't Come Home A-Drinkin'" and a handful of other songs were banned by some radio stations.

Each of "them good ol' dirty uns" became top sellers, including among them a song she held from release for five years for its advanced subject matter, a song about birth control's liberating effect, "The Pill," an idea cooked up by two male songwriters.

> If the women were disc jockeys there wouldn't be a fuss about it . . . A preacher in Kentucky preached an entire sermon on it. The next day the entire congregation went out and bought it . . . The preacher said I was spreading sin. I didn't have to spread sin—Eve started it. If truth's to be known, Adam started it.

"The Pill" was one of the best laughs of the year; banned in Boston and stations in the Midwest, the more controversy it aroused, the more popular it became, to the glee of Loretta.

Loretta Lynn symbolizes the courage and outspokenness of the country woman. She sings simply, touchingly, with hard edges and melting slides. An accomplished singer, she is set above many another capable vocalist by her bright temperament. She sings different types of songs, but she will never bend to sing one that would portray her as a weak sister.

In the midsixties America was bombarded by changes. The war in Vietnam was causing unrest at home. Country remained intact without attracting a younger audience; it was held by an older, hawkish group of conservatives while the young student population listened to folk protest and British rock, and the black population was asserting its cultural independence. Country was representing a region of America where human rights went begging, where blacks were not allowed service at lunch counters or choice seats on public transportation, where boys with long hair were in danger of being beaten by gangs who objected to long hair.

It seemed that country music then was talking out of both sides of its mouth with its heartfelt sentimentality and so many crocodile tears. Purported good intentions could not blot out the fact that in the southern part of the United States people were being attacked and killed for demanding constitutional rights. Country was not to escape the stigma of that connection till after the Nixon administration foundered.

The country singers of the sixties—Dottie West, Jan Howard, Connie Smith, Jeannie Seely—remained cloistered. But country style was too good not to be heard outside Dixie.

The spell was broken not by established country artists, but by the arrival of Bobbie Gentry's "Ode to Billie Jo," not in itself a country song as the old-timers would see it.

The song had all the accouterments of a country ballad, a simple guitar figure, a narration, the accent and setting down-home Mississippi. An ambiguous story line tipped off country regulars that "Ode to Billie Jo" wa'nt country. Loretta Lynn pointed out:

> Nobody did understand it—what did they throw over the bridge?
> If a story don't really tell something—country people like a story.
> They want to know how it starts and how it ends.

The author of "Billie Jo" was born in Mississippi, in exotic Chickasaw County. She left for California, where she eventually majored in philosophy at UCLA; she brought a new point of view.

Bobbie Gentry was closely questioned about the mysterious fate of Billie Jo. Why had he jumped off the Tallahatchie Bridge? What had they thrown into the river?

She intended to illustrate "the indifference of man to man" in this fascinating mood piece. But for the mystery, Bobbie Gentry will not reveal it. She told Judy Hugg:

> The fact that the two of them threw something off the bridge is purely symbolic. Yes, I did have something specific in mind, but I didn't say what it was for a reason. And I still haven't, for the same reason.

She represented country to all but the country audience. Eventually, she showed her true pop colors in Vegas, where *Variety* praised her "orb appeal" and her "choreo, 88ing, thesp."

Many of her later songs had the same cinematic quality as "Billie Jo," but nothing she wrote came to match the popularity of "Billie Jo," which eventually was made into a film.

For an "authentic" country singer there's Tammy Wynette, the queen of heartbreak stereotype: a sad Goldilocks with a sob in her voice, ever true to her faithless redneck brute, her weepers sung sadder than if she were in traction. A million leave-takings are in that broken voice, an earful of dismay poured out in songs of divorce, infidelity, questions of child custody. But not as if there were no remedy for the pangs of heartbreak.

She sings about that gray area in human life that could be made rosier, given only a little human kindness. If it's pain she sings of, it is the pain inflicted by lovers who could remedy it by only choosing to. The situation is never hopeless; a divorce is preventable, a drunk is redeemable, and kids wouldn't pipe up with those darndest things if their parents hadn't given them occasion to comment on their strange behavior.

She is a secular singer, but a lady. Affronted by a lover, her response is not Loretta Lynn's indignation, or Dolly Parton's wistfulness. She is pained but serene.

Personally, Tammy Wynette has a sunny disposition, quite different from the songs she sings. Her material is passed on by Billy Sherrill, the Nashville producer whose redoubtably commercial sense of what constitutes a successful country song is legendary. He chose "D-I-V-O-R-C-E," "Stand by Your Man," and a score of others that forever linked her with the country weeper, because they were commercial.

"Stand by Your Man" was a choice not because it reflected Tammy Wynette's character, but because it fulfilled the expectations of her audience, magnificently—to become the biggest seller by a country woman singer till then.

Tammy Wynette is no dupe of the cunt country syndrome. With wealth and success well in hand, the question of women's liberation is for her an academic one. There is no problem singing "Don't Liberate Me, (Love Me)" while she can say what she wishes, do what she wants, and go where she pleases with no one to forbid her. "Stand by Your Man" may be a hymn of stay-at-home wives, but she is not one of them; nor does she particularly care for the Grammy-winning song. It is requested by the audience who want to hear that song or another one like it.

Another turn for country music came when Jeannie C. Riley sang Tom T. Hall's "Harper Valley P.T.A." Country was changing its conservative ideas with this song attacking hypocrisy. The heroine of the song ("my Mama"), who has become the butt of malicious gossip in Harper Valley, appears at the Parent-Teacher Association meeting to give the righteous wags a proper tongue lashing; she'd had enough. The idea tickled the public fancy, but Riley herself did not follow up with more popular songs; some claim that she is "too country" to appeal to a wide audience.

In the early seventies country artists were coming from different backgrounds, no more the cotton picking farmlands of the South, the mountains and hollers of Appalachia.

After the sixties, Brenda Lee, one of the best stylists in popular music, shifted her emphasis to country. Her style had gone from the teen wail "I'm Sorry" through the novelty "Sweet Nothin's" and "Dum Dum" to the haunting "Johnny One Time," which she sang in '69.

Country went pop in 1970, erasing the final traces of *aw, shucks* provincialism. The performers and audience began taking themselves seriously, seeing their music as a legitimate art form, the peer of any.

A California-based country singer with a cool voice and a talent for passionate love songs, Lynn Anderson crossed from country to pop in 1970 with "(I Never Promised You a) Rose Garden," a Joe South song written five years before. Her producer-manager-husband considered it a man's song and felt it would not be good for her career, but "Rose Garden" not only brought her to network television and won her a Grammy, but connected country music solidly with the television audience. Country had come of age; the country woman because of that song was given another alternative to the soft-headed idiot persona she had had with the cunt country material.

The following year Sammi Smith sang Kris Kristofferson's sophisticated "Help Me Make It Through the Night" in her husky honky-tonk alto. The song was country; frank, emotionally true. Probably not one of the first open invitations to bed in country music, but certainly one of the best. Country was on its way to being slut and slanderous.

People became aware by then of yet one more queen of country music when Dolly Parton, who had quit the shadow of her duo partner and producer Porter Wagoner in 1968, was introduced to the contemporary audience by Maria Muldaur, who sang Dolly's "Tennessee Mountain Home" on her popular album. As an ex-jug-band

New Yorker, Maria sang a more "vulgar" version than Dolly's. Maria's version appealed to people who had been raised on folk music.

With a bright Appalachian mountain soprano, an endearing lisp, looking like an ice cream soda in her extravagant Marie Antoinette wigs, Dolly Parton seems like a send-up of the American pop singer archetype, and sounds like no other singer in popular music.

Her songs differ in theme and mood, from the tongue-in-cheek "Dumb Blonde" by Curly Putnam, to the old "Muleskinner Blues," which not only portrayed the diminutive singer as a macho drover, but featured a spine-chilling yodel, to heartbreakers with a recitation like "I Will Always Love You."

An intensely emotional style makes Dolly Parton's weepers as devastating as Tammy Wynette's, sometimes edging her past the queen of heartbreak with her "dumb" childlike timbre and the overwhelming effect of her resounding biblical imagery.

One of the favorite country themes is the leave-my-man-alone song, where the singer addresses the "other" woman. There are worlds between Loretta Lynn's versions, "Fist City" or "You Ain't Woman Enough to Take My Man," where Loretta contemptuously offers the would-be usurper a belt in the mouth, and Tammy Wynette's cautionary songs, offered as a good piece of advice. In Dolly's version, particularly the distraught appeal to "Jolene," the rival is a beauty beyond compare, an awesome pulchritude with hair of flaming auburn, skin of ivory, and eyes of green emerald. Dolly begs her not to take her man. Jolene, please!

Dolly Parton's songs are more realistic than either Tammy Wynette's or Loretta Lynn's. She is asked by her audience about people and situations that only exist in her songs, because they are exceedingly vivid. There are no subjects within the range of human feelings that she would not touch; she would not want to seem as if she were above them.

Her songs are filled with revealing details, emotions, times, and places. The atmosphere of "Tennessee Mountain Home" is built around crickets singing, the calm of summer nights, and the sweetness of back porch romances. She blends splendor and tatters in the unlikely "(My Life Is Like Unto) A Bargain Store" and reveals love to be the riches of the poor in "Coat of Many Colors."

There are different country vocalist traditions in other parts of the country, although country and western music are usually considered the same genre. In Bakersfield, California, a pioneer tradition exists. To that area of the country former Oklahomans had moved during the dust bowl period and brought country music. It evolved there separately from the Nashville style. Texas had a strong big band tradition that became western swing.

A current western swing style band with vocalist and rhythm guitarist Chris O'Connell, Asleep at the Wheel, offers another role for a country female vocalist: a member of the group just like everyone else. Chris O'Connell is no Nashville belle, and she rejects the tradition of country, cunt country, smutty country innuendo that either glorifies or debases women:

> . . . As for "I've been shit on all my life" songs, they'd make me look like an asshole—especially in this band!

Ideas of women in country were changing with the younger arrivals. Their style of dress became more casual, with less frills and gingham. Lynn Anderson appeared as a vision in ruffles and a bustle on "The Lawrence Welk Show" to ease her entry to television. But Tanya Tucker, a personable young singer who at fourteen held all the promise of becoming a major talent, went onstage in leather jumpsuits:

> I don't want to look like every other girl singer. I want to have an image that's special.

Leather suits . . . A *Rolling Stone* interviewer probed, was she intending to become a sex symbol?

> Sex symbol? That's pretty cool. I don't think I want to be that, though.

Her songs seemed to be too mature for her years; carnal songs, rape and murder stories, weird tales of misfits and crazy people. Billy Sherrill was producing and again he had an uncanny ear for what would appeal to the public imagination: "Delta Dawn," a story about a crazed woman of forty, "What's Your Mama's Name?" where a man searching for his child is arrested for child molestation, "Blood Red and Goin' Down," a child sees her father murder his unfaithful wife and her lover.

There was a fascinating contrast between Tanya's deep, precociously worldly voice and the youthfulness revealed by her phrasing. Her relaxed simplicity placed little depth in the lyrics, which were tasteless sung by a young girl but might be certifiable if sung by a mature woman with a voice like Tammy Wynette's or Sammi Smith's. Shocked or bemused, the audience listened. Tanya Tucker performed well. Other than her excellent voice and ample talent, she didn't differ from girls her age; she looked young, acted young. Tanya Tucker will become one of the great American singers.

Country was going along its usual business in the early seventies, oblivious to changes in popular awareness that would eventually affect its unmoving solidity. New elements were seeping in, yet conventional styles were still being echoed by newcomers who sang in the traditional country manner.

To rival Tammy Wynette's kid songs, Barbara Fairchild wrote and sang the "Teddy Bear Song" and other kid material. Jeanne Pruett, a country songwriter for a decade, sang "Satin Sheets," written for her by a new songwriter, yet drawing from the "Raggle Taggle Gypsies" folk theme about the woman who, pampered with gifts and every amenity, is not happy with the rich man who provides them.

The country façade was still intact. Outsiders were not easily accepted as "country," even though it was easy to duplicate the style note for note and turn for turn. Country music was still centered in the South, in Nashville, and smaller centers existed in other parts of the country. Bakersfield, California, was not as acceptable, yet more legitimate to hard country loyalties than the country western forms on the other side of the blanket: Austin and Houston, Texas, Macon, Georgia, and other small centers of progressive country style.

The rights of foreigners to country music were questioned, from the Australian Diana Trask and Olivia Newton-John, the Canadian Anne Murray to the American progressive "longhairs" brought up in the breach between their parents' country music and the new generation's electric rock music.

Like any other musical style, country is a technique that can be duplicated, and the real reasons for the jealousy, for accusations of not being "country" was a reluctance to share economic benefits.

Being from a small town in the South, from a poor rural white family was not all it took to sing country. Nor is it necessary to share the political and social sensitivities of the people to the south of the Mason-Dixon line.

In 1974 occurred a debacle for country music.

Country was just being recognized as authentic Americana, a country music boom was enriching the regulars when outsiders suddenly began to run off with money, glory, Grammy and Country Music Association recognition. The CMA named Olivia Newton-John Female Vocalist of the Year, and that year's N.A.R.A.S. Grammy awards named Anne Murray top country artist.

The high, breathy voice of Olivia Newton-John, a Welshwoman brought up in Australia who began as a folk singer and had some success in England with "Banks of the Ohio," with a country arrangement of "Let Me Be There," not even written by an American, exposed the dangers of crossovers. They could flood the market with ersatz country! Who would object if it wasn't "authentic"?

Most offensive was that neither Olivia Newton-John nor Anne Murray subscribed to the country lifestyle, to country outlook, its culture, nor were they early trained to the love of its heroes.

Established country entertainers took umbrage. They met at George Jones and Tammy Wynette's house to form the Association of Country Entertainers:

> . . . to preserve the identity of country music as a separate and distinct form of entertainment

whose membership was limited:

> . . . exclusively to those persons who make their living as country music entertainers and who identify themselves primarily as such.

About fifty country performers joined. Loretta Lynn demurred:

I'm staying out of it. I don't want no part of it. They're hollering 'cause Olivia Newton-John got that CMA award. Well, I didn't hear no hollering when Lynn Anderson got it for "Rose Garden," and "Rose Garden" was a lot more pop than the song Olivia Newton-John had out.

Some of the members of the new association were later to aspire to cross over into pop themselves. Country was already crossing into pop during those years, but not Dogpatch styled country. The charms of *aw, shucks* country had long since faded. Outlanders like Olivia Newton-John, Anne Murray, the jazz diseuse Diana Trask, Helen Reddy with an occasional eclectic choice among her album cuts were acceptable to a wide audience when they sang country material because they lacked the southern drawl of the American country singers. The outsiders could not be connected with the American peasantry. Yes, there are class systems in America.

It could do no harm to have a singer of the distinction of Diana Trask sing country. Barriers were falling. She had been told years before, "You ain't country," but audiences came to see her more and more.

A college education was no barrier to acceptance in country music. In 1975 Donna Fargo went from a job as a schoolteacher in California to become part of the singing and songwriting establishment of country with "Happiest Girl in the Whole U.S.A."

That year the Opry was fifty years old. An economic recession narrowed the size of the audiences so that only top drawers could have ample box office receipts to insure their survival.

Country could never be the same again. It no longer lagged as far behind pop music, it was no longer isolated, a mixture was taking place. Linda Ronstadt drew her contemporary audience with country material like "I Can't Help It If I'm Still in Love with You," a Hank Williams song, bringing a new influence to both pop music and country. She also brought a new sound as a singer by developing into a style that had more in common with La Lupe or a Latina vocalist than any North American singer. The ¡Ay! of Mexico is in her voice.

Also new to the country audience, Emmylou Harris arrived in '76 with a self-consciously country album, *Elite Hotel*. Her grief-stricken timbre appealed to country sensibilities and to others who were beginning to discover country music, and she did not have a southern drawl to repel the large U.S. audience in the North and West.

Known for an obscure but striking abuse song, "Turn Around and Love Me," Rita Coolidge began appearing without her husband Kris Kristofferson onstage and in recordings. Jessi Colter, who usually appears with her husband, Waylon Jennings, made an impression with "I'm Not Lisa," a study in mistaken identities.

More Canadians eased toward U.S. acceptance with country material. One of the best was pop singer Suzanne Stevens.

Another change came for Dolly Parton when she was accepted by the contemporary audience. When she came into her own, she produced her own album and sang pop material, real pop—Barry Mann and Cynthia Weill's "Here You Come Again."

The new audience lionized Crystal Gayle, Loretta Lynn's younger sister, and welcomed Stella Parton, Dolly's sister. Tanya Tucker's older sister, LaCosta—an excellent singer—returned to singing.

Younger writers entered Nashville. Linda Hargrove, who writes subtle and forthright songs, began to develop into one of the most interesting writers in country. The rules of lyric simplicity for country songs were still in force:

> People don't expect you to be clever, just to deliver an honest idea
> . . . My songs are becoming simpler and more basic.
> I'm not saying be trite when I say be simple. That was the hardest thing to learn, to say something complex simply.

When Jimmy Carter won the presidential election, his call to simplicity and old-time virtues like the ones touted in country music were in the air. The lovely southern drawl was no longer seen as a liability. Country, U.S.A. was legitimized almost to being chic. That couldn't last, but it was a far cry from "Honky Tonk Angels."

IX
WOMEN OF HEART
AND MIND

PERFORMERS who emerged as singer-songwriters in the late sixties were folkies. They were city people who had experienced the
popularity of concern and protest songs and ended by making their
own statements. During the folk period, the search for grass-roots
folk singers led to the hollers and back rooms of the Southeast.
Through hearing folk music, listeners grew used to the sound of im-
perfect voices, off-key singing and down-home mannerisms. The
whisky wheeze had the cachet of authenticity. Glottal phlegm got 'em
gigs; drawls and twangs stood high in the ranks of the folk picking
order.

When songwriters began singing their own songs, the people who
had listened to Appalachian a capella chants heard and approved the
voices of Paul Simon, Bob Dylan, and Leonard Cohen for the pith of
their lyrics. Standards were relaxed for men, but the woman writer-
performer had only the pristine sources of Joan Baez, Judy Collins,
the ardor of Buffy Sainte-Marie, the perfections of Odetta's sonic
booms, and the purity of Jean Ritchie. For women, the aspirations
remained high. Style still counted as much as content.

Buffy Sainte-Marie was one of the first to break from the folk repertory to her own songs. From the beginning of her career, her songs came from original elements. Her style is the most varied in tempo and spirit of the singer-songwriters. Joni Mitchell was discovered by Buffy Sainte-Marie and Judy Collins, before gaining her own audience.

The early singer-songwriters of the sixties, Janis Ian, Melanie, Carly Simon, were beholden for their development to the folk movement.

Not till the appearance of Carole King as a performer in the early seventies did the singer-songwriters arise from other genre roots. Meanwhile, each genre of popular music had its own creators who performed their own songs.

As songwriters, the women are not in a category of their own. The best of them, Joni Mitchell, Janis Ian, Dolly Parton, the musicians, Carole King, and, on a smaller scale, Melissa Manchester, Chi Coltrane. The lyricists, Cynthia Weill, Dory Previn, Carole Bayer Sager, are the elite among songwriters. So strong is their influence on popular music that the music reflects their artistic development.

They in turn reflected the influences on their society. Their songs differed from the expressions of topical concern that were prevalent in the late folk movement, and dealt not with politics but with individualism. A popular approach to self-examination was in the air in America more than anywhere else in the world. Confessional lyrics were acceptable. Sometimes a psychologist appeared somewhere in the background of a writer whose ministrations had aided the artist to express what was "really" in her heart, resulting in a psycho-analytic style, a truth-for-truth's-sake which had a surprisingly consistent language, as if the writer had gained useful idioms from the vocabulary of Freud or Jung.

Philosophical jargon has little connection with the fragile emotions of songs. When the lessons of psychology, Marxism, feminism, Buddhism, and Christianity, wrong or right, have been assimilated, their banalities fall away. Ideas become actions, actions words. When ideas are taken from reality rather than imposed on facts, a writer creates her own expression. A good song about a woman's awareness will not resound with feminist dogma, since the best poets speak in their own voices.

Writing about their own lives, the singer-songwriters supplanted the three-minute Tin Pan Alley rule for popular songs, increased audience attention span so that it demanded to hear whole albums, not only singles, and incidentally made of the music industry a megadollar structure.

The way for a gentler style of music opened at the end of the sixties. Political demonstrations were abandoned as a means of social change after the events at Kent State, Jackson, and the stark reality of death even at a free rock concert in Altamount. An entire generation broke stride, with the realization that Woodstock had been a pipe dream and no new order had been born there. Unarmed civilians could not stand against shooting troops, individuals could not escape being destroyed even while working for social change, and finally, within the very resistance itself, among the outcasts who might be counted allies against the establishment, there were mindlessly destructive elements.

The wave of introspection that followed made it possible once more for lyrics to become important, lyrics that are a more articulate expression than simple yes and no vote at the ballot box, or anger against anger of civilians and government forces on a city street.

Lyrics were heard, and gentle ballads, which were always the strength of the female vocalist. The audience was older by then, since a population shift had taken place, and a woman fares better before a mature audience who doesn't see her with hostility as the authoritarian figure and agent of oppression: Mother.

Writers who had plugged their records behind the scenes to well-known singers began to emerge after Carole King's success to a much greater extent than the women earlier who had written and sung their own songs.

Peggy Lee, the dueña of the pop circuit, showed that it was possible for a female vocalist to perform her own material. La Lee was not prolific, but her lyrics had a charming style.

Nina Simone, who brought sass to the Village Vanguard in the late fifties, might have frightened a potentially huge audience by her stark portrayals of black social issues, years before every black woman was expected to support black awareness.

Since in a system where being "good" was rewarded by the proverbial pie in the sky, bad is good, and that "bad" Nina Simone shines in the black firmament among the "baddest."

Some singers decided to try their hand at songwriting as fashion dictated. Profit was a motive since a singer and a songwriter each share a percentage of song and album profits. If one does both, then the richer she. Important artists have written good songs, though perhaps not classic pop standards: Janis Joplin, Tina Turner, Barbra Streisand, Helen Reddy, and other women who are performers rather than writers.

When singer-songwriters became a fad, there was pressure on a performer to write. Critics and public assumed that a writer-performer possessed emotional authenticity that outvalues the credibility of a mere vocalist. Later the idea was quietly dumped. There were as many writers who could not perform as there were singers incapable of writing.

Songwriters usually have a recurrent mood or theme. Dory Previn is eaten by doubts, Joni Mitchell beset by contradictions, Janis Ian nonplussed by her perceptions, Melanie is optimistic, Carly Simon witty, Chi Coltrane robust, Wendy Waldman serene, and Phoebe Snow whimsical.

Some are stronger composers than lyricists: Carole King, Melissa Manchester. Others are lyricists first: Dory Previn, Carole Bayer Sager, Cynthia Weill. Some are given to a constant mood. Chi Coltrane is capable of writing forceful rockers and fragile ballads. Janis Ian is versatile too; though she's best known for wrenching ballads, she also writes light satire, city blues, and schmaltz. Phoebe Snow encompasses absurdity and pathos.

The singer-songwriters in the United States reflect social and political currents in American society. Janis Ian began by speaking for the unenfranchised young, Carly Simon for the guilt-ridden rich, Buffy for native Americans, and Cynthia Weill even from the safety of the Brill building, spoke for the urban masses.

The popular assumption was that women songwriters, their voices heard at last, would sing for womanhood about the female awareness, baring the hearts and minds of their sex, pointing the way to an entirely new world view. Nothing of the kind.

A new awareness among men and women was brought about in the seventies by the women's liberation movement, but it did not cause an immediate change in the tenor of popular music.

Change was not quick. Women songwriters rarely express any specially female awareness, nor do they stand in the way of patently silly ideas about their own female nature. They wrote the usual songs about finding meaning in their lives through a lover, or womanhood. The tautology escaped even some of the greatest pop minds, but reason is optional for a good popular song.

In most areas, the new army of women hardly made a difference. Few had the interests of other women in mind when commercial decisions were to be made, and more seemed to be gained by conservatism in the industry than by suddenly presenting a radical change to the potential buyer.

Women songwriters had the same technical means to write as men. They were fostered in the same conventions, banalities, and formulas. They worked with the popular idioms forged in earlier times by a different society, before women supposedly came into their own.

During the height of the women's liberation movement, a few songs made feminist statements—Helen Reddy's "I Am Woman" was the best example—but there was no sudden surge of feminist material in the commercial scene. The mass of the writers huddled in the precarious safety of moon-June-croon tunes.

If exploitative, destructive, or silly themes find success in popular music, it is because there is an audience for them. They reflect the attitude of great numbers of people, taking them from where they stand, not from where they "should" be in the opinion of other groups of people. Popular songs are anarchic; they are a matter of free choice to the listeners, if only there is courage and imagination among the writers.

New ideas affected people, new consciousness opened the way cautiously, since popular music does not lead but follows the awareness of the people for whom it sings. Popular songs are supported like a flag by the people who grasp their meaning. Popular songwriters are the reporters of the emotional life of their people, collecting news of the heart. The statements that were sent and received were the important ones, singing is believing.

Before 1970, women who sang and wrote their own songs had small followings. Most were little known; Blossom Dearie resembles no one, with her thin voice and tinkle-tune piano. More commercial, Jackie De Shannon had been writing and producing songs for years, but she was not known till she sang a Bacharach-David song that became a hit.

It was not easy to be accepted among musicians. There were invisible barricades. Shelby Flint, whose first exposure came in 1962 with "Penny in My Pocket, Angel on My Shoulder," found that part of learning the craft of songwriting was to think in male terms:

> I got into sometimes writing from a man's head. It probably didn't work out so well, because the things that felt most I would write from a situation that I was really in. I mostly would write when I was unhappy (*laughs*).

In the year of misogyny, 1966, there were women writing and performing, but they were not given much credit, since they could only be second-best according to prevailing popular ideas. Consequently, few of them were heard. They were assumed to be silent, just as the rose that blooms unseen in the forest is said not to bloom, since no one witnesses its beauty.

Women who did write were aware of special strictures. Norma Tanega was one of the few writing and performing that year, but she felt the special limits set upon her:

> I had to be very careful about how I became sexual . . . which I thought was shitty . . . I had to be careful about how I have "your body close to mine." I couldn't crush you and rumple you, baby darlin', because that would make me aggressive. What I meant to say is "I grab you, baby!" That's the way it first came to me . . . I had to slant it to "here he comes, he's gonna take me over, folks!" I had to be careful. I can't remember what I thought, because I put it out of my head.

In 1967 popular music changed. Rock was adopted as the voice of a new generation. Janis Joplin was discovered at the Monterey Pop Festival, and with her a novel ideal for American womanhood, the debauchée. The hex on female vocalists of 1966 was dispelled, and while songwriters began singing, the same audience that lionized Janis Joplin greeted Laura Nyro with a Bronx cheer. That year Bobbie Gentry wrote "Ode to Billie Jo" and Janis Ian "Society's Child."

No other song had faced that racial issue, *what if your daughter married one?* A teenaged white girl! A black boy! Her mother closes the door to him; it was dynamite, even though the girl acquiesces. She obeys her mother, accepts her judgment, since she is, after all, only "society's child."

Radio stations banned it from the air for fear of offending listeners. It might have gone unheard, but it was rescued by Leonard Bernstein, an olympian from the classical genre who invited Janis to play the song on his television program.

Then it was heard everywhere. It was a teenage lament. It was not written by the adults in the Brill building, the songwriters' factory at 1650 Broadway in New York. A real young girl had written it and she had the promise of a brilliant writer. Because of the promise, more than the song's actual merit, Janis received an inordinate amount of attention. The obverse of the success of "Society's Child" was a horrendous trauma. Hate letters, razor blades, broken copies of the record came in the mail. She had trodden hard on racist sensitivities.

Janis Ian's songs at the time were bitter to the point that they could only have been developmental, the natural depression of the late teens. Her producer was Shadow Morton for "Society's Child," who had played Svengali to the Shangri-Las. He brought out some of her adolescent strength, but she was too original an artist to go teen. Her songs were protest songs, concerned with a rapidly changing minority: teenagers.

While working with Shadow Morton, she met Brooks Arthur, then a young engineer who was working with Brill building teams at the time. Arthur would appear later in her career, and fortunately did not shoot his creative wad promoting the "dumb" sound of the teen groups. As for Janis Ian, for a number of reasons, it was not her moment yet.

Rock-A-Bye, Baby

In '67 my parents got divorced, I quit school, and fell in love, and "Society's Child" hit. It was a lot at once. The thing I think I built up was just—nothing could bother me—I was tough enough to handle it. Then I found out that being tough is jive. Being strong in that way really fucks you in the end because you find out that you can't handle it, that you need other people to help you out. By that time you've got such a rep for being snotty, at sixteen . . . that there really isn't anyone around to help you.

She withdrew, a drug problem intervened to assure her a four-year hiatus: a dozen joints a day, a couple of pipefuls of hash, four or five Seconals:

There's a thing where you don't want to die, but you want to be in a coma till all of it goes away.

Janis Ian was to return years later, but she did not take part in the change in popular music from the sixties to the seventies. She remained in the background while other songwriters, singing their own songs, asserted their personal vision and changed the hit formulas of popular music.

Joni Mitchell began to be heard around 1968, and became the most important innovator of the women songwriters in American popular music. She reflected her time, from the tentative folk days to the peak at Woodstock to the heartsickness of the midseventies postwar period. Her songs, albums, and image are under her control. She creates, designs, produces, and directs like a film auteur, not a pop singer.

A look at her album covers tells of the changes with passing time. She pictures herself au naturel inside the cover of *For the Roses* ('72), and later in *Hejira* ('76) she's a well-kempt lady in mink with a two-lane blacktop where her heart should be. For *Don Juan's Reckless Daughter* ('77) she's in drag and blackface; another album was a collaboration with Charlie Mingus. Each album is committed to one idea, an opera, without the dramatic structure.

Eventually she quit the Judy Joan Joni trinity, metamorphosed to a bitch-goddess. No maid of constant sorrow she, but soul-sister to

Mae West. Her songs changed from sentimental idealist to romantic realist, with a dash of bitterness to keep from cloying.

As with most of the female vocalists, nothing really stirred for Joni Mitchell till after 1966. She was neither a folk singer nor a member of a rock group. While the press groped for comparisons, the record executives pondered the problem of drawing dollars from this unusual singer who wrote her own songs like Juliette Greco, yes, but she wasn't like the French singer. Nor was she British, or American enough to qualify as the Girl Next Door. She was not politically or socially concerned with usual American causes. She was Canadian.

Matters hardly improved in 1968 when Warner Brothers advertised her as "99% Virgin." Women were pretty much a joke while rock music was in vogue, since they were assumed to be wimps, she told an interviewer, according to Kobe Atlas:

> They said I didn't have any balls . . . A man in the promotion department criticized my music for its lack of masculinity.

But she endured, apparently with better survival instincts than the rock heroes who became casualties a couple of years later.

Not only was her music considered "feminine," but her voice was a noncommercial soprano that she used with the flexibility of a paintbrush, soaring to pristine highs, plunging to woody lows, skipping the middle. Her voice was drawn out in opposite directions, audible evidence of the dualism of Joni Mitchell. One of the finest vocal somersaults in popular music is the switchback in "Nathan La Freneer," an alley-oop describing the sordid main drag of a city.

With age and many cigarettes, her voice deepened. The highs appeared less often, the vibrato came under her control. After a grand tour of seventy cities, an even darker tone appeared, and a subcurrent of desperation, a sobbing breathlessness. But the note of wry humor did not disappear.

By the time she made *Hissing of Summer Lawns* ('77), her existence had taken on the accessories of the upper bourgeoisie, and it would have been in worse taste to affect poverty than to acknowledge her own wealth and the different life she led than when she was a folk singer on the coffeehouse circuit. With that album she was for a season the Gucci of popular music—all status and no taste. Piddling effervescences of the better singles lounges appeared in her songs. Determined to explore the chantoosie's bag of tricks, she tried on a mannerism that told of exhausted passion, a sort of panting gasp, and the joking tone of Billie Holiday, the supple nuance Helen Morgan had intoned from atop a piano. The way she sang told of manless woman, lonely, love-hungry woman, the successfully "dumb" woman who is actually a man-trap.

The so-called new Joni arrived with *Court and Spark* ('74) and continued to develop aferward, into all the branches of the other woman, the predatory woman, the eagle-eyed cocotte. The new worldly sophisticate was a woman of a decade or more of dropped relationships behind her, taking a dimmer view of romance than a skittish girl in the throes of her first longings, jetting hither and yon in her Paris dress, flaunting her deluxe ennui.

Joni Mitchell as a songwriter is the mistress of the outsider theme, a topic of exquisite anguish. She writes of being forced to flee. The wall dividing her from the simple joys is built of her own principles. It separates her from fulfillment, which she suspects is in any case illusory.

The theme that underlies each of her concept albums is the question of freedom, of choice. In *Hejira* she flees bad love affairs in search of a good one, and in every album, *Court and Spark, Hissing of Summer Lawns,* she inspects the traps that she almost fell into, or the traps that have caught others, or the ones she is thinking of allowing herself to be caught by. She is fully knowing and wary of being caught in the oldest of snares, the love trap. Even when she writes a torch song, she lights her cigarette on the torch, a slight pause before moving on. She is the poet of the dilemma, taking off rather than seizing it by the horns, "typically feminine" caprice.

She nearly disqualifies herself as a pop songwriter by the clarity of her vision. She is never befuddled. Male characters are caught in illusions about themselves; the pastoral Michael, the rough Carey, the cynical Richard, intellects, artists, executives, a series of poseurs whom she encompasses in her final triumph as Woman. Ultimately she conquers them by invoking her superior rank. She assumes the throne of the greatest authority of all by seeing them as little boys to whom she is comforter, nurturer, and above all Mother, the final authority.

Love, the almost exclusive preoccupation of popular music, is her topic, and men are her objects. To write about lovers is a charming flattery, but like most women Joni Mitchell was not schooled in gallantry, and so her turnabout is not entirely fair. She focuses on their foibles. They are fatuous, they strut with swaggering conceit, they are mildly narcissistic, and ultimately they turn away from her.

Matching lovers to songs became a parlor game, and she began covering her tracks when *Rolling Stone* awarded her an "Old Lady of the Year" prize, comeuppance for a woman who dared deal with men in songs. If she was quick to kiss and tell, they were quicker to pounce on each peccadillo, locker room revenge for uncloaking her lovers' psyches to public view. Though she may see herself as a daughter of Don Juan, the press pegs her more accurately as the less sympathetic Casanova, tales of whose romantic conquests were published.

In a song the last word is hers. She is ever searching for another lover, but note well: one of her own choosing. They may come and go, but songs remain. She accepts the changes. She creates out of turmoil and confusion.

When she writes champagne blues, songs of resignation or disappointment, it does not matter that they are written by an independently wealthy woman who is at the top of her craft, an artist who has gained the respect of a huge audience. There are still barriers. A woman in a man-run world waits, by a jeweled telephone, for the summons of a lover. Milk-white and wealthy though she may be, she is hobbled as tightly as a foot-bound Oriental concubine.

The woman in "Cactus Tree" has ideas of her own about her life. Lovers who call and write are puzzled to find her occupied, "busy being free."

The idea of a woman's place in the world was changing through the sixties. Joni Mitchell had only to look around with her normally clear intelligence to recognize this fact. She was no crusader, and there had been other songs about women choosing not to become involved with lovers, long before "You Don't Own Me," and even before "I Never Will Marry." Like the laird's wife who left house, land,

and money to run off with the raggle-taggle gypsies, Joni Mitchell fled not one, but many men in "Cactus Tree" and gave her reasons in "Woman of Heart and Mind," to the lover who sees her as any of the female icons of Mother, Sister, Girl. She is not accusing her lover of inconstancy, coldness, or tyranny, but of losing her in his illusions. She will not play his game.

She is not speaking only for herself, but like every popular singer she is amplifying an inner feeling of her listeners who are silent, and the more the lady in the song can prevail, the greater the fund of choices for their body, mind, and heart.

Though she may fail egregiously, she never lapses lower than high mediocrity. She leads the meandering current of popular music, whose rules she has changed so that when a new songwriter is told she won't succeed by writing about unheard-of topics because it simply "isn't done," she asks, what about Joni Mitchell?

The singer-songwriters of the seventies locked with the troubadour tradition, a brilliant one for men, but not for women, who had no more than a few minor lyrics from an occasional nun in her cubicle.

The greatest female lyricist before the singer-songwriters in the twentieth century was Edna St. Vincent Millay. Though not a songwriter, her style permeated the Greenwich Village air and her spirit, reckless, carefree, romantic, pointed the way to emancipation. Indirectly, Joni Mitchell, Joan Baez, and Judy Collins were affected by Millay, poet and flapper.

To express their personal sensibility, women had much to overcome. Among the most difficult obstacles were those set by the religious tradition, particularly Catholicism, with its doctrine of "immaculate conception" that led to the assumption that any other kind of conception, ergo sex and, by extension, women, is dirty. It is not difficult for such absurdities to go unchecked in a society of the religious that concentrates power in the hands of celibate males.

The Judeo-Christian tradition has preserved the most powerful literary heritage of the western world—a Bible with a marvelously rich collection of characters and stories, full of blood, fire, and sin. Dory Previn has an Irish Catholic background, and she draws her imagery from that symbolism; from familiarity with grotesques, which are part of the baroque mentality illustrated by the Church when it holds up demons to frighten the faithful. She rattles skeletons in every closet.

No one has written so revealingly and so well about madness, the day-to-day crises and the loco escapades: fleeing the men's magazine paradise of a would-be seducer, who is so rapt in the paraphernalia of the singles scene that he takes no note of her departure in "Cold-water Canyon"; screaming in the car in "20 Mile Zone"; hearing the inner voices of "Mr. Whisper"; and noting the charms of our illusions, from mythical kings to Jesus. She is most serious when she is most amusing, and for debunking the legends so astutely she might have been burnt at the stake in the not too distant past.

The best of the women writers, Joni Mitchell, Janis Ian, Dory Previn, are accused of indulging in gloom and self-pity. Not one of them sees her own work in that light, since they are dealing with the facts of their lives. Dory Previn consciously avoids self-pity:

There are certain things which could be interpreted by people who are into self-pity as self-pity, but I never wrote any of them with that idea in mind. I'm talking about for example "I Dance and Dance and Smile and Smile" perhaps.

Like the Lark of Christian legend, she is intrepid. She reveals exceedingly private experiences:

When I wrote the first album, I told a friend of mine about some of the subject matter, "Mr. Whisper," about the voice of insanity, "Daddy in the Attic," about incest, "20 Mile Zone," about freaking out. And this woman said to me, "Dory, you can't reveal that about yourself . . . I won't let you do it. As your friend, I ask you please, don't, don't put that out in public . . ." Well, it's within the realm of my experience. I said at the time that not only was it time for things like "20 Mile Zone" to be written, and things about insanity, but I thought in about two years they'd be cliché, and they are. Everybody knows about it and everybody talks about it.

Sympathetic human warmth, humor, tolerance, the Christian virtues of trust, hope, and charity are in Dory Previn's songs, and because she writes about human beings, many of her songs are comedies. She writes about illusion and reality, the idols, who are falsely perfect and shatter, the heroes, who have weaknesses, and are soft and mortal.

Her persona is protean; she ventured beyond anyone in commercial popular music when she wrote "Don't Put Him Down," a song about male sexual impotence. Private, unheard of, taboo—a natural topic for Dory Previn in a society where taking up the cudgels for a man's defense causes more discomfort than relief. A woman defending a man's impotence in the macho system of rules renders him doubly impotent, spotlighting his incapacity, where conventionally the pose of manhood is to be too strong to accept the generosity of a woman, and it is his role to protect her. It would have taken a superman to write "Don't Put Him Down," a statement that for a woman requires only compassion for a man.

If women are finding a voice, and we are . . . we have more to say right now. We have this new platform, all these things that haven't been said. Men have said almost all of it from the singular male point of view.

The impotent male is oppressed, though, in the midst of what seem to be privileges, and that is the topic of concern for Dory:

Oppression is oppression, pain is pain, and it's just heightened by the degree and sensibility. What I have experienced is very akin to the extreme experiences of the oppressed, the minorities, because I was oppressed, for whatever reasons—those are immaterial. I was oppressed because I was not supposed to be my father's child. That's oppression; that's not having a place in society, in your family.

I was oppressed because, as a Christian, I only see a male trinity. Where's the woman? Where's the sister? Who's the mother? I see a male god, his son, *His* son, and a holy ghost . . . Who sits at the left hand of God, is the chair empty?

She fully expected to be stricken by catastrophe or die when her first album was released, retribution for having acted against male authority; looking around at the example of some well-known women writers who annihilated themselves by withdrawing to a reclusive life or by writing under an assumed name.

Catholic ritual is so dramatic that it remains in the imagination even if the faith itself is gone. Melanie Safka was also a Catholic who as a child intended to take the veil, to "marry" Jesus. She retained a sense of mass ritual that appears in one of her most powerful songs, "Lay Down (Candles in the Rain)," a lie-in for peace where she joined demonstrators in Central Park to hold hands and lie down on the muddy turf, combined with an incident at Woodstock where she performed.

It had begun to drizzle as she took the stage, and the crowd were asked to light candles for warmth.

As it started to pour, people kept lighting up the candles more and more. The people in the audience were feeling that they were making light, everybody was getting very excited. When I was looking out there it was like this hall of light that went on for ever and ever. It was raining, and everything was flickering, beautiful. I was sharing in this experience with all these people because I was on the stage when it was happening.

It seemed the closest that a woman may come to celebrating mass. Melanie's themes of alienation, loneliness, a mild Slavic nostalgia, bittersweet longing, are optimistic at the core:

I'm not trying to "sell" a particular idea. There's no one thing that I'm pushing, the lyrics tell what I'm feeling. I sing songs for peace, honesty, songs calling for divinity in people. Sometimes a concert is a place to do that.

She is a singer with a heroic buoyancy in her voice, a girlish voice with the bite of a teen stylist like Brenda Lee, and yet within the "dumb" framework of "Brand New Key," Melanie's most commercial song, she did not underrate the intelligence of the new audience, the group that had grown through the sixties. Like most of the other singer-songwriters, she emerged from the folk genre and started out singing about the hardhearted and murderous women, criminal females like Barbry Allen and Mary Hamilton, women at odds with the world, the strength of the folk themes for women in that generation. At the beginning of her career, the force of women's image was too strong for her. After initial success, she felt confined, trained by her experiences and controlled by other people's image of her as the "vegetarian, beautiful people, flower power girl who loves cows and kisses them in the field."

Her career ground to a halt when she decided to have children.

> The way I was pregnant— I was really pregnant, I wasn't like fashionably pregnant . . . When you're pregnant, a lot of your creative energy comes out of you in the child. After I had the babies, I got a creative surge and I wrote a lot.

While Janis Joplin wailed at the 1967 Monterey Pop Festival, bringing rockdom to its knees, Laura Nyro was met with snickers and embarrassment in a less auspicious debut there.

She was a natural magnet for opprobrious epithets, a stark tragedienne who, though hailed as a new songwriting genius, was christened the "Bronx Ophelia." Her loose songs were bursts of inspiration, quotations from American pop songs. They were held together by her audience, who grasped the thin thread of common culture and her idiomatic constructions, which, from another viewpoint, would have seemed to be no more than word salads.

At the start of her career she made *Eli and the 13th Confession,* a concept album around the growth of a girl to maturity in thirteen songs, hopscotch style through anguish and elation. Old rock 'n' roll from doo-wop groups, the symbols of the Catholic Church, the rhythm of New York City flashing by like stations from a subway car, and a mood of giddy, muddled infatuation were gathered like a bouquet of flowers.

Acceptance by the public and a comfortable record deal changed the influence on her music. The new elements were gross and unassimilated when she began to reach outside American pop and the music of the Tri-City area.

Whatever the new influences upon her were—a new way of life, her travel to the Orient, a settled existence, prosperity, emotional fulfillment, maturity—what suffered most was her symbolism. For a westerner, there is nothing that can outdo the glamour of the Christian symbols, to rival the impact of the crucifixion, not even the ritual of hara-kiri; after all, Jesus returned for an encore. There are no madonnas or Magdalenes, there is no pietà.

Laura Nyro toed a thin line between affectation and genius, then produced nothing for four years. The longer she went without creating an affecting song, the more it seemed that her talent had been precocious, erupting from the anguish of immaturity, and that her need to write vanished when she found her niche in life. Then the fragile talent appeared to be a series of mannerisms with no real depth. She marked time, her audience grew older, and during her absence from 1972 to 1976 other women emerged.

An artist who stops working ceases to be one. It is one of life's petty rules that you are what you do, and though it is possible for a short while to do little, inactivity tells on skill.

It is not surprising that the most commercially successful woman singer-songwriter is also one of the most professional. Carole King, even when she dissociated herself from her husband and collaborator Gerry Goffin and broke ties with the Brill building structure that had confined her, never stopped working. Her influence shifted popular music to its base on the East Coast, but when she moved to California, she drew inspiration from a new blend of sensibility and life-style.

There is a certain earthiness associated with West Coast culture. It is a rough pioneer culture that blends pastoral themes with the popular American culture that was created in the film capital, Hollywood. The East Coast style is sharper, haughty and polished, and comes out of big city mentality.

Carly Simon is one of the East Coast stylists. She will probably never live down her reputation as a rich girl, heiress of Simon of Simon and Schuster publishing. So what. The image had a double trenchant. Since she had the advantages of wealth, critics assumed she was without talent or "soul" for not having suffered enough.

She was different. The others had taken the habit of singing in natural voices, almost speaking their lyrics, while she sang with a pop-flavored slickness, and seemed confident and well preened by comparison, more to the commercial mold.

A sparkling new ideal of womanhood was she: tall, rangy, big mouth, big teeth, a vitaminized almost-six-feet of her. That brassy honk of a glass-smooth voice implied the cool impersonality of prosperity; the wealthy can afford to be jovial, it seemed to say. What if beggars curse them? We are soon to be home sipping a drink beside a cool swimming pool, safe from the swelter of a reeking city.

And—oho!—the capriciousness of that spoilt rich girl . . . The song that first brought her public notice was a collaboration of hers with screenwriter and film critic Jacob Brackman. "That's the Way I've Always Heard It Should Be" was an older sister to "Society's Child," where the heroine ungraciously accepts an offer of marriage because that's what is done, even while she sees her parents and her married friends at each other's throats like caged animals.

There were obstacles for her as well, as any woman finds in any career. Inevitably there were pimping businessmen around to tell her, "Honey, if you're nice to me, I'll make you a nice record."

Before she found her own way with clever songs, airy humor, acquired a phobia of clichés, and decided to ceremoniously eschew banality, Carly Simon was a folk singer, part of a duo with her sister Lucy. They appeared on "Hootenanny" and played the Bitter End and other coffeehouse circuit venues. That was in 1962, and it wasn't till 1971 that Carly Simon began to hit her stride. That year was considered a bad one, by some critics, for American popular music; not surprising, it was a year when women were emerging.

Carly Simon had other difficulties, for all that she was supposed to have poise and self-confidence because of a wealthy upbringing. She has a phobia about flying, and performing before an audience, and the end result is timidity, not the best attitude when so much depends on being able to appear before people. She married James Taylor, a brilliant writer-performer himself, who dislikes having her perform, deducing from his remarks in *Rolling Stone* referring to Carly and the audience: "She's a piece of ass. It bothers me. If she looks at another man, I'll kill her."

The quotation is out of context and open to all kinds of interpretations about the state of James Taylor's and Carly Simon's sanity and their relationship, which is their province, but it does not go far enough with respect to Carly Simon and her audience. She and any other performer is only a piece of meat on the stage when she fails to fulfill the role of an artist there. When she succeeds, she is a goddess, she is a reflection of the audience itself as they would desire to be.

Besides this, more than half of her audience are women, and for either sex the singer is the subject, not the object, of desire.

Carly Simon's career has been managed by Arlyne Rothberg, who, going with the grain of her client's personality, protected her from the public.

That she appeared and was successful, or that she withdrew, and that people responded to her or did not notice was all significant; but Carly Simon was not exclusively a singer-songwriter, she was a collaborator, and though the concept of "That's the Way I've Always Heard It Should Be" and of other songs were approved by her, she did not write the lyrics. There is no reason to assume that she could have written those lyrics when the fact is that she did not; she did not initiate and follow through many of the songs she is most frequently associated with, including "Attitude Dancing," "I Haven't Got Time for the Pain," and "Slave," which were written in a breezy, urbane style by Jacob Brackman. She often collaborates with others to compose songs. When she writes alone, her songs have a different personality: "You're So Vain," "Anticipation," "The Right Thing to Do," "Legend in Your Own Time." They're arch, they show a delight in wordplay.

Interpreting her personal message by the songs she has popularized would skew the meaning of what is being said by Carly Simon. "Slave," a supposedly tongue-in-cheek song, put Carly Simon steps ahead of the hoi-polloi. She was portrayed on the album cover and on sepia billboards à la Tina Turner, evoking the familiar Sheena Queen of the Jungle thrasher. To point this out is petty, but no thinner than the commercial ploy represented in offering this new image of Carly Simon.

Was it caprice, cheek, arrogance? Was it Carly Simon or a riddle? The song telegraphed the message that when the burden of personal liberation has been shouldered, the bonds of slavery are a lark by comparison. When you have it all, submission is a trip. Having tried the alternatives, there is a choice. The ideas were provocative, but it was not a time of great passions where women's ideas were concerned. The song was not noticed, and did not become a weapon against women who were attempting to emerge from the very bondage that Carly Simon seemed so lovingly to embrace in this song. As a venture, it went so far ahead of the crowd that it caught up with the rear guard.

The lyrics were authored by her male collaborator, and Carly Simon was not entirely making her own statement, but rather abdicating in favor of composing the music.

Many of the singer-songwriters concentrate more on the music than on the lyrics. Carole King herself is most effective as a composer, while her lyrics lack conflict, resolving into a complacent flatness that ends in saying nothing at all, giving them a lack of cohesive direction that she would never allow in her music, where an easy resolution would take her melody nowhere.

It would be unfair to attribute credit to Carole King for the lyrics of "Don't Say Nothin' Bad About My Baby," "One Fine Day," and "He Hit Me (But It Felt Like a Kiss)" when the songs were a product of a collaboration. She dots her songs with references to the inadequacy of her words, something a writer should never do. If words don't suffice, then she should work harder, to find words that do.

By 1972, it seemed that the field was full of women. There were more changes. Women gained a wider audience, though businessmen were still cautious about developing female talents. Two very interesting women surfaced, Christians of different musical persuasions: Judee Sill and the magnificently talented Chi Coltrane.

Someone claimed that Chi Coltrane played piano "like a man" when her exuberant "Thunder and Lightning" was released. They might have noticed instead that she played like no other pianist at the time except a few old Chicago blues thumpers. She did not play with delicacy because, like the blues piano players, she was self-taught, and flung the strength of her arms and shoulders into the keyboard, often breaking the bottom strings. She picked up her musical knowledge in choir practice.

> The things teachers teach you, they teach you out of a book, and the books are available to anybody who wants to get them; you can get them at the library, you can buy your own at a book store.

Not having been channeled into conventional thinking about music, she set fewer limits on her own sources:

A horn of a car outside that's between two notes, it can be music, or the sounds on the street, the shuffling of feet, the talking or laughter in a room: there are some notes hit that do not fit into the scale . . . you hear different voices.

Musically, she has the freest, most unburdened gift of all the singer-songwriters. She has no fear. She is not tied to a persistent mood that limits her to one type of song, she is as adept at sweet ballads as hard-rocking dance tunes, that are full of rhythm and energy. She is the best performer of the singer-songwriters, since she can sing fire and brimstone or pure piety. Her voice has the "dumb" reckless abandon, the snarl of rock, the cry of the blues, the artful fades of pop. The only consistently recurring theme in her music is elation.

A myth of her fiery temperament grew from a fabrication by a road manager who found it useful to get things done. The story got back to Chi, who considered herself an angelic sort:

"Let me tell you, you'd better fix it because Chi Coltrane is going to tear this place apart when she gets here—she'll refuse to go on!" He'd scare them that way into fixing it and he could come to me and say it's going to be okay. "Wait till Chi hears about this! Ohhhh, she's gonna just . . ."

The reputation persists, even though she is one of the most unflappably professional performers, remaining calm in the panic of backstage disasters.

Most singer-songwriters dread going onstage, or at least draw from another personality for their performances than they do for their writing. The 'Trane welcomes a chance to take the stage:

They think they're there to see you and they don't realize a lot of times you're there to see them too.

A more languishing religiosity illuminates the songs of Judee Sill, whose following is minuscule but passionate. An overexcited writer claimed that her music made his asshole quiver, which warned people off her music rather than attracted any to it and was, in any case, the sort of lofty writing that told more about the writer than about his topic. She wrote songs in a western jazz style, shot through with

229

biblical references, and now and then an exquisite ballad like "The Kiss." But on stage she disgraced herself by belching loudly, although those who knew her reputation were neither surprised nor offended.

She might have driven home the point that women's sensibility, if such a thing exists, is far more extensive than it is given credit for being, and a female style of music really doesn't exist:

> Music, because it's a gift of the muses, which comes from the original kingdom, and not heaven or earth or the hereafter or any of the things that we know or imagine about, it goes beyond. It comes before the separation of the sexes, so that it's whole.

By 1973 a new wave of singer-songwriters arrived who had not undergone a baptism of fire in the sixties. Janis Ian re-emerged, changed. She returned at twenty-three, the scattered energy of her adolescent rebellion focused on new emotions, the bitterness vestigial, the brutality of her cutting sarcasm transformed into refined poignancy.

Folkies from the Village days had regrouped in Los Angeles by then, Len Chandler and John Braheny held weekly songwriters' nights at a storefront theater in Hollywood, and writers exchanged tunes. Janis Ian performed "Jesse" there and broke the spell that had excluded her from the music scene.

"Jesse" reached the canny ear of Roberta Flack, who sailed it up the charts, and Janis Ian was a commercial songwriter once more. She joined producer Brooks Arthur for a run of excellent albums: *Stars, Between the Lines,* and *Aftertones.* It might have been easier, but returning after a past success did not ensure acceptance. If it was difficult to grow up while working, there were other difficulties for her as an adult woman:

> They start jiving you that you can't do this and you can't do that —you can't use a minor seventh till you know about root chords and yada yada . . . Some dude who's writing your lead sheets tries to tell you that you don't know . . . so he can be one up on you.

All else being equal, a woman is assumed to be more ignorant than a man, a simple putdown. At another extreme is the classic assumption that she will be available:

There was this guy in Seattle who took liberties, as it were, and I, having never had to deal with things on that basis, didn't know whether to say fuck off or slap him or start to cry or what. It made me feel like I was being raped . . .

I went back and said: "This person may be very important, but I can't deal with it. Somebody should cool him out." They said, "Hey, you're a chick—you know—this happens all the time to women. You should really be able to deal with it." It became *my* problem, not his . . . some cat starts putting his hands on you . . . Jesus, *fuck* man, I'm trying to build a career and here are these people saying the equivalent of, well, if this cat wants to have you on the floor, don't yell, don't rock the boat, don't make waves!

Her songs were, by new standards, sentimental, regressive, and promoted attitudes that were against the better interests of women, so said the doctrinaire fringe of the women's movement who demanded adherence to its principles by every woman writing. Janis' "You've Got Me on a String" was singled out and she had to come to her own defense:

I kept trying to explain to the guy that it didn't matter if it was woman to man or man to woman or two women or whatever; but that was something people went through.

Almost everyone's been through that. I've never gone through that before. It was a trip for me to be so in love that I would do anything . . . I always thought that was bullshit. But then, there really isn't anything that comes close to feeling like nothing, y'know.

If a theme persists throughout her work, it is the feeling of being an outsider. "Jesse" finds her urging a lover to come home; "At Seventeen," she's the high school outcast; "Stars" is a view of the loneliness of fame; and "In the Winter" is a chance meeting with a former lover, a song that could have been sung by Edith Piaf, such is the mettle of the undaunted yet vulnerable heroine.

Janis Ian had recently returned to performing when she wrote "Stars." She needed audience support to sing it, for the song was autobiographical and revealing. She shooshed noisy groups in the audience and refused to sing till silence was maintained. She was high-handed but sincere, and the room finally quieted. Whether the crowd was willing to listen, shamed into silence, listen they did to seven minutes of "Stars," without a contest of wills between performer and audience.

> It's weird when you do it onstage. People either come backstage and say, "Boy, it was really nice that you opened yourself up that way," or they come back and say, "How come you do such a bummer of a song to close your show?"

Being excluded, even from the simple human contact of dancing, is an obsession in several of her songs, with dancing as a metaphor for life: "Dance with Me," "When the Party's Over," "At Seventeen," "I Would Like to Dance," "Slow Dance Romance," and "Will You Dance."

While Janis was conceiving the most poignant of her songs of isolation, "At Seventeen," the topic was being discussed in consciousness-raising sessions of the early women's movement. Coincidentally, the song was a summary of a political issue:

> It's about having curly hair, straight hair, but any way you have it, it's wrong. When you're done singing it everybody knows you felt ugly, and everybody can relate to that.

After 1973 there was a deluge of women singer-songwriters, but they specialized in performing, or writing, or composing. There were great voices among them, some of whom had emerged earlier, like Terry Garthwaite and Minnie Riperton; and beautiful voices, like Bonnie Koloc and Cheryl Ernst. Composers and musicians were Melissa Manchester and Joan Armatrading. Writers who sang were Carole Bayer Sager and Sarah Kernochan. Singers who wrote were Kiki Dee and Nona Hendryx, and Joan Baez returned stronger than ever with ballads that had gone from sensuous to voluptuous. Grace Slick was more incisively surreal than ever. Still in the background were more excellent writers: Harriet Schoch and Maxine Sellers, Anna and Kate McGarrigle, Patti Dahlstrom, Judi Pulver, Claire Hamill.

By 1974 the work had been done. There were writers who were not even aware that barriers had once existed for women, and did,

and do. One of the most promising new singer-songwriters, Wendy
Waldman, was one of the fortunate ones:

> I'm a composer. I can do a lot of things that men can do. My
> music is different because it comes out of my experience. I'm trying
> very hard to make that clear enough so that I will not have to bend,
> because to bend is to surrender up yourself.

There was awareness of womanhood fostered by the feminist
movement, but the ideas about self-respect and identity were the run
of everyone's inspiration, a matter of individual choice. Wendy
Waldman writes for herself:

> When I realized that I had a self, that was my own, unique, just
> me and the universe . . . that in a million years I could not write
> enough music to please all the men in my life, and even if I did, all
> those songs would never say my own private dreams and my own
> special unique existence, which is mine and which is a private thing
> that every woman and every man has inside . . . I shifted from—
> well, I'll keep trying to please my father—whomever, in different
> forms; my husband, my producer, my manager, to—I will find out
> who I am, and simply make that statement, and those who can, will,
> and those who can't, won't come for me. And that's all.
> I gave up trying to buy the world with love. I can't love, I can't
> get, I can't live for other people's love.

Although 1973 was a turning point politically for women in
America, only Melissa Manchester hung on beyond the year of her
debut. Evie Sands also appeared with a record, but she had been
writing songs long before. Both these women are stronger composers
than they are lyricists. Composers express ideas, interpretations of
life, their form translates into moods, emotions, but there can be no
sex stereotyping there, any more than there can be sex in numbers.

Melissa Manchester collaborates with lyricists often, and though
she concentrates more on the music of her songs, she is assumed to
be expressing an inner area of her private soul. A writer from
Women's Wear Daily asked Melissa if she had experienced pain in
her own life, and drew the bright-eyed reply:

Oh sure, but it's nothing compared to what I'm going to have. It's just inevitable, isn't it?

As Melissa's career developed, it was noted that lyricist Carole Bayer Sager had collaborated on many of Melissa's most successful songs—"Midnight Blue," "Home to Myself," and others—and she also had an impressive history of hits for major artists. Although she has a voice that could set frogs a-croaking, her words are the most refined, advanced pop lyrics of her generation. They are in a class with Cynthia Weill's.

None of the writers admits to having appropriated any of the feminist tracts that were distributed so freely in the late sixties, even though many of them were written in anonymous collaborations by excellent writers and thinkers: Susan Brownmiller, Ti-Grace Atkinson, Ellen Willis, Shuli Firestone, and others. There was an effect of their writing on lyricists, since the new feminist ideas were powerful enough to color popular opinion. Some pop writers had literary cover versions of those mimeographed sheets distributed by the Radical Feminists and the Redstockings. Some only rephrased the ideas in lyric form, some took off into new directions because of them.

The effect of the women's movement on Carole Bayer Sager's writing was not a conscious choice but a matter of falling in step with it:

I share many of the same feelings of women who want to stand up and be counted, so therefore I've always supported the women's movement.

A lyric can reach the heart, not only the mind, of people, which is what feminist politics is all about.

But some lyrics don't mean a thing. Joan Armatrading arrived from Britain in 1975 with lyrics that mean close to nothing, and her songs are none the worse for it. Like Bonnie Raitt and Ellen McIlwaine, she played a fine guitar, a fact that was important, since women were not considered to be disciplined enough to become distinctive instrumentalists.

That year Phoebe Snow was loosed on the scene. A dark complexion and a headful of Afro frizzies assured her the cachet of minority talent. People thought she was black, but it was soon evident that she

DORY PREVIN   JONI MITCHELL

BUFFY SAINTE-MARIE

CHI COLTRANE

WENDY WALDMAN

CARLY SIMON

CAROLE KING

VALERIE SIMPSON

PHOEBE SNOW

PATTI SMITH   HOLLY NEAR

THE DEADLY NIGHTSHADE

FLORA PURIM

MINNIE RIPPERTON

TERRY GARTHWAITE

had more in common with Janis Ian and Lesley Gore—white, Jewish, from New Jersey—than with Billie Holiday, her erstwhile prototype.

She had an unusual voice, with a schtick vibrato and a warm, jazzy style. She was from the latest generation of Greenwich Village musicians who took jazz, not folk, as their roots. Her songs were assumed to be the work of a darkly neurotic, high-strung, moody woman. When she tramped out onstage, the personality that finally emerged was prankish:

Isn't it a gas to go out there and hit them with all the funniness, when they think that I'm the girl who wrote "Sometimes my hands are so clumsy . . . I drop things . . ."—this depressed neurotic chick—and I go out there and go "Hi, everybody!"

By the middle of the seventies, the singer-songwriter trend had run its course. The fact that a singer-songwriter was expressing a personal sensibility ceased to be important. Everyone was expressing some kind of sensibility. Beautiful voices and personal singing styles, since they also express a sensibility, again became important.

It was a couple of decades away from the first stirrings of the folk movement. It had taken an entire generation to run through the folk ideals of the troubadour.

Women singer-songwriters had shown a new face of womanhood. If songs do educate the heart, there are still people who are destined to live out the prophecy of the songs they hear, and while the songs are servile, the place of their listeners will be among the meek, subsumed to whatever forces draw the reins.

The social changes that culminated in the women's liberation movement were more than rational systems without any effect on people's lives. The changes went directly to the emotional life of women so that they were not aware of the intrusion of feminist ideas into their lives, only that they had personally made certain choices, and the freedom that was so natural erased any awareness of previously not having had the choice, which is the essence of liberation.

The songwriters who performed their own music reflected the world around them. They were articulate and aware, and, once having made their statement, they could no longer find shelter in the security of the "dumb" sound. The heart of the American popular song will have reason, though every generation has it to learn again.

X
BYE, BYE BABY

TIME to say goodbye to the girls, to oooweee baby, the old baby of the songs. Goodbye to picture-ladies, footstools and dishrags, the women in popular songs. Goodbye, demeaning stereotypes, adieu broads, farewell chicks and all the funny mirrors of women that reflect them puny, silly, naïve, and a little stupid.

Adiós, clichés of pigeon, ragdoll, and just-a-victim-of-her-man. If they show no signs of leaving, it is we who must back away through time and turn to other women for a clearer vision.

There are women who were never "baby." Some of their voices are so original that no category in American popular music can contain them. They seem to be fewer still, since few of them have much in common with each other and speak to small audiences. Then there are others who are in the center of the wealth and fame of celebrity.

The major record labels have distributed music by women with an alternative point of view. Helen Reddy's "I Am Woman" proved that championing women's rights could be economically feasible. But it never happened again. Instead, while the women's movement focused ideas about women that had only appeared in a diffused manner before, women began to express themselves with a new freedom.

When a woman sings about herself, it is a feminist act in spite of irate demurrers by artists who feel that no movement could claim their talent, the talent they have worked so hard to develop. Without the women's movement, some of them might well have kept their talent to themselves.

Record companies in 1971 saw an area with economic potential that had not yet been mined: women, an idea that could be sold. From another point of view it could be said that the recording industry had exploited little else, women as an audience, women as a product. That year the number of women signed to recording contracts doubled. The record companies were searching for "another Carole King." She was never found. Other women were.

Women became important artists in the seventies. They were listened to. The seventies were a romantic decade, and, for worse or better, romanticism promotes feminine attributes, or what have come to be known as attitudes and ideas amenable to women. Many of the new performers were aware of women's issues, and the business world could see how lucrative it could be either to support those issues or to rail against them publicly. The controversy could generate energy (money!).

Vocalists, including those who said that all they wanted was to have a good time, to see people happy, to make good music, were aware of their ascribed role as speakers for the inner soul of women, and many of them became conscious about their choice of songs.

This is true of any great artist, but the women's rights movement placed one more principle in circulation, that women were not to be portrayed as second-class human beings.

Then for others, all thought of political or social consciousness evaporated at the prospect of a hit single and the dollars and ballyhoo it would bring, even though they had to return to the poisoned source of the doormat-dishrag ditties to find the hit, the dreary backlash of women who wished to be girls.

"Dumb" girls continued popular, weepers, as ever, irresistible. For many popular singers, to speak out at all meant speaking in the old language of pop music, the empty moon-June-croon tunes, and many of the artists already signed to record labels had bought the values that the record labels represented. The women's movement was, after

240

all, a political movement, and one must guard against having one's individuality co-opted by a group.

A career still depended on some sort of accommodation with record labels, and artists with nothing to lose, or already at the top, could risk making a feminist statement. They tried to walk the line between the record label's conservatism and the emerging consciousness of the audience. It was a gamble, though once a singer had made contact with an audience, it would defend her from the record company by acclamation. A record company does not argue with success. The record company had to be convinced to promote, distribute, invest. Many established artists were too comfortable as they were. Besides, the system had recognized *their* exceptional talent, so anyone as *gifted* should also find no sexist barriers to their careers.

In the fickle world of pop music, no one is ever comfortable for long. New statements seep in from the streets into the music, into the instant plebiscite of the charts and jukeboxes.

Carole King's genius had been discovered by the industry copycats after she had worked there for more than a decade. She emerged along with the singer-songwriters, and incidentally during the high tide of the women's movement. Her talent is as a composer, not a lyricist. Her lyrics verge on lousy, though they are appealing in their "dumb" simplicity.

For evidence of a new female awareness, since it is not enough for one individual to emerge to endow an entire class with distinction (and anyone with nothing better to do might set out to prove that Carole King's music was something she copied from male forms), the only real proof to be looked to is found in the lyrics.

There is no dearth of old songs that express disaffection with a woman's status: "I Wish I Was Single Again," "You Don't Own Me," and songs written anonymously or by men. Women agreed with the sentiments of a song, sang it, loved it, but did not write it.

There is no question of whether or not they *could* have written it; they didn't and therefore they couldn't. Something prevented them.

For all the critical ennui, political detestation, stylistic outrage that Helen Reddy's "I Am Woman" has inspired, the doggerel set to a martial air by a male composer was authored by a woman.

For making that simple statement she was thought—by outsiders—to be the drum major for the women's liberation movement. To Helen Reddy went the well-deserved credit and the profit, since she presented the other point of view.

Carly Simon sang "That's the Way I've Always Heard It Should Be," but she did not (translation: could not) write those lyrics, which were written by Jacob Brackman.

Dory Previn, after heavy duesmanship in the music scene that dated back as far as Carole King's, wrote with an intense personal vision. She wrote as any independent thinker writes, not what she would be expected to write, and not what she ought to write by the standards of any group, but what she did write, which is something better than would fit any group's expectations, which are always less than a human being is capable of, since they reflect the norm of a group. That is the value of an artist to a society that sets artists apart as either gods or outcasts.

Some of the burden of expressing the inner feelings of her audience can be avoided by doing away with lyrics and becoming an instrument like the skat-singing Ella, Sarah, and Carmen. The Brazilian Flora Purim, and Urszula Dudziak, the Polish vocalist, are both vocal instrumentalists.

A song without words is like a woman without a face. Why not ply that lyric? Wordless songs create a suggestive void for which there is no compass. Fortunately, most singers who forego lyrics do so with a reason, and are aware of the tyranny of words. Flora Purim performs exquisite wordless songs, but this is a musical imperative, since she is sensitive to the use of words:

> I would never sing "baby." "Baby" is a very weak way to say, a very common way . . . a jive way to approach a lady: "What's happenin', baby?" It's really jive. It's jiver than saying, "I love you" . . . I couldn't do that. I would be jiving right in front.

Major labels had the most success with singers of conventional appeal, particularly when the conventional appeal was the unconventional, as was the rock 'n' roll fundamentalism of Patti Smith, unconventional elsewhere but as fitting as Br'er Rabbit in a briar patch on the rock stage.

She portrayed a familiar heroic phantasm, taking male models for her show, for want of good female imagery: Jim Morrison, Keith Richard, spiced with "Gene Vincent poses, Billy Lee Riley moves," a little Mick Jagger moue, frosted with the surly truculence of the city streets, which are the cradle of rock sentiment. Kids see that phony feminine stuff is corny. They want to look up to somebody cool. The guys are cool. Girls are stupid.

I was always under the impression that girls were silly when I was younger.

Girls are silly. They're sissies, and sissies can't survive on the street. They're a pain in the ass. To walk the streets, you had to be tough, you had to have attitude. Why should anyone want to identify with girls, with "baby," with dishrags and doormats? Where's the logic?

I'm lucky. Most girls related to, like, say, the Beatles or the Stones because sexually they aroused them, they moved them as guys.

Those guys, after they finished moving me as guys, they moved me as artists, and so I was able to transcend just that little sexual giggle, and relate to those people on a more brainiac level and steal from them, and become something myself because of them.

But most girls don't know who to turn to, to develop themselves. They can't develop themselves in terms of comparing themselves to Jim Morrison or Lou Reed or something.

Patti Smith is a diseuse and a poseuse, her performances are excellent, her raps are marvelous, her interviews make good copy, she is a writer, a poet. The performer-as-shaman theories see the singer as speaking for the unconscious desires of an audience and such mumbo-jumbo is not lost on Patti Smith. These theories are schoolboyish but do no harm, they are part of the aspirations of an audience. Patti Smith says what has been said before, but *that* she says it is extraordinary, because she is a woman. It really shouldn't be necessary for this to be said, since a performer appeals to anyone, regardless of sex, androgynously, homosexually, heterosexually. Patti Smith isn't the first woman to draw her inspiration from male performers; Tanya Tucker and Suzi Quatro both take their greatest influence from Elvis Presley, but Patti Smith does it assiduously, studiously.

No woman had the panache to take that punky attitude in quite that way before. No smile, no shuffle, just a provocation from a south Jersey punk in black chino pants and torn T-shirts, antithesis of girl, amalgamated poolshark and hitman:

> It's all class y'know; black silk shirt, black clothes, a white tie.

Uh-huh. She took the "dumb" sound, made of it a cultural landmark, gloated over it, rubbed their noses in it, and was adored. She can do a voice like Brenda Lee, Melanie, and the "dumb" sound of the Ronnettes, the Marvelettes, the Crystals:

> They were so great because they were such strong vocalists, they didn't exactly have a lot upstairs, but . . . I merge that kind of singing with brainiac stuff.

While her hit single collaboration with Bruce Springsteen ("Because the Night") was on the charts, she was giving poetry readings, and while *Seventh Heaven, Witt, Kodak,* and *Babel* were on the bookshelves, *Horses, Radio Ethiopia,* and *Easter* were in the record racks. Patti Smith reflected the longing for intellectual legitimacy in her audience, an aspiration to transcend vulgarity and to achieve art, to make the popular classic.

It is the status that eludes the street punk, though not the performer who creates these dreams, since you can be sure that no musician, however rude, is a true street punk; the work's too hard.

For conscious and deliberate that she may be in going beyond Janis Joplin, shouting, flailing, and spitting on the stage, in "dumb" abandon, yet wary of the dangers of performing, of allowing a merger of the stage illusion with her life, and not willing to be victimized for the sake of a good show, "Fuck yourself up when you're onstage, but offstage, take your vitamins," she did take a wrong step off a stage and hurt herself seriously. These are the dangers of the stage trance when one approaches it en amateur and takes leave of reality.

Earnestness and conviction are good, because without them there is no reason to go on a stage. Patti Smith can be considered crude, but the reason she is doing what she does is because she wants to, intends to do it; she has reasons:

> I'm really relentless about what I do. Nobody tells me what to do
> . . . I stand behind my material and ain't nobody going to fuck with
> what I do. I do what I do.
>
> I don't do it for ulterior motives. I don't be profane to shock. I'm
> not out to shock nobody, I'm just out to make people aware that
> there's so much out there, there's so many levels that you can move
> through, there's no reason to stop.

Which doesn't mean she's above appropriating a cliché:

> Ultimately, I want to make everybody horny.

But she thinks of being a visionary, of having a vocation, a mission:

> I can relate to Joan of Arc and all those kind of people that get
> pulled by something beyond them, I understand what that feels like
> . . . people that are really sensitive feel the desires and needs of
> other people. That's what a good performer's all about.

Patti Smith is as much as Laura Nyro a product of American culture from that special part of the Northeast, the Tri-City area, the mixture of the city, black, Italian, Jewish elements whose only common trait is hope.

> I don't think America will ever have a totally mellow period. I really love America for this reason. It's always in a state of rebellion.
> It's a country that never really relaxes. We'll always have something
> because we're not a country that's ruled by dogma. We don't have
> Mohammed on our shoulder, we don't even have Jesus.
>
> We're not even a Christian country anymore, it's too split up. The
> cool part of America is ruled by rock 'n' roll . . . Instead of Messiahs we always had big rock 'n' roll stars. We always like live heroes . . . We like to see who we're worshipping.

From the lap of respectability on the rock scene, Yoko Ono performed a few experiments that had little connection with the music of the nostalgic and backsliding rock genre of which she became a part by association with John Lennon.

Her experiments were a luxury, and were ignored, since she was mostly known as "the girl who split up the Beatles" and served as a focus for racist and sexist envy. Either she brought adult sexuality to the boyish camaraderie of rock, which ruined the game, or she supposedly exercised a Svengali power over Lennon, this witch, this scarlet divorcée who appeared nude with him on an album cover and might actually have considered herself his equal.

Something called art rock came about fully a decade later than she had attempted it, and an appreciation of Dadaist jollity, in what is, after all, an absurd world, developed. For Yoko it did not go very well when she rolled onstage struggling to get herself out of a laundry bag for the Plastic Ono Band. The rock audience finds it very difficult to laugh, or to reflect on absurdities. It is a boyish, serious, conservative, peer-pressured audience set deeply into its codes of behavior. It is macho, and it is against macho ethics to descend (or ascend) to humor.

Rock ideals are heroic and tragic; the only laughs are sardonic, the only wit is satirical, the only humor is ironic. Rock music is treated with an almost obsequious seriousness by its audience. To bring humor or "meaning" to it is like trying to jolly a sulking adolescent to whom nothing is funny, and who, in any case, speaks a foreign language: I am a rock, I am an island.

Yoko's feminism found no support there. Among the rocks, who cares what girls want? They'll take what they're given and be glad of it. Rock is for the guys. She was talented, she was abrasive, she didn't get a chance to develop her talent in anonymity before appearing before a very large, hostile audience. She was very interesting.

Her "Woman Is the Nigger of the World" gained her no friends in rock 'n' roll, and among women it was a hot potato; it verged on being offensive. The song was more like a putdown than an assertion of women's worth. What upstanding feminist woman would agree to being characterized as a "nigger of the world"? The song was an awkward plea for understanding to an unsympathetic audience couched in a peremptory tone, and appealing to a sense of justice that did not exist there as far as women were concerned.

An audience might have gathered for her eventually, if she had persisted, and if she had been able to connect with her own group.

There were other originals. Some of them came from conventional stock, like Carole Bayer Sager, who would have passed in the Brill building, so polished was her style. She collaborated with Melissa Manchester to write "Home to Myself," one of the rare women's statements of independence, a gentle song about being alone and not disliking it. Like all her songs, it was marked with poignancy and a sense of dramatic detail.

In keeping with the fad for writers to record their own material, she put out an album that loosed a froggy voice on the airwaves that had all the Weltschmerz of an extinct avian species. The very badness of her voice ingratiated her to a loyal following who valued her wrecked pipes as if their ragged texture were gotten through some brave virtue during the war, as testimony of the wisdom of a misspent life and a capacity for abysmally deep feeling, a voice nurtured only on coffee and cigarettes.

If her voice had received the unendingly repeated airplay given to top ten hits and grated on the ears of all, a pity it were indeed, since her vocalism would have outworn the welcome so well deserved by her songs. Carole Bayer Sager is among the most accomplished lyricists in pop music, a writer who can be classed with Cynthia Weill and Dory Previn. Her songs deserve to be interpreted by the finest voices.

When San Francisco was at its apex as the American music center, in the low period during the late sixties, the Joy of Cooking was one of the City's most popular groups. The group was centered around two women, Toni Brown, who wrote songs and played the keyboard, and Terry Garthwaite, guitarist and vocalist. Toni writes undeluded songs about life, love, and womanhood. Terry is one of the most interesting singers in America.

During the times of Janis Joplin and Grace Slick, the idea of female instrumentalists in a rock style group seemed bizarre, even though the Joy of Cooking was very popular.

It took a cavalier, cranky attitude to separate the women from the music and attack their right to perform, but it did happen. A backstage visitor told them, "If I close my eyes, I forget that women are playing." The remark wasn't made by an outright lunatic. It expressed an undercurrent of hostility toward women on the rock scene. Also, it was not an isolated opinion. An interviewer commented that he found it hard to accept the fact that a guitar was being played by someone wearing a skirt. Ignorant, but still a popular misconception of what constitutes musicianship, or sex.

Terry Garthwaite still plays an instrument when she sings, and she has developed her vocalism by assimilating techniques from Oriental and African sources. Each of her vocal excursions is a tour de force, a delight for anyone who listens with pleasure to the human voice.

The major labels didn't diverge excessively from the lucrative mainstream in backing Patti Smith, Helen Reddy, Carly Simon, Yoko Ono, or the Joy of Cooking. They could have done better with some others, whose borderline success gave them little influence on the direction of popular music: Shelby Flint, whose lyrics glow with passion; Norma Tanega, who composes exquisite melodies and is given to whimsical lyrics; Maxine Sellers, whose charm is her tough skepticism; Harriet Schoch, whose songs of seasoned psychology approach wisdom as nearly as can any popular song; and if only more had come of the records put out by Sarah Kernochan, whose songs are delightful little movies on vinyl. The recording industry finds it difficult to promote an original in a field where every new song has to follow or resemble something that came before, to be familiar enough to be popular.

Unfortunately, there have been many distinguished women artists on major labels whose moment slipped by and left their talent unencouraged, undeveloped, so that very few people ever became aware of them. The business is loath to wager on a woman's success.

The press is not likely to champion a female performer, since many writers are bound by habit to a genre approach that disqualifies a new artist who does not sing in the old idioms, with the old techniques and attributes.

A female performer is not allowed to fail and yet continue to compete. Women are not allowed to make fools of themselves, though many a fool is only a hero manqué. Failure as a learning experience, or trial and error methods are not permitted, since women either succeed or leave the field. But people slip through the toughest barriers with their message, and there are always surprises.

One of the delightful ones was the Deadly Nightshade, a trio of women signed to a small label having access to the distribution of RCA.

If there is a great deal of humor in feminism, it is because the essence of feminism is comedic. Comedy consists of flinging something unexpected at someone unaware. This is where the Deadly Nightshade excelled.

The 'Shades took some accepted "feminine" compromises to a sexist system to their logical, nauseating conclusion. "Nose Job" was their "Wishin' and Hopin'" (remember: "Wear your hair just for him"). The lady of the song bids for a cool lover's heart by having her nose altered. Now will you love me?

On the brighter side, sweet indeed is the revenge of the lady executive in "Dance, Mr. Big, Dance" when she interviews her former boss for a position and finds him lacking in basic typing and filing skills. However, the sexist dragonette suggests, the job can yet be his if he wears a tighter shirt.

The 'Shades are funny, sociable, and sing an eclectic mixture of their own material along with well-chosen early Motown, Philadelphia girl groups, jug-band, and country. Clearly they've made a careful study of their girl roots. Helen Hooke plays fiddle, Pamela Brandt bass, and Anne Bowen vocals and washboard.

They appeared in rural country and western bars in the Northeast for several years before signing.

> Real people and women's stuff mixed into a concept for us. It became important to us to involve the audience personally in what we were saying, and talk about real situations in a song. One whole strain of influence in country-western is from Mother Maybelle Carter. [HELEN HOOKE]

In spite of country and washboard paraphernalia, their sound is not authentic "dumb." The 'Shades are not street kids who doo-wopped on the corner; they got their degrees.

> We wouldn't have gotten together if it weren't for the colleges. We

used to laugh at them, put them down like everybody puts them down, but women are really encouraged to succeed . . . People get down on you a lot. They want to push you around, be the person behind the star. Our colleges, Smith and Mount Holyoke, just taught us that we could succeed.

They gave us enough confidence in what we know that, maybe our feelings get hurt, or maybe we're weak sometimes, but we know we're good.

They also gave us basic skills, how to think in a straight line, how to deal with the men who went to the schools who end up in power; they talk that jive talk that goes on in the business.   [HELEN HOOKE]

The 'Shades put a clause in their contract with the label to guarantee them approval of their own advertising and promotion, so that no material issued would allow exploitation on the basis of sex or offend a feminist sensibility:

They knew that every other band that was women had gotten all screwed up. It had not been done right. They knew something was happening out there and they didn't know what it was. They knew that we'd been playing for three years already, and we had some idea of what it was. We had done all our own bumper stickers, posters, T-shirts and controlled our own band for years, so they were perfectly agreeable.   [ANNE BOWEN]

They knew that if they tried to hype up the feminism that the first people to be turned off would be the feminists.   [PAMELA BRANDT]

The women's movement is an idea. Many people who would consider themselves allies of the women's liberation movement would not agree on the details of the new rights, and many who abhor the thought of a women's movement will support most of its ideas. At the present level of technology and freedom from material want in America, there is no avoiding the issue of equal rights. But popular mentality moves slowly and the music industry reflects this slowness, magnifies it. The best way to convey a new musical idea is to control recording and distribution.

Many musicians have formed their own labels. They do so because they don't want to compromise their style to make it suit the formula for a hit, or their audience is small. Betty Carter, the finest of the independent jazz vocalists, issued records on her own Bet Car label, and Daffodil records was the vehicle for the tiny voice of Blossom Dearie.

In their case, one gets the feeling that if a good record deal came along, there would be no reason for them to refuse it. The New Miss Alice Stone Ladies' Society Orchestra releases their own records; the Alices are the most fun since the Deadly Nightshade, and they have the most bumptious stage show. Schtick, Tuba, and bizarre are the Alices. Nothing would keep them from being on a mainstream label.

There are others who have, in addition to their music, a political mission, and are wary of being co-opted by large recording labels that would bury their message. Holly Near has her own label, Redwood records, and a number of women share the work on Olivia records. Malvina Reynolds released her work on her own label, Cassandra records.

Among songwriters, Malvina Reynolds was the small voice of conscience before the bandwagon of the folk movement of the late fifties took off. She began writing in the forties, first recognized as a result of "Little Boxes," a song about a cheap housing development of "ticky tacky" houses on a San Francisco hillside. The song brought "ticky tacky" into architectural textbooks and perhaps a blush to a thoughtful land speculator somewhere, but the ticky tacky houses outlived Malvina. Never mind, she had her share of successes too.

She wrote her songs to be political tools, handbills. She allowed them to be used with no royalty payments and no restrictions for advocacy purposes, a gift to the future which she hoped would be a better one for all.

There was always another cause, another protest, another issue, another idea to be championed. She appeared at picket lines, demonstrations, fund-raising benefits.

I'll always come unless it's some little thing that's not well organized. If it's anything on the colonial nations, the plutonium thing, ecology, the rights of kids, I'll write a song or have one appropriate to the occasion.

There wasn't a humanist cause in three decades that she didn't support. She was for the poor, the oppressed, the young, the environment. She attacked bureaucracy, arbitrary power, waste, clichés. She abhorred fascism, and also the sort of fascism in purportedly religious movements such as Moonism, an aspect of cultism that she was among the first to point out. The California farm workers, Women Against Violence Against Women, the Anti-Nuclear Initiative, the peace movement, the women's rights movement all found her support. She protested pollution, Joe McCarthy's hearings, HUAC, the Shah of Iran's regime, Nestlé. She protested Archie Simonson, a Wisconsin judge who condoned the gang rape of a young girl by attributing it to social permissiveness and women's clothing, absolving the actual rapists of their responsibility.

Malvina was no muddle-headed lil' ol' lady in sneakers who feared to offend. She was effective. She was tireless. She would not go limp. Fights were to be waged, or hope would go down to unconscionable defeat. There is indeed a "common enemy" whose existence she would not ignore, an enemy that could not be educated or appeased.

> Do you think that the people who financed, with millions of (our —taken from us through profits, power rates) dollars, the defeat of proposition 15, which would have slowed atomic plant building pending modest inquiries as to safety, waste disposal—do you think these people, who are inflicting death and deformity on unborn generations for profit's sake, ever experience anything like human caring or support that would affect their power and direction? I have not put "enemy" into the universe. They have.
>
> I am not looking to receive "friend" from them. The power to harm and kill must be taken from them.   [SPORADIC TIMES]

She wrote songs for a purpose. For children, she wrote *Funnybugs, Giggleworms,* and *Tweedles and Foodles.* For women she wrote "We Don't Need the Men," "Rosie Jane (pregnant again)," and one of her last songs was about teenaged pregnancy. There was a song to save whales from extinction, another for trees and wildlife. There was "What Have They Done to the Rain," a song about nuclear waste, "Little Boxes," and other songs about the conditions of human life, "The Day the Freeway Froze," "Boraxo," "DDT," and her song about protesting, "It Isn't Nice." Songs that are useful.

Bye, Bye Baby

There is something about singing that unifies and lifts the spirit,
and brings our cause to the attention of passersby in an ingratiating
way. [SPORADIC TIMES]

Olivia records is a collective of women founded in 1973 to record
and distribute music written, recorded, produced, and engineered by
women. The group is intended to train women in the music business,
to give them access to privileged work not readily available to
women in the recording industry.

They hope through music to reveal an aspect of women that has
not been given full play in the past: "feelings, thoughts, interests,
and experiences of women interpreted by women, about the side of
women's lives that does not deal with men or ask for their approval."

When the concept of women's music is narrowly interpreted, it
refers to songs with gay themes; perhaps the best known of these is
Meg Christian's "Love Song to a Gym Teacher." Most of the material on the Olivia label has universal appeal. Women work in the
process of making a record in all phases that are under Olivia's control. There are independent distributors of Olivia records throughout
the country. They too are women. The operation has succeeded.

Olivia has remained an all-woman organization even though by
excluding men they have lost useful help. The decision was a political one, and not without precedent, since there was no question of
reasons when blacks found it necessary to retrench among themselves and exclude whites as a means of gaining strength.

For a group wishing to develop women's competence, it is useful
to do without male help, which in this culture has meant taking a
woman's hands off technology and showing her how it works by
doing it for her. No surprise—she didn't learn to use the technology.
There is no way to learn to use a tool without touching it. One blow
of a hammer to the thumb is worth a thousand nails driven by someone else.

Then, the importance of a man's approval, or the devastating
effect of his disapproval, or the drag of his indifference, or the dis-
traction of his ego, backed as they are by the entire force of female
upbringing, is disproportionate to its importance where women are

253

concerned, and irrelevant to their progress. Therefore the best way out of dependency for women is to refuse male help entirely.

The Olivia collective set out to create a non-sexist, non-racist, non-ageist, non-exploitative company. They wanted to express the new women's culture, and help define it.

Olivia's principles were applied in an exemplary manner by performers, technical and business women involved in their recordings and live concerts.

Live concerts organized by Olivia and their agents always offer childcare and are wheelchair accessible. For some concerts an interpreter for the deaf is provided. The professed social awareness of Olivia is not just lip service; they actively support causes which concern women. In answer to a California legislative campaign to deprive homosexuals of rights to housing and jobs, Olivia released a collection of gay songs, *Lesbian Concentrate*. The title is a fillip directed at Anita Bryant—a former singer contracted to the Florida citrus industry to advertise their product—for her part in the campaign against gay rights in Florida's Dade County.

The unusual aspect of this record, other than its political direction, is that part of the proceeds from *Lesbian Concentrate* went to the Lesbian Mothers' National Defense Fund, a group that helps women in child custody cases where sexual preference is an issue.

Olivia records released albums by Cris Williamson, Linda Tillery, Meg Christian, a Bay Area rock group Bebe K'Roche, Teresa Trull, and distributed women's records from other small independent labels.

Cris Williamson, who earlier released an album on Ampex records, is a songwriter and singer. She has a rock style, but she makes a distinction between rock and women's music:

> When I sing rock 'n' roll it's very into sexuality, that kind of hard, driving, male-oriented—I consider it male-oriented because it's a male form, developed from the male side of me . . . It had a lot of force involved in it.

The material she sang on Olivia projects had a gentler feeling. Part of the awareness of women's culture are theories that try to isolate male elements from female ones, ideas that have yet to be solidified, but there are attempts at a definition of women's music. What is essentially female in women's music? Cris Williamson finds the key to the difference is the subtlety she finds there:

> I love subtlety. A lot of men's music and arrangements fills in all the spaces. You've got available space and—okay, fill it up.
>
> For me, I like to indicate, and I think maybe women do this a little better. Perhaps all we have left is subtlety. We haven't, as women, had a lot of outlets, so we can only do it with touches here and there for explaining ourselves.

The music that came from her new awareness returns to a spirituality that she believes existed before male-centered religions took over:

> People tell me what spiritual experiences they have when they come to my concerts, women's concerts. There's a real gathering, and I feel sometimes when I look out and see all these uplifted faces, that we are participating in an ancient ritual again.

The work at Olivia, with its women, was not like work in the conventional music industry.

> Olivia records are more concerned that it not be sexist, ageist, or oppressive to women or to anyone. It's a clean operation in that sense.

One of the most promising artists on Olivia is Linda Tillery, a singer with a gospel and rock background who earlier sang lead vocals for San Francisco's Loading Zone and released one album on Columbia.

At Olivia she produced Bebe K'Roche, and then her own album. The atmosphere at the women's label was a different experience for her as well as for the others.

> Women's creative energy is triggered off by different things . . .
> For me, it's the need to be felt, and the need to be understood and the need to be listened to, heard and respected just for what I do.
>
> I feel like I have all these reasons for which to cry out: in rage, frustration, compassion, hatred . . . As a woman it has to do with

internalization. I take them in differently than men do, so the way I'm going to spew them out is certainly going to come from a whole different place, having not had the advantage of male privilege.

I don't know what it feels like, to be secure in that way. I can't imagine what it would feel like to carry that kind of cocky attitude and express it through my music. Not just cockiness, but to be secure in that I have the power to make the world in some way turn upside down if I want it to.

Women who are aware of the message about themselves that leaps from a song choose their material thoughtfully. They will no longer sing the old staples of the pop music scene, hangdog ballads of unrequited love. As conscious songwriters, they avoid writing them, or perpetuating the stereotype of the clinging, helpless woman. Linda Tillery would not sing a "kick me daddy" song:

I would never, *ever* sing a "kick me daddy" song, because I have never, *ever* lived a "kick me daddy" life. And if a daddy ever *kicked* me, that'd be the last kick he'd ever lay in his *life*.

Politically conscious performers have not all found it necessary to exclude men from their work. Holly Near has collaborated on songs with Jeff Langley, a friend since high school. But like the women of Olivia, she will not sing dishrag songs.

We consciously write love songs that don't say, "I need you, I can't live without you, you can beat me and I'll still love you" and all those kind of things that have gone in love songs. To write a love song that doesn't say that is a conscious act and therefore a political statement.

She often tours with Cris Williamson and songwriters Margie Adam and Meg Christian. They appear in support of organizations or causes, or at women's prisons. Her work is "conscious entertainment," and she sees herself as a cultural worker, an artist with a message. "Cultural workers," she notes, "have skills that can soften the blow of ideology."

Women's music is not so well defined a concept for Holly as for the others, since she addresses herself to the music:

Is there such a thing? How do you go about it after having years of influence from a male-dominated society on you—how can you ever decide what you would have done had you never heard all that —had you not been told that I-IV-V was the blues, and that you have to have verse-chorus, verse-chorus?

If you look at other cultures who did not have that kind of influence, have different musical scales, is there such a thing that is a connection between women, just as there might be between races or between cultures or between nationalities?

No. If women do not control their society, they will not dominate its music. Whatever is most widely diffused will be the creation of the group that controls everything else. The people who submit abdicate their right to self-expression. They will not be heard as often, as loudly, and they will not be known as well as the people who take the initiative.

If certain forms of music are not available to women, they will not express themselves in that form. If certain instruments—brass, percussion, electronics—are not considered proper for them, they will not learn to play them. If certain styles, rock or instrumental jazz, are dominated by men, women will find it harder to be involved in them.

Being in certain places, doing certain work where they don't belong, according to the opinion of a larger or stronger group of people, is a dangerous situation any individual would hesitate to enter. Music is an idiom, but it is circumscribed, stereotyped. To drag in the ragged comparison to the black awareness movement once again, it was once a backhanded compliment to blacks to say that they had rhythm. Some do, some don't. Is it better that they should dance well than become doctors and engineers? Women are categorized into types that are so pervasive in popular thinking that they are hard to see as false. Some women may have gentle qualities and a capacity for tenderness, but not all, nor are these qualities absent in men.

It's not necessary to read characteristics such as gentleness and lyricism as feminine. An artist is capable of expressing a range of feelings not denied to anyone, but not usually expressed in the course of a day by most people, or perhaps in the course of a lifetime.

Women have been ballad singers because the ballad form is quiet, demure, and a little sad. The ability to sing a ballad is not linked to gender, nor is the ability to shout; it is connected to culture.

Experience determines one's mode of expression, and now the lyrical content of songs is beginning to change. The musical styles will change as women claim wider experience, or as all musical styles change. In the future, more women will be involved in the changes.

By choice, Holly Near writes love songs that speak from a point of view that is eye to eye equal to her lover.

"You Can Know All I Am" is a love song. It's saying, "I will show you and give you access to who I am, but I can't change my life for you, give up the things that are important to me, my life work, or my beliefs, or my center for you."

Her songs are not only accepted, but needed, requested, wanted by her audience, who respond to the emotion in them.

People respond. We don't have to have the whole world know who we are. We have lots of people who really like and respect our music, and our music is of use to them.

People want songs to speak about their own lives . . . There are heroes and heroines all over this land who are struggling to stay alive day after day.

Rosalie Sorrels, Barbara Dane, Joanna Cazden, Casse Culver, Alix Dobkin, there are many more alternative singers and writers; Miriam Cutler, who writes witty songs for the Alices, Vicki Randle, another beautiful voice, Hazel Dickens, who wrote "Don't Put Her Down, You Helped Put Her There," Peggy Seeger, who wrote "I'm Gonna Be an Engineer," and groups gathered with a purpose beyond making music: the Chicago Women's Liberation Rock Band, the New Haven Women's Liberation Rock Band, and the Berkeley Women's Music Collective.

Women's music gathers an audience that supports the hope of women to have greater goals for their lives than they have in the past. This audience wants a self-reliant and strong ideal. They are sensitive to women's issues and humanist causes.

The ties between this audience and its artists are strong. At some concerts, particularly those of the Olivia collective, the artists meet with the audience after the performance to hold workshops that break down the mystique which puts performers in a position of power and their audience into a submissive role. The situation dispels the dream image that operates whenever someone performs before a group and is magically transformed into its leader.

This audience is not treated like a mass of childlike volatility, but is expected to react responsibly, even to not littering the concert hall. The members of the audience are considered individually and collectively answerable for their positive or negative responses. This is an important awareness that might create resistance in groups of people to being manipulated. This is an important innovation attempted by the women's music movement.

All is to the good in encouraging audience participation and shunning old female stereotypes, and the women's music movement by its exuberance may overflow the bounds of music and entertainment. The claims that women's music is gentle, tender, womanly may open the door to other stereotypes.

Women's music is supposedly strong and beautiful. It is to be hoped that all good music shares this characteristic, all music that can move a human being.

Despite some befuddled romanticism about women's collective unconsciousness, it is true that there is no more earth-moving music than a song, a popular song sung at the right time by the right people for a proper reason: the "Marseillaise," "We Shall Overcome," "I Am Woman," or why not "Cactus Flower," "You Don't Own Me," "Love Song to a Stranger" or even "Angel of the Morning"?

The women's music movement offers an alternative to the kissy-poo exploitation of the recording industry. It is certainly more responsible toward its audience, wishing to do it good. Sometimes, the more political the intent of the singer, the less musical her direction, since doctrinaire songs are the slaves of ideas, and can exclude craft, freedom, and variety of emotions. Singers and songwriters who do not fall into the trap of dogma yet sing with a new consciousness are exceptions in this genre, as in any other.

Production companies that arrange concert tours connected with the women's music movement share the socially conscious intent of

Malvina Reynolds, Holly Near, and Olivia records. Women on
Wheels and Once in a Blue Moon, California concert production
companies, print their flyers and programs in both Spanish and English. Wise Women Enterprises, based in Maine, organized tour stops
to include performances at the area women's prisons. Childcare for
women's music events is provided because it is recognized that
women with children find it hard to leave their homes.

These production companies are part of the movement for
women's rights. A leaflet from Women on Wheels says:

> Women on Wheels is a women's concert production company. All
> of the people creating our concerts are women, women who share a
> vision of a culture which speaks realistically about women: about
> their potentials, their strengths, their loves and their struggles. With
> each contribution of our talents to these productions, whether it be
> in graphic design, sound, ushering, performing, childcare, lighting,
> leafleting, or whatever, we are expressing our faith in the importance
> of this growing "women's culture." We feel that in order to fully
> and truly change the status of women in this country, a redefinition
> of women must be reflected within popular culture and mass media.
> "Women's culture" is a seeding for that redefinition and we at
> Women on Wheels are proud and excited to be a part of it.

Women's music festivals have been held on college campuses in Il-
linois, California, and elsewhere. There are publications, groups, and
individual activists who promote and exchange information on
women's contribution to music. The late Helen King and other
members of the Songwriter's Resources Service in Los Angeles are
some of the strongest allies of women in music. There are teachers,
organizers, and supporters such as Karlene Faith, Kristin Lems, Kate
Millett, and others. Women's studies departments at universities are
beginning to encourage research in the field of women in music.

If the American popular song and its singers still portray some
silly ideas, it is because America wants them, creates them, deserves
them, and has not rejected them. Good and beautiful songs are also
heard.

A singer is not a leader. To follow an artist is to run in circles, since a singer is our own image, depicting us as we would wish to be, speaking for us, expressing our feelings and our ideas, but does not create the world in which we live.

These have been most of the women whose voices are heard in America, its message to the world. These are the most popular voices. If you listen, then the song's for you, and the singer is one voice. Yours. And her songs have only one message, after all. They say—have courage, you are not alone.

CLASS ACTS

I am grateful for the help from my friends and family, and people, and organizations, many of whom are not mentioned here, and a very few who are. In no particular order:

Sherry Rayn Barnett
Sam Emerson
Chris Van Ness
Tichi Wilkerson Miles
Jerry Wexler
Jeff Barry
Brooks Arthur
Florence Greenberg
Wendy Weil
Nona Hendryx
Susan Schwartz, my editor
Diane Matthews, my other editor
Marcia Nasatir
Kathy Wagner
Patti Wright

Cleo Thompson
Pat Siciliano
Janice Azrak
Bob Mercer
Cynthia Bowman
Marsa Hightower
Jean Powell
Vicki Wickham
Helen King
Joan Bullard
Marian Massey
Marni McCormick
Liza Williams
Diana Gould
Melly Peterson

Joan Eisenberg
Todd Everett
Lee Cadorette
Jane Alsobrook
Shelley Selover
Judy Paynter
David Brokaw
Kyo Sharee
Sue Clark
Gail Roberts
Charly Coplen
Barbara DeWitt
Bryn Breidenthal
Sally Stevens
George James
Grelun Landon
Muriel Decunzo

Ronnie Lipton
Bobbie Cowan
Jack Rael
Arlyne Rothberg
Beverly Magid
Eliot Sekuler
Evan Archerd
Norm Winter
Marv Greifinger
Lorette Murray
N.A.R.A.S.
S.R.S.
R.I.A.A.
The Singers
Glenn Rounds
Kathy Reinoehl

The members of record company press departments, managers, agents, and independent members of the recording industry who helped with information and shared their knowledge with me, as well as, last of all, the Victims of Vomit, who deserve a space of their own in my affections, to keep them from contaminating the thanks I give to the others.

INDEX

Index

Index

Index